Developing Teaching & Learning in Africa

Decolonising Perspectives

EDITOR
Vuyisile Msila

Developing Teaching and Learning in Africa: Decolonising Perspectives

Published by African Sun Media under the SUN PReSS imprint

All rights reserved

Copyright © 2020 African Sun Media and the editor

This publication was subjected to an independent double-blind peer evaluation by the publisher.

The editor and the publisher have made every effort to obtain permission for and acknowledge the use of copyrighted material. Refer all enquiries to the publisher.

No part of this book may be reproduced or transmitted in any form or by any electronic, photographic or mechanical means, including photocopying and recording on record, tape or laser disk, on microfilm, via the Internet, by e-mail, or by any other information storage and retrieval system, without prior written permission by the publisher.

Views reflected in this publication are not necessarily those of the publisher.

First edition 2020

ISBN 978-1-928480-70-9
ISBN 978-1-928480-71-6 (e-book)
https://doi.org/10.18820/9781928480716

Set in Futura Lt Bt Light 11/15

Cover design, typesetting and production by African Sun Media

SUN PReSS is an imprint of African Sun Media. Scholarly, professional and reference works are published under this imprint in print and electronic formats.

This publication can be ordered from:
orders@africansunmedia.co.za
Takealot: bit.ly/2monsfl
Google Books: bit.ly/2k1Uilm
africansunmedia.store.it.si *(e-books)*
Amazon Kindle: amzn.to/2ktL.pkL

Visit africansunmedia.co.za for more information.

This book is dedicated to the memory of a colleague,
Professor Gregory Hankoni Kamwendo, a protagonist of decolonised education.

May he rest in peace. The decolonisation debates continue.

Contents

Foreward i
    Steve Sharra
Preface v
    Vuyisile Msila

Basic Education

1   Basic Education and Decolonisation in South Africa: Preparing Schools for New Challenges 1
    Vuyisile Msila

2   Indigenising Mathematics in Schools – Why Ethnomathematics Matters 21
    Monicca T. Bhuda and Thabo I. Pudi

3   Decolonising Science: Challenging the South African Classroom through Indigenous Knowledge Systems 43
    Philip M. Ramadikela, Thabo I. Pudi and Hamza O. Mokiwa

4   Inclusive Education Without Resources: A Policy Approach for Sub-Sahara Africa 59
    Maxwell P. Opoku and J-F.

Higher Education

5   The Dislocated Rural Student: Calls for Decolonisation 79
    Berrington Ntombela

6   Humanising and Decolonising Adult Basic Education and Training (ABET) in South Africa 103
    Luvuyo L. Lalendle, Vuyisile Msila and Sizakele Matlabe

7   Fostering Collective Teacher Efficacy Through Values-Based and *Ubuntu*-Inspired Leadership: Implications for Decolonisation 125
    Terefe F. Bulti

8   Reflections on Programming in an Afrocentric Distance Education Certificate Programme: A Case Study 149
    Zamo Hlela

9   Heutagogy, Decolonisation and Rethinking Knowledge: Voices of University Teachers 165
    Luvuyo L. Lalendle and Vuyisile Msila

New Epistemologies and Society

10 Decolonising Epistemologies: The Paradoxes of a Self-Colonised State 187
   Philip M. Ramadikela, Vuyisile Msila and Teshome Abera

11 Lost in Translation? Revisiting Language Decolonisation Project in
   Nigerian Education 205
   Oluwaseun O. Afolabi

12 Transforming Leadership: Towards the Advancement of Decolonisation and
   Social Justice 225
   Itumeleng I. Setlhodi and Philip M. Ramadikela

13 Western Thought and African Presence in Biblical Interpretation 243
   Joseph A. Agbogun

Index 261

Foreword

Steve Sharra

Decolonising Teacher Education in the New Decade

At one minute before 8pm on the evening of 22 May in 2018, I got a WhatsApp message from Professor Alfred Matiki, then based in Gaborone where he was teaching at the University of Botswana. He said he had just heard that Gregory Kamwendo, a mutual friend, had been shot dead in South Africa. I had not heard anything. Matiki had received a phone call from a relative in Durban, but there were no further details.

In the subsequent days, it was confirmed that Professor Kamwendo, Dean of the Faculty of Arts at the University of Zululand, had been shot dead in his car in front of his home in Empangeni. It was a crime that was to shake his university, leaving everyone aghast.

Prior to becoming Dean at the University of Zululand, Kamwendo had been Dean of the School of Education at the University of KwaZulu-Natal (UKZN). He went to UKZN from the University of Botswana where he taught for many years and headed the Department of Languages and Social Sciences Education. He left the University of Botswana just as I arrived there for a sabbatical position in December 2014. He reassured me of an environment that would be intellectually fulfilling – it was.

Hankoni Gregory Kamwendo was a Malawian sociolinguist and language educator, and was a leading scholar in language education, on and on the decolonisation of African education. He researched and published extensively on how to bring African languages into African education systems. This book is dedicated to Professor Kamwendo's memory is a befitting honour and testimony to his scholarship and academic leadership on the continent.

Developing Teaching and Learning in Africa: Decolonising Perspectives continues the legacy of the work of Kamwendo. It is a particularly important book because it tackles the question of decolonisation from the perspective of the education of African teachers. Much of the decolonisation debate has focused on higher education in Africa, but this book argues that the debate is important for teacher education as well, starting with basic education.

As Msila persuasively contends in the preface, the decolonisation agenda will not achieve its transformative purpose unless it pervades the whole education system. This means transforming the curriculum in the schools as well as the curriculum in institutions that educate teachers. Teacher educators in universities and colleges will need to be at the forefront of this agenda. It will be meaningless, Msila points out, to transform the curriculum but leave out teacher educators. Worse still, bring that curriculum to student teachers who are unprepared for transformation.

The book provides both depth and breadth on the most important topics in decolonising education. The authors are committed to bringing Pan-Africanism, the African Renaissance and *Ubuntu* philosophy into the classroom. They demonstrate that it is possible to explore indigenous mathematics with both student teachers and learners. They also show how and why we must be inclusive in our approach, and ensure that both teachers as well as students with disabilities are empowered to contribute to their own education. We must challenge perspectives that see students with disabilities from a medicalised and economic liability perspective. Rather, human rights and local resources must inform inclusive education.

Teachers must be equipped to address the place of indigenous African languages in the classroom and in the education system. Teachers must have a broader view of knowledge production and the historical, political, and social contexts in which this process is mediated. Indigenous knowledges have a place in a globalised world and are key to reclaiming African identities pushed to the margins by colonialism and neo-colonialism, imperialism and neoliberalism. Teacher educators need to tackle negative attitudes towards indigenous knowledge from teachers, curriculum specialists and education policymakers.

Developing Teaching and Learning in Africa: Decolonising Perspectives uses case studies from across Africa, making it a resource that should be used in various parts of the continent. The authors take on topics surrounding issues such as high university fees (#FeesMustFall), colonial symbols on campuses (#RhodesMustFall), indigenous languages in African education, indigenous knowledge, inclusive education among others. In this way, the book provides a thorough overview of debates that dominated education discourse in the decade that started in 2010 and ended in 2019. In the coming decade, the imperative will be to embed these debates in the education of teachers in Africa, and in curriculum reforms.

For the continent to progress towards the African Union's *Agenda 2063*, national educational systems will need to play a central role. It will be impossible to propel the aspirations of the Africa we want without teachers who are well educated and intellectually equipped. The Continental Education Strategy for Africa, the first ten-year strategy for revitalising education in Africa, puts teachers and teacher education at the top of its strategic objectives. Revitalising teachers and teacher education on the continent will require intellectual, financial and material resources, and this collection offers itself as one such resource.

With this volume, Vuyisile Msila continues with his leadership on research and knowledge production in Africa's education systems. His 2016 book *Africanising the Curriculum*, co-edited with Professor Mishack Gumbo, introduced indigenous perspectives and theories into the discourse. Msila and Gumbo followed up with *African Voices on Indigenisation of the Curriculum*, published in 2017. In the same year, Msila came out with *Decolonising Knowledge for Africa's Renewal*, placing him firmly on the frontiers of intellectual leadership on matters to do with reshaping African knowledge production for emancipation.

This book continues the legacy of the late Gregory Kamwendo, who envisioned an Africa in which indigenous knowledge and African languages played a vital role in educating the continent's young people. In this new decade, African scholars, policymakers and teacher educators are called upon to fulfil the promise of the Africa envisioned by Kamwendo and other African thinkers who believed in the power of knowledge to change society.

Steve Sharra, PhD
Lilongwe
Malawi

Preface

Liberating Education

Vuyisile Msila

Context

The complex discourses of decolonising education in Africa continue in as many conscientious citizens still lay their hopes on the doors of educational institutions to solve the ills of the African societies. Since the advent of colonisation, African education has been in search of relevance and meaning even though colonial damage has grown immensely over decades; this makes it challenging to obliterate colonialism. With the epistemic violence, that has been a sine qua non of colonial and apartheid education – African education was always accompanied by de-Africanisation, deculturalisation, dehumanisation and distortions to misrepresent the truth. All these are concepts discussed in a number of ways in this volume. To redress many anomalies that came up because of colonisation, progressive educators speak of a dialogic education to confront cognitive injustice in learning sites.

In his seminal work, *Pedagogy of the Oppressed*, Paulo Freire (1970) emphasises the need for education to be a dialogue rather than follow a banking model or approach where teachers' sole viewpoint is fact. Freire's dialogic teaching reduces learner withdrawal and teacher talk in the classroom; dialogue calls for a teacher's skill of intervention and tact of restraint "so that the verbal density of a trained intellectual does not silence the verbal styles of unscholastic students" (Shor, 1987:23). Shih (2018) explicates the premise of Freire's dialogue under a few themes that include; (i) each person having the right to speak, (ii) the fact that dialogue cannot be an act of one person, (iii) the idea that dialogue is not hostile and polemical argument, (iv) humility, (v) love, (vi) hope, critical thinking, and (vii) faith. The search for a decolonised system of education is a search for critical education that is not only dialogic but relevant to the entire continent of Africa as well. Various chapters in this book demonstrate revolutionary forms of introducing decolonised models that should transform traditional learning sites that use the West as the sole benchmark for knowledge generation. Additionally, decolonised education is opposed to the unbending methodological paradigms of traditional learning sites that use the West as the exclusive vessel for knowledge or the centre. Decolonised systems seek to decentre the Western knowledges without marginalising them. In his book, *Moving the Centre*, Ngugi Wa Thiongo (1993) argues a need to move the centre in two ways – between nations as well as within nations. Wa Thiongo maintains that this is the basis of liberating world cultures from aspects such as class, race, and gender. Moving the centre between nations implies that the centre will be moved from its assumed position in the West to a multiplicity of spheres in all the cultures of the world. Furthermore, moving the centre within nation means moving away from all minority groupings to a centre situated among the working-class people and where equality is supreme.

Teacher education needs to be conscious of the needs of today's classrooms to be able to experiment with anti-method pedagogy that decolonises knowledge and de-Europeanise the vision of education, as we know it. This volume of essays challenges us to rethink thinking behind teaching as well as learning and explicate what is meant by a decolonised system of education and which knowledges are relevant. On the subject of rethinking knowledge, Ndlovu-Gatsheni (2018:24) argues:

> Rethinking thinking is fundamentally a decolonial move that requires the cultivation of a decolonial attitude in knowledge production. It is informed by a strong conviction that all human beings are not only born into a knowledge system but are legitimate knowers and producers of legitimate knowledge. Rethinking thinking is also a painstaking decolonial process of 'learning to unlearn in order to re-learn' …

Eurocentric and apartheid education have necessitated that teacher education and schools should constantly and consciously address the miseducation and dehumanisation aspects of education in the past as well as in the present. Thomas (1998:84) cites Mazrui (1967) who contends that African and third world people ought to be co-workers in the revival of culture:

> "To escape death and isolation, and to nurture the latent African genius". African societies have to pose several questions when it comes to the goals of education in post-colonial Africa. Among these are the questions on language, on attainment of a national spirit, on magnification of African cultures and on education that acknowledges the noble idea of an African Renaissance."

As a Change Management practitioner at the University of South Africa from 2017 to 2020, I have come across several colleagues in conferences from a few institutions of higher learning where decolonisation has been a subject of discussion. I have observed two extremes in the various debates as South African institutions endeavour to manage transformation and decolonisation paths. On the one hand, are pedantic demagogues who refuse to move until concepts are clarified – many critics have said that academics easily fall into this trap. This group is meticulous about explication of terms and delineation of processes in higher education transformation. The explication of terms is very vital, for we cannot continue with debates without a common understanding. However, this demand can be a delaying mechanism to derail transformation and decolonisation process as we continue an unending intellectual exercise of semantics while we experience inertia and un-transforming environments.

On the other extreme are those who are impatient about the sluggish transformation and decolonisation of education institutions. The latter group maintains that the long-winded development of theory is stalling the process of change hence we need to see the actual changes effected at all education institutions. However, ideally, we should demand a middle ground where there is an understanding of theory for practice. No one can develop any curriculum models without the necessary theory. Kwame Nkrumah spoke of the need to apply the weapon of theory when he stated, *"Action without thought is empty. Thought without action is blind"*. Nkrumah postulated this maxim as he articulated his consciencism philosophy, pointing out that in the process of developing decolonisation thinkers, we need both thinkers and implementers, the doers (Nkrumah, 1969).

The creation and sustenance of responsive campuses for example, need thought as we redesign and reincarnate the higher education institutions, thus enamouring Africa's future. Children need schools that would prepare them for the building of their communities and their country in an age when Africa is faced with insurmountable challenges. The chapters in this book focus on the challenges facing teacher education programmes, teachers, learners and schools at a time of volatile changes. The book examines how we may need to think about redesigning teaching in basic education, adult education and in institutions of higher learning as we contemplate decolonisation of knowledge. In this preface, I explore a few sub-topics, which include the development of teaching in Africa. Secondly, the focus is on why enacting cultural decolonisation can transform institutional cultures embedded in education institutions. Finally, the focus is on the complexity of decolonising institutions and what constitutes this process. Among other factors, there is much need to examine teacher education programmes whenever people discuss decolonisation and transformation in education.

Developing Teaching in Africa: What about Teacher Education?

Stokes (1997:217) argues that teacher education needs to be consistent with a "progressive, democratic vision" and that teachers should ensure that in their classrooms, they constantly examine their cultural identities as they enhance critical consciousness among learners. Stokes (1997:217) adds:

> A critical teacher education should problematize the lived experience of children, women, and men throughout this society, and simultaneous positions of domination and subordination – contradictory experiences of oppression and complicity with privilege. At the intersections of race, class, and gender, each participates in multiple positions of power and powerlessness.

Decolonising teacher education is an imperative step towards the attainment of the objectives of a decolonised system of education. Teachers should be part of rethinking the curriculum and ensuring that it will be meaningful to the lives of all learners in their classrooms. Furthermore, decolonisation requires teachers who would be able to educate themselves about domination and subordination especially if they are to be able to avoid the reproduction of present conditions (Stokes, 1997). Teachers should also be able to draw a balance between theory and practice. Therefore, when we speak about *Ubuntu* in the classroom, what do we mean? What do we mean when we speak of education as a political act? What does it mean to reframe the pedagogical practices? Why should educators enhance community links with their classrooms? These and many other questions are key when we examine the decolonisation of teacher education in Africa. Teachers need to constantly self-reflect as they question their own identities, posing questions as to what they are teaching and why they are teaching it. Furthermore, how the content is taught is very vital for decolonisation of knowledge is not about transforming content only, but about pedagogy itself – the way teachers teach and learners learn matter. Teachers should no longer be passive but must ask questions about the knowledge they facilitate in the classroom at all times. Some of the questions to pose continuously are:

o   Whose knowledge am I teaching?
o   How would it change the colonial or traditional practices?

- How will the curriculum benefit my learners and me?
- Does the curriculum have an effect on power relations and culture?
- What is my role in curriculum planning?

Numerous other pertinent questions that can be posed are not answered in this preface but in the various chapters in this book. We need active teachers who are activists for transformation and leaders in new pedagogical practices that embrace democracy, social justice and cognitive justice. It is crucial for teachers to use education in helping learners understand the links between education and the learners' communities. The idea of relevant education can never be over emphasised, and it is important for education to enable learners to establish their own identities. It is also of utmost importance for teachers to see education as embracing all rather than alienating – constant revision of content is central here.

The current education system presents challenges for teachers to change what they teach and how they teach, especially when one understands how many teachers were taught as learners, then as teachers in initial teacher education programmes. Many may struggle to integrate indigenous and Western knowledges. In fact, Heleta (2016) argues that there is a need to transform the Eurocentric curriculum that bolsters Western dominance and white privilege. I am certain that teacher education programmes, teachers and most importantly teacher unions can all play a vital role in this regard. The union is a critical stakeholder and needs to be in the forefront of education transformation with other stakeholders.

> (South) Africa must tackle and dismantle the epistemic violence and hegemony of Eurocentrism, completely rethink, reframe and reconstruct the curriculum and place South Africa, Southern Africa and Africa at the centre of teaching, learning and research.
>
> Heleta, 2016:1

Teachers need to be proactive and as they examine their practice and posing essential questions about their pedagogical practices. They ought to understand the humanising aspect of progressive education as well as its conscientising role. Paulo Freire (1970) used both these concepts to illustrate the imperatives of liberating education. Yet, transformative teaching must also work with ways of transforming culture.

Culture Impact on Knowledge

At the centre of colonial and apartheid education is culture, which has always been manipulated to reflect the empire or *die volk's* might. The British were always clear about their intentions hidden in education whilst apartheid education was very open about education's intentions and that was to create children who would reinforce the master-servant relationship (Kallaway, 1988). Decolonisation ought to play a huge role in examining, understanding and transforming the culture reflected by African education. In understanding the basic tenets of decolonisation, cultural decolonisation should help demystify our quest for a liberating education. Relevant pedagogy and meaningful learning will be guided by cultural decolonisation. Colonial and apartheid education has denigrated African cultures over the years whilst demeaning indigenous knowledges. Ndlovu-Gatsheni (2018) writes about ways in which colonisation led to culturecides, historicides, linguicides and epistemicides: "Africa is one of those epistemic sites that experienced not only colonial genocides but also 'theft of history' (see Goody, 2006), epistemicides (killing of indigenous people's knowledges) and linguicides (killing of indigenous people's languages)" (Ndlovu-Gatsheni, 2018:3). In addition, culturecides refer to the killing of the indigenous peoples' cultural practices and historicides, which is the killing of the indigenous peoples' history.

Cultural decolonisation changes thinking and enhances the belief in African cultures and identities rather than cultural dominance of Europe. Cultural decolonisation in education will also help rehumanise those who were dispossessed and oppressed. Decolonised scholarship, curriculum and teaching will be able to magnify this role of culture in the classroom. The language debates have become very critical in the cultural decolonisation debates.

As people rebuild education, institutions need to plan their cultural reconstruction. New cultures need to inform scholarship, curriculum as well as ways of teaching. As pointed out above, generally, the current university in Africa is based on culture and values of Western education. Nkrumah perceived African culture as the basis of African-centred education and was despondent to see the University of Ghana a resemblance of Oxford and Cambridge (Botwe-Asamoah, 2005). Furthermore, Botwe-Asamoah (2005) argues that Nkrumah maintained that an African university could not serve the society unless it is rooted in the indigenous social structures and cultural institutions. The experiences of the African people mattered to Nkrumah and he struggled because when he emphasised Africanisation of education and claimed that English should no longer be a determinant for promotion in secondary school, he was accused of lowering the education standards. It is however striking that Nkrumah's observation in 1960 Ghana could be the truth in numerous African education institutions six decades later. The struggles that Nkrumah observed were also experienced by his contemporaries such as Julius Nyerere. Nyerere (1970:130) highlighted the need for a relevant Africa focused Tanzanian education when he stated in October 1961:

> We are in the process of building up a Tanganyika nation. Valuable as is the contribution which overseas education can give us, in the end, is we are to build up a sturdy sense of nationhood; we must nurture our own educated citizens. Our young men and women must have an Africa-orientated education. That is an education, which is not only given in Africa but also directed at meeting the present needs of Africa.

The application of education to suit the local circumstances is crucial to Africa and that is why Nyerere talks about education meeting the needs of the African continent. Epistemic violence means that colonial and apartheid education brought education that alienated the African from his/her environment. When we talk of epistemic violence, we refer to the cultural hegemony that dominated over the decades of colonial and apartheid domination. The colonial invasion was a conscious reproduction of the imperial culture upon students as we magnified the Western culture in all aspects of education institutions. We cannot forget the fact that the universities in Africa were built to nurture new colonisers. Much of the epistemic deafness we find today among academics and society is due to the internalisation of the culture of domination that is rooted in our institutions. Today, the cynicism we witness in the society is mainly due to internalised aspects of Western culture. It is because of our beliefs in Western science and Western scholarship that we tend to neglect the local as we frequently underscore globalisation, perceiving the decolonial project an antithesis of progress. I believe that the first priority for the decolonisation of knowledge is cultural decolonisation.

Over the past decade, decolonisation has filled our society's agenda. Various role players have seen it necessary to search for answers of how we can reshape the African society. This is not new although the recent student upheavals in South Africa in the form of *Fallist Movements* have made many to reopen the debate and investigate the questions around decolonisation and Africanisation of knowledge. The university has been entangled in this on-going debate about a decolonised society.

Green (1998) points out that post-apartheid South Africa needs to restructure its entire education system to meet the needs of the previously excluded and drastically under-educated majority. A new form of academic culture is also needed to build new and meaningful norms for creating fecund basis for a decolonised system. Shared governance is necessary in institutions – bring together various academic committees to make necessary decisions in transforming what happens in lecture halls. Empowered faculty will be able to build relevant curricula that address how education should be. However, the dilemma for institutional leaders this time is serving the interest of all role players. Leadership in higher education institutions in South Africa has shifted, being less about power and more about comprehending the ambiguity that binds higher education institutions. In fact, the current South African higher education institution has become more complex and many are not simply hierarchical structures. Madeleine Green (1997:46) argues:

> Because organisations are complex webs of seemingly chaotic interrelationships, patterns and connections can be discerned only over long periods. Organisations are networks of people and problems; webs of culture, habits, myths, and formal and informal authority. The predominant image is one of overlapping circles rather than a pyramid. Furthermore, organisations (including institutions of higher education) are part of a complex network of other institutions and entities: depending on the country, they may include ministries, other government agencies, intermediary bodies and voluntary organisations.

Because universities have multiple centres of power, they need meticulous, progressive leaders to lead the decolonisation project. Leaders need to spread a shared agenda as the institutions transform its operations. Higher education leaders need to understand the super-complexity of the institutions of higher learning to be able to shape new cultures. It takes wise leaders to lead the process of change. Others argue that even when academic leaders are not change agents, higher education can change without strong leadership because some leaders consciously or unconsciously maintain the status quo. Irresistible pressure from inside and outside may change the institution. However, it is better to have a guided change that will not be traumatic and messy.

There is no adequate theorisation on the decolonisation of schools and other basic education institutions in South Africa. This leaves a gap in the debates for transformation of higher education institutions. We cannot discuss decolonisation at higher education institutions without any reference to basic education otherwise many initiatives to transform education will falter. With the high failure rate and low levels of literacy and numeracy in a country like South Africa, experts need to revisit research in language of teaching and ways in which to decolonise the curriculum including learning areas such as mathematics, natural sciences and technology education. Decolonisation goes a step further to just focusing on pass percentage; it examines and transforms the content of education.

How Do We Decolonise?

Decolonisation will not happen without a huge necessary disruption. Without this disruption, we will always find ourselves where we have been over the years. The problem we have today in stalling education transformation is created by the fact that we are not ready to confront the meaningful overhaul of education. In seeking education for liberation, there is no way we can avoid education as well as revolutionary consciousness. Revolutionary consciousness is linked to critical consciousness that people such as Paulo Freire espoused. Education should challenge the status quo and enable the people to take charge of their lives. The call for a decolonised education is to challenge the status quo as the way we teach children is gradually transformed. Education should be conscious raising in the context of decolonisation both the teacher and the learner should understand the role of African epistemologies in the process.

It is after the attainment of this critical consciousness that we can be able to find and pursue the role of social justice education. In pursuing the principles of social justice, the youth should drive the society's agenda for revolutionary education. For many families, education has never addressed the consequences of oppression hence some may talk about the need for a relevant socially just education. Many young people still ought to see education as that which encompasses a humanising pedagogy and a liberating practice. Given our background in South Africa, we should have thought more about the role of education in responding to social ills. In Africa, we need education that would respond to not only to poverty but also to various other ills left by colonialism. Socially just education should be compulsory for all classrooms and classrooms should reflect a free society. President Zuma addressed the Pan African Youth Congress on 28 November 2014. In his address, he acknowledged that, although there are African countries that have made some progress in socio-economic development, the majority of African youth still face unemployment, underemployment, inadequate access to education, health care, and housing. Furthermore, Zuma added:

> Agenda 2063 is premised on Pan-Africanism and the rebirth of the African Continent. It promotes restoration of values of human solidarity, *Ubuntu*, self-pride, self-determination, non-sexism, non-tribalism and the celebration of our diversity. Youth programmes must consider these values both in content and in form. You must individually and collectively espouse these values in your conduct in order to propel the African continent onto a higher development trajectory. This is even more important because you, the African youth, represent the future of Africa.

Donaldo Macedo (1993) portrays the *Pedagogy of Big Lies*, in which he explains what schools do; that is to promote a pedagogy that propagates the inability to think critically. This is literacy for stupidification; stupidification results to education for domestication. Macedo (2000) (in Chomsky) writes about teaching tasks which lead to dumbness; where teachers treat learners as *tabula rasas*. The latter is an education alienated from the learners' realities. Colonial and apartheid education entrenched this kind of education, a pedagogy of lies where education was manipulated by colonial governments. Furthermore, Macedo (1993) argues that we all need an education system that conscientises because it will be conscientisation that will be an antidote to education for barbarism as Tabata (1980) referred to apartheid and colonial education. We need to ask ourselves a perennial question of how we can ensure that education serves the historically disadvantaged, and how can it conscientise perpetually, thus ensuring that learners become lifelong learners who are critical in their approach to living. Learners who are made to internalise big lies in education are always inward looking for they are made to believe that there is only one rigid reality. Education based on big lies incarcerates instead of liberating the mind, it obscures instead of unmasking knowledge. When people use concepts such as African Renaissance, one sees their hope in bringing meaningful education that heralds new ideas and intellectual revival especially among young people.

President Thabo Mbeki maintained that real African Renaissance would be attained when there is conscious move to end greed, dehumanising poverty, obscene opulence and corruption, all factors which give rise to coups d'état and instability (Mbeki, 1998). Mbeki pointed out that African Renaissance is the hope of a decolonised Africa. This means that decolonisation gives Africa a face, a vision and hope.

The progress of the country's success should start with the transformation in education. The youth in Africa will change their societies through different forms of education. Education needs to disengage with its colonial and apartheid past. In his inauguration as Chancellor of the University of South Africa, Mbeki (2017) underscored the need for relevant, emancipatory curriculum. To this end, we cannot disregard the Indigenous Knowledge Systems, which will be critical inembedding social justice in education. For several decades, education in Africa tended to overlook the traditional experiences that can make the learners to be adept in life.

A socially just education from schools can be the basis, a foundation of education that demonstrates Africa's renewal for youth development and the future. The call for a decolonised system is synonymous to the call for a rehumanising education that caters for the local African contexts. As we talk of decolonisation, we require an education revolution that would change schools. These schools would enhance the African identity Eskia Mphahlele (1974) talked about. Our schools for example, need to learn to speak the indigenous languages. Cheik Anta Diop (2000) argued that African Renaissance could be attained through the African indigenous languages. This is an idea that is supported by Wiredu (1987) who writes about the need to develop the African indigenous languages. He goes on to point out that, the weakness of African philosophies is that they are communicated in colonial languages. The latter weakens their cause and commitment. Ali Mazrui (1980) also examines the technological superiority of Europe and explicates how English and French were in the forefront in the development of black political thought. Like Wa Thiongo and several other African thinkers, the colonial languages marginalised the indigenous cultures as they entrenched colonialism. In Anglophone, Francophone and Lusophone Africa, the Africans' education shunted the Africans away from their identities and cultures. In addition, in seeking to be global the African is moving away from these swayed by Western hegemony and there is a tendency for education to be formulated by experts who are captives of the Western knowledges. Africa should also be the centre; it should also be the point of reference in Africa. The Africans need to master the local, the regional the Continental before they can gain control of the world. Thomas (1998:83), writing about Ali Mazrui contends:

> In order to combat Western cultural hegemony and the Third World's growing cultural dependency, he makes a strong case for regional autonomy. He postulates that Africans [...] have as much to offer to world culture and global peace as did their English, French or Italian counterparts. On this point, Mazrui (2005) reaffirms the clarion call by Du Bois for African and Third World peoples to become co-workers in the kingdom of culture; to escape death and isolation, and to nurture the latent African genius.

Our schools can create a planetary system by employing a variety of knowledges. It is the argument of several chapters in this book that we need an Africa that uses a variety of knowledges as it decentres the exclusive use of Western epistemologies. This implies that there should be epistemic justice that would combat epistemic violence of yore as knowledges compete on an equal pedestal without using the West only as a measure of knowledges. However, decolonisation needs disruption, for without an overhaul, we cannot speak of true decolonisation.

As we disrupt the education, system we need to answer the question of relevance, for decolonisation of knowledge without bringing in the debate of relevance is futile. We should be able to answer the questions of what we do, how we do it and when we do it. Up to now for example, Africanisation has been more of a political project where we have looked at street name changes and re-examination of the colonial and apartheid symbols. We need a system of education that would embrace the following four factors rooted in conscientisation for a decolonised system:

1. **Critical pedagogy** refers to a progressive philosophy of teaching that focuses on contexts, histories and power relations.
2. *Indigenisation* refers to bringing the marginalised indigenous cultures, histories and people to the centre.
3. *Relearning* is about the conscious effort to disengage with colonisation and learn the implications of decolonisation. It goes with unlearning the past as part of the decolonising process.
4. *Disruption* calls for acknowledging the urgency of transformation. It seeks the upheaval of the status quo to lead to social justice and cognitive justice.

Each of these needs to talk to the idea of relevance and empowerment of the learners and teachers. We do not want to continue producing learners who have a cognitive dissonance. We need to continue asking ourselves as to what it means to be educated. Are learners who do not know themselves educated? Education in Africa should not be congruent to exclusive Western knowledge. How do we achieve relevant education that would eschew cognitive dissonance? We need a system where the learners start with their own before they expand their knowledge. This is the idea that Wa Thiongo (1993) discusses that a decolonised education starts with own languages before one can use other languages and knowledges to enrich one. In one of his most recent works, Ngugi Wa Thiongo (2014) writes about *globalectics* – an area that embraces interconnectedness and equality. This concept refers to a way of thinking and relating to the world, particularly in the current era of globalism and globalisation. Furthermore, Wa Thiongo opines about the ideal of building a better understanding of humanity between the global North and South – he explores a question of how we should ensure that the world has a meeting point. Many African thinkers have expressed this in several ways. Mwesirige (nd) cites Mazrui who contends that there are five strategies of taming Western-oriented imperialism disguised as globalisation and he referred to globalisation as simply villagisation of the globe. The five strategies are indigenisation, domestication, diversification, horizontal interpenetration and vertical counter-penetration. The African institutions of learning should respond to these in a move to better Africa. A decolonised curriculum encompasses a number of critical strategies and these may include; re-education of faculty/staff, relooking at prescribed works, privileging African ways of knowing as well as bias towards African pedagogies e.g. language, folktales, praise poetry, African worldviews. Furthermore, decolonisation needs to come with rethinking of culture, relooking at systems and strong leading of relevant change. We need to examine models past and present, successful and not to explore what we can glean from such. However, there are many challenges on the path towards decolonisation of education. One of the most critical challenge when it comes to institutions of learning and decolonisation is preparing teaching staff to unlearn knowledges that they might have embraced as unbending truth. True decolonisation needs solid plan and vision and there are several lessons South Africans can learn from the experiences of other African states.

As intimated above, the decolonisation project needs to seriously explore the rethinking of teacher education. In fact, without visionary teachers at higher education institutions and in schools, there can be no renewal of education and African education's future will continue to be blurry. As attempts are made to build responsive campuses, the initiatives will come to naught without empowered facilitators who understand their role in decolonising education. There are serious concerns though; that in institutions that purport transformation, faculty is still made up of individuals who are not ready to change or are not even keen to change. We also know the disastrous results of Curriculum 2005 in South Africa, which tended to deskill the first group of post-apartheid teachers. Amongst the pitfalls of this ambitious system was that teachers were not given time to understand and embrace this with understanding. On the eve of introducing a decolonised system in schools, we need educators who will not only understand decolonisation but also believe in it. Conscientious teachers will have to look at history and understand how African knowledges were severed to be able to re-member them with a decolonised, relevant system. This collection of chapters focuses on three vital aspects; developing ways of knowing, ways of teaching and ways of learning en route to decolonising education.

This volume's title is *Developing Teaching and Learning in Africa*, and it underscores the equal importance of both learning and teaching in decolonising learning sites. The Education transformation is futile if we enhance one without deepening the other. Education institutions that overhaul the curriculum and scholarship without inspiring teaching and learning are unlikely to attain successful transformation. In addition, what this book wants to achieve is to heighten the need to debate practical alternatives on the path towards the decolonisation of knowledge. The book is divided into three sections, Basic Education, Higher Education and New Epistemologies and Society.

In the first chapter, *Basic Education and Decolonisation in South Africa*, Msila focuses on how and why basic education in South Africa needs to be decolonised. Moving from roots of mission education and apartheid education the discussion explicates the reasons for moving the learners and their teachers away from the barbarism inherent in past education systems. Msila acknowledges the varied meanings of a decolonised system; some have referred to decolonised systems of education as forms of service-learning, implying that true decolonisation will integrate meaningful community **service** with instruction and reflection to enrich the **learning** experience. Others see the huge responsibility of decolonisation as negation to epistemic violence and colonial or Western knowledge domination in education. Although the society has haggled in defining the concepts, there have been several instances where consensus has been achieved. In concluding the chapter, Msila looks at Eskia Mphahlele's work at Funda Centre in Soweto and arguably his work here was the first breakthrough as to how people could practically decolonise education in South Africa.

Bhuda and Pudi's second chapter deals with the integration of ethnomathematics into school curriculum. The chapter, *Indigenising Mathematics in Schools: Why Ethnomathematics Matters* examines how mathematics has been utilised over decades in Africa as part of everyday life. However, the Western knowledges may not recognise the existence of mathematics in African cultures hence like many other areas there might have been the marginalisation of mathematics used by traditional societies. The authors claim that it is essential to use diverse ethnomathematical ideas in order to construct a curriculum that accommodates African indigenous learners of diverse cultures. Thus, teachers as agents of change ought to embrace and implement this policy by contextualising mathematics learning to the learners' cultural ways of life, learning, being and doing. In their argument, they demonstrate that there are contradictions and paradoxes in ethnomathematics although the school systems have to accommodate ethnomathematics. In South Africa, there are current reforms in mathematics education, which emphasise the need to empower learners mathematically, socially, and epistemologically.

Chapter 3, *Decolonising Science: Challenging the South African Classroom through Indigenous Knowledge Systems*, Ramadikela, Pudi and Mokiwa explore debates on ways in which Indigenous Knowledge Systems can enhance science classrooms. They argue that Western knowledges have always dominated in science classrooms because generally few people have really argued for indigenous knowledge systems' usefulness in these classrooms. The authors argue that it would be improper for African learning sites to exclude either Western Science or 'African' science supported by Indigenous Knowledge Systems. Progressive, conscientious educators who promote social justice and critical pedagogy among their learners will bring the two together for the benefit of all learners.

Opoku and J-F in chapter 4 also pose critical questions in the chapter entitled, *Inclusive Education Without Resources*, among these questions are whether inclusive education can provide equal opportunity to students with disabilities to access education at all levels of schooling without resources. These authors maintain that the question is relevant to sub-Saharan African countries because they have numerous challenges, which range from lack of funds to shortages in facilities and resources. These counties have few special schools. The chapter highlights various deficient processes and practices utilised in Sub-Saharan Africa in implementing Inclusive Education.

Ntombela's *The Dislocated Rural Student: Calls for Decolonisation* (chapter 5) focuses on the South African students' struggles for a decolonised education in 2015 and 2016. However, the author also looks at how these struggles have been usurped by other role players as the students are relegated towards the back. Ntombela explores how this has happened. Furthermore, the chapter interrogates the multiplicity of academically colonised subjects. It does so by profiling a typical student in a 'rural' university and shows how the university dubbed 'rural' dislocates such a student by way of appealing to universal discourses of academia. Although the notion of a rural university appears straightforward when viewed from geographical location, there are nuances that disturb such a label. It remains, nonetheless, that geographical location all by itself cannot absolutely measure the state of rurality of a university; students on the contrary, even though they may not absolutely take the label of rural, have among them those whose lineages and rootedness is rural. These lineages can be linguistically and rhetorically explained. The dominant Western thought continues to view Africa as an expanse of rural landscape whose preservation is for the gaze of the inquisitive tourist. Therefore, the reconstruction of rurality is hardly for the betterment and humanisation of rural residents than a curious traveller enticement move meant to commodify the people and their lived experiences. Ntombela argues here that decolonisation is essential for students in institutions, especially those located in rural communities.

In chapter 6 *Humanising and Decolonising Adult Basic Education and Training (ABET) in South Africa*, Lalendle, Msila and Matlabe examine the role of a decolonised adult education in South Africa. They trace the history of adult education in South Africa from its inception to the present and explore how this has evolved over the decades. These authors apply Paulo Freire's theory of critical pedagogy as they examine the gaps in the current models of adult education.

Bulti in chapter 7, *Fostering Collective Teacher Efficacy Through Values-Based and Ubuntu Inspired Leadesrhip:Implications for Decolonisation*, skilfully demonstrates in practice how decolonisation can utilise both Western and African knowledges in running excellent institutions. He reveals values that are critical for building Collective Teacher Efficacy in well run schools. The discussion demonstrates the importance of values such as servant leadership, integrity, humility, selflessness, compassion, and respect as utilised in 'Western' literature. Yet, the same concepts are reflected when one examines African models of leadership such as *Ubuntu*. Therefore, Bulti demonstrates why eclectic approaches in decolonising leadership would be critical in Africa institutions. He does this as he explores the invaluable nature of Values-Based Leadership (VBL); he explicates VBL as a leadership model meant to contribute to institutional success, particularly in terms of establishing a desired relationship among the working staff, and between leaders and followers. Values-Based Leadership is defined as "a relationship between a leader and followers that is based on shared strongly internalised ideological values adopted by the leader and strong followers' identification with those values".

Hlela's chapter 8 entitled, *Reflections on Programming in an Afrocentric Distance Education Certificate Programme: A Case Study*, raises the argument that frequently programming or curriculum formulation in the African context is too often drawn uncritically from Western theoretical frameworks such as humanism, andragogy, constructivism is usually problematic. All these frameworks are informed by individualistic conceptions of learners and learning, shaped by industrial and post-industrial political economy, liberal democratic politics and consumerist culture. Hlela argues that common among these curriculum designing is how knowledge is portrayed as universal and applicable in all contexts. However, this knowledge tends to overlook local socio-cultural context or local histories. Such programmes (Western thought and knowledge) are thus imposed to African 'territories' of learning (supposedly undeveloped African thoughts and knowledge) just like the colonial template only this time Africans impose the template upon themselves through disciplinary power. The chapter presents and documents history of the certificate programming since its first offering; it also explores the extent to which a distance education Certificate Programme locates itself within Afrocentrism in relation to content and programming and concludes that it remains at infusion phase. The chapter presents five tenets of an Afrocentric programme.

In *Heutagogy, Decolonisation and Rethinking Knowledge: Voices of University Teachers* (chapter 9), Lalendle and Msila commence their discussion from the 2015/2016 student uprisings in South Africa, which initiated debates that enveloped, and conscientised the entire society on the ills of the past hegemonic system of education. The students were organised under the banner of what was to be referred to as the 'Must Fall Movements'; #FeesMustFall and #RhodesMustFall whose effects spread across the country as students demanded liberatory education as well as open access to institutions of higher learning. These authors state that these calls for a transformed system of education soon led to the calls for a decolonised system that would end epistemic violence in institutions of higher learning. Apart from access, there was also exploration of student success which also enabled role players including students, to initiate debates on the formulation of innovative teaching and learning strategies that would serve the society with meaningful and relevant education. This chapter uses a case study to examine the effect of the self-determined nature of heutagogy congruent to what some referred to as liberatory, decolonised methods. In doing this, university teachers are interviewed on their experiences on Heutagogy as a liberatory method of teaching.

In chapter 10, *Decolonising Epistemologies: The Paradoxes of a Self-Colonised State*, Ramadikela, Msila and Abera explore the interesting case of Ethiopian history, a country that was never colonised by the European powers but became complicit in its own colonisation. The Ethiopian traditional education was based on a rich history, which could be traced to the Solomonic dynasty, and was highly supported by the Ethiopian Orthodox Church. The school was then religiously based provided in not only churches but also monasteries as well ancient. After the Second World War, the Ethiopians intensified attempts to modernise their education using external advisors from Britain and the United States of America and that is when major changes were introduced including the English language as medium of teaching and learning.

This chapter explores the path followed by a state that colonised itself thus creating several complexities as Eurocentric view minimised the importance of language, culture and epistemologies. The arguments in the chapter support a need for a dynamic model where the traditional educations system should not be marginalised instead it should be developed and combined with the Western models of education. The present system is a burden to learners who have to struggle with not only language of learning and teaching but a system that disregards Ethiopian.

Afolabi in *Lost in Translation: Revisiting Decolonisation Project in Nigerian Education* (chapter 11) examines the mantra on decolonising Nigerian education. Scholars have carried out several projects on how to decolonise teaching, such as the Fafunwa Education Project, and learning in Nigerian Education System, yet nothing has changed. Afolabi questions the paradox of using a colonial language, English, to debate decolonisation. He says this has posed a huge challenge to Nigerian languages in which students are taught and learn through a colonial language. He also examines the lack of an enabling environment to teaching, learning, and the political will that compounds the challenges of Nigerian education. The chapter raises questions, which include what prospects are there for African languages in teaching and learning? What challenges colonial languages pose on Nigerian education? Finally, the chapter examines the reasons behind the failure of the call for decolonisation and how the English language can be decolonised.

In *Transforming Leadership: Towards the Advancement of Decolonisation and Social Justice* (chapter 12), Setlhodi and Ramadikela focus on leadership and decolonisation. These authors write about the need to undo the teachings and learning of education as they pose pertinent questions: (i) how does one erase or unlearn what one has learnt and internalised over time? (ii) Why is it imperative to decolonise – what can be done to reconfigure acquired knowledge, skills, values, beliefs as well as habits) and (iii) does unlearning imply total negation of colonial teachings? Whilst raising these probing questions, these authors emphasise that decolonisation and transformation are not synonymous. The authors claim that decolonising implies freeing selves from imperialist ideologies and imposition, and it underscores the reclaiming identity and following our distinct makeup to bring about social justice.

In the final chapter, Agbogun focuses on the *Western Thought and African Presence in Biblical Interpretation* (chapter 13). The Bible has over the epochs been explained in particular ways that appears to suit the Western narrators. Agbogun argues that the exegesis from the original Bible was drawn from a text what was originally written in Greek or Hebrew languages. The Bible then has this complexity of being drawn from particular cultures with antiquated expressions. The synoptic gospels have similarities in most of the narratives of Jesus' life and ministry. The cumulative result and conclusion of the life and ministry of Jesus are suffering, death and resurrection, which translated into the completion of salvation and redemption for humankind according to the Bible. Decolonising the interpretation of the Bible means imagining the African perspectives within the stories of the Bible. Agbogun pushes for the contextualisation and highlighting the Bible's relevance. This chapter also demonstrates how Western knowledge has misled people in biblical interpretation as it defines Africa and Africans in the New Testament.

References

Botwe-Asamoah, K. 2005. *Kwame Nkrumah's Politico-Cultural Thought and policies: An African-Centered Paradigm for the Second Phase of the African Revolution.* New York: Routledge.

Diop, C.A. 2000. *Towards the African Renaissance: Essays in African Culture and Development, 1946-1960.* New Jersey: Red Sea Press.

Freire, P. 1970. *Pedagogy of the Oppressed.* New York: Continuum.

Green, M. 1998. *Transforming Higher Education: Views from Leaders Around the World.* Phoenix: American Council on Education/ORYX Press.

Heleta, S. 2016. Decolonisation of Higher Education: Dismantling Epistemic Violence and Eurocentrism in South Africa. *Transformation in Higher Education*, 1(1):1-9. http://dx.doi.org/10.4102/the.v1i1.9

Macedo, D. 1993. Literacy for Stupidification: The Pedagogy of Big Lies. *Harvard Educational Review*, 63(2):183-207.

Macedo, D. 2000. *Introduction to N. Chomsky's Chomsky on Miseducation.* Lanham: Rowman & Littlefield Publishers. https://doi.org/10.17763/haer.63.2.c626327827177714

Mazrui, A. 1980. *The African Condition: A Political Diagnosis.* London: Heinemann.

Mazrui, A. 2005. Pan Africanism and the Intellectuals: Rise, Decline and Revival. In: T. Mkandawire (ed.), *African Intellectuals: Rethinking Politics, Language, Gender and Development.* London: Zed Books.

Mbeki, T. 1998. *Africa – The Time Has Come.* Cape Town: Tafelberg.

Mbeki, T. 2017. *Speech of the TMF patron Thabo Mbeki, on the occasion of his installation as Chancellor of the University of South Africa.* Unisa Campus, Pretoria, 27 February 2017.

Mphahlele, E. 1974. *The African Image.* New York: Praeger Publishers.

Mwesigire, B. *5 strategies for de-Westernising globalisation by Ali Mazrui.* [Online]. Available: https://bit.ly/2Avseil

Ndlovu-Gatsheni, S.J. 2018. *Epistemic Freedom in Africa: Deprovincialization and Decolonization.* London: Routledge. https://doi.org/10.4324/9780429492204

Nkrumah, K. 1964. *Consciencism: Philosophy and Ideology for De-colonization.* London: Heinemann.

Nyerere, J.K. 1970. *Nyerere: Freedom and Unity/Uhuru na Umoja.* Dar es Salaam: Oxford.

Shih, Y. 2018. Rethinking Paulo Freire's Dialogic Pedagogy and Its Implications for Teachers' Teaching. *Journal of Education and Learning*, 7(4):230-235. https://doi.org/10.5539/jel.v7n4p230

Shor, I. 1987. Educating the Educators: A Freirean Approach to the Crisis in Teacher Education. In: I. Shor (ed.), *Freire for the Classroom: A Sourcebook for Liberatory Teaching.* Portsmouth: Heinemann.

Stoke, W.T. 1997. Progressive Teacher Education: Consciousness, Identity and Knowledge. In: P. Freire, J.W. Fraser, D. Macedo, T. McKinnon & W.T. Stokes (eds.), *Mentoring the Mentor: A Critical Dialogue with Paulo Freire.* New York: Peter Lang.

Tabata, I.B. 1980. *Education for Barbarism Bantu (apartheid) Education in South Africa*. London: Unity Movement of South Africa.

Thomas, D.C. 1998. From Pax Africana to Global Africa. In: O.H. Kokole (ed.), *The Global African: Portrait of Ali. A. Mazrui*. Trenton: Africa World Press.

Vilby, K. 2007. *Independent? Tanzania's Challenges Since Uhuru*. Dar Es Salaam: E & D Vision Publishing LTD.

Wa Thiongo, N. 1993. *Moving the Centre: The Struggle for Cultural Freedoms*. New York: James Currey.

Wa Thiongo, N. 2014. *Globalectics and the Politics of Knowing*. Columbia: Columbia University Press.

Wilson, H.S. 1994. *African Decolonization*. London: Hodder Arnold.

Wiredu, K. 1987. The Concept of Mind with particular Reference to the language and Thought of the Akans. In: G. Floistad (ed.), *Contemporary Philosophy: A New Survey*. Boston: Martinus Nijhoff Publishers. https://doi.org/10.1007/978-94-009-3517-4_7

Zuma, J.G. 2014. *Address by President on the occasion of the 4th Pan African Youth Union Congress*. The Presidency. Republic of South Africa.

Contributors

Vuyisile Msila – Editor

Prof Msila is a former head of the Institute for African Renaissance at the University of South Africa. He has Masters degrees from Michigan State University, Nelson Mandela University and Vista University. His PhD is in Educational Management. He is currently a director at Unisa's Leadership and Transformation Department. Msila's interests include Africanisation and decolonisation of education, Politics of Education as well as Education Leadership. His previous books include *Ubuntu: Shaping the Current Workplace with African Wisdom* (2015) as well as *Africanising the Curriculum: Critical Theories and Perspectives* (2016).

Teshome Abera

Dr Abera has a PhD in Sociology, MA in Philosophy, EMBA in Industrial Relations and Project Management. He has published journal articles in the areas of Ethiopianism and Indigenous Knowledge Systems. His two books are Globalisation, its Challenge on Democracy and Effects on Africa (2019) as well asd Michel Foucault Power Knowledge Nexus (2012). Currently, he is serving as an assistant professor at Addis Ababa Science and Technology University.

Oluwaseun O Afolabi

Dr Afolabi holds a PhD in Peace and Conflict Studies Programme, Institute for Peace and Strategic Studies, University of Ibadan, Nigeria. He is a lecturer at Lead City University, Ibadan, Nigeria. He has academic publications of book, chapters in books and reputable journals. His current research interests include education, church history/conflict, religious conflict, conflict management and resolution.

Joseph Avwerosuoghene Agbogun

Reverend Agbogun was born into the family of Chief Samuel Agbogun of Ekpan-Ovu. His education qualifications include Bachelor in Religious Education from Seminary (2010), Bachelor of Arts in French (2004), Bachelor of Arts in Religious Education (2014) and Master of Arts in Religious Studies (2020) all from Delta State University, Abraka in Nigeria. He became minister of religion in 2006. He has published several journal articles.

Monicca Thulisile Bhuda

Ms Bhuda is a culture activist, an indigenous scholar and a lecturer at the University of Mpumalanga. She holds a Bachelor degree (Honours) in Indigenous Knowledge Systems (IKS), a Masters degree in Indigenous Knowledge Systems, both from the North-West University. She is currently a PhD candidate in African Indigenous Knowledge Systems.

Terefe Feyera Bulti

Dr. Bulti (PhD) has been working as a lecturer, researcher and leader in the sector of Ethiopian higher education institutions for the last 18 years. He is currently a president of Hope University College (Ethiopia). In the past, he was a Department Head at St. Mary's University, Faculty Dean and Associate Vice President. He also served at National Aviation College as Executive Dean. He received his PhD degree in Education Management from the University of South Africa. He earned his first degrees from Addis Ababa University specializing in Business Education.

Zamo Hlela

Dr. Hlela holds a PhD from the University of KwaZulu-Natal (UKZN). He is in the discipline of Adult Education in the School of Education at UKZN. He teaches curriculum studies, learning theories, research, community development at undergraduate and post-graduate level. His area of research interest is in the advancement of Afrocentrism in education. He is currently involved in a community engagement project that seek to develop a model for documenting histories of indigenous people from an Afrocentric perspective.

Luvuyo Lumkile Lalendle

Prof. Lalendle is an Executive Director in Planning and Quality Assurance at University of South Africa (Unisa). His career as an academic and senior administrator span over three decades. He has a PhD in Higher Education and Lifelong Education from Michigan State University. His publications are mainly on transformative discourses in Higher Education.

Sizakele Matlabe

Dr Matlabe holds a Doctor of Education Degree at the University of South Africa (UNISA), Master of Education, as well as Bachelor of Education degrees in Adult Education from University of North West Mafikeng Campus. Matlabe, is a Senior Lecturer in the Department of Educational Foundations, College of Education, at UNISA. She is a research project leader in *Researching Widowhood in Southern Africa*. Research interests include Widowhood, Adult Education, Higher Education and Open Distance Learning.

Hamza Omari Mokiwa

Dr Mokiwa holds a Doctorate in Curriculum Studies from the University of South Africa (UNISA). He is currently a Senior Lecturer at UNISA where he supervises; Masters and Doctoral students. He is a visiting researcher at the Illinois Institute of Technology (IIT), USA; and Josiah Kibirah University College of Tumaini University Makumira, Tanzania. His research interests include Science, Technology, Engineering and Mathematics education, decolonisation of education, as well as classroom practice.

Berrington Ntombela

Dr Ntombela holds a DPhil degree in English Language Studies. He currently works as a Senior Lecturer and Head of Department of English at the University of Zululand. Before joining the University of Zululand, he worked in the following places: SABIS University of Erbil in Kurdistan-Iraq as Head of English Department; Caledonian College of Engineering in the Sultanate of Oman as Senior Lecturer, and Higher College of Technology in Muscat, Sultanate of Oman as Lecturer. His research interests include linguistic imperialism, discourse analysis, semantics and ELT. He has published a collection of poems under the title *Hither and Yonder River*.

Maxwell Peprah Opoku

Dr Opoku holds first degree in Political Science from Kwame Nkrumah University of Science and Technology. He was appointed as Graduate Teaching Assistant at the Centre for Disability Studies, Department of Community Health. He was awarded scholarship by the African Union to study Master of Governance and Regional Integration at Pan African University, Cameroon. He also holds a doctoral degree in Education at University of Tasmania. His interests include disability research, special education, gender as well as inclusive education research.

Thabo Israel Pudi

Prof Pudi obtained his D.Ed degree in Technology Education from UNISA and his Masters degree in Critical and Creative thinking skills from the University of Johannesburg. Pudi's publication record spans several journals both local and international on various topics including technology and politics. He is the formerly sub-editor and editorial board member of the *Africa Education Review* journal. Pudi is also the author of three books in the series, *Stories of the liberation struggles in South Africa*.

Phillip Mahlodi Ramadikela

Dr Ramadikela is currently a school teacher at Kgadime Matsepe high school in Pretoria, South Africa. His qualifications include Higher Education Diploma (Postgraduate) (Unisa), Hons B.Ed (Education Management) Master of Education, as well as Doctor of Education in Education Management. His research interests include parental involvement, professional development of educators and professionalisation of educational leadership and management.

Itumeleng I Setlhodi

Dr Setlhodi heads quality assurance and enhancement in the college of education, University of South Africa. She also supervises Masters and Doctoral students in Educational Studies. Setlhodi holds a Doctor of Education and her research interests are in values education, educational leadership, Africanisation of education and practices, as well as gender and education.

Steve Sharra

Dr Sharra is a Malawian author, teacher educator, curriculum theorist and education policy expert. He holds a PhD in Curriculum, Teaching and Educational Policy (Michigan State University), and an MA in English Education (University of Iowa). He has taught at primary, secondary and university level in Malawi, Botswana and the USA. His research interests and academic publications are in education, peace studies, Pan-African studies and uMunthu epistemology.

J-F

Dr J-F is academic Coordinator and a Lecturer in Human Development at the University of Tasmania, Australia. A developmental specialist in child/adolescent mental health, psychiatric and psychological disorders. He has worked as a registered schoolteacher, private consultant as a criminologist for juvenile justice, guidance officer and educational psychologist.

Basic Education

Chapter One

Basic Education and Decolonisation in South Africa: Preparing Schools for New Challenges

Vuyisile Msila

Introduction: The Flight from Barbarism

In 1980, the educator I.B. Tabata wrote at length about a system of education in South Africa whose main objective was to indoctrinate and short-change learners; this was Bantu Education for blacks, a system Tabata referred to as *Education for Barbarism*. This system was devoid of epistemic freedom and laden with indoctrinating policies that separated the white child from the black child. The Bantu Education Act was based on segregation, legitimised apartheid policies, and extended the audacious objective of colonised education whilst breeding a system of education meant to demean the black child through knowledge that made the black community inferior. Apartheid education assumed that "whites should be separated from blacks (as a 'nation') and that Afrikaans-speaking children should be separated from English-speaking children (by mother-tongue schooling)" (Christie, 1988:165).

In fact, Peter Kallaway (1988) points out that education for blacks under apartheid was a means of restricting the development of the learners by distorting school knowledge to ensure control over the intellect of both the learners and their teachers. Furthermore, Kallaway opines that apartheid education not only domesticated but indoctrinated learners as well in order to entrench the master-servant relationship between whites and blacks. Based on the Christian National Education (CNE) ideology, knowledge taught in apartheid classrooms, legitimated white supremacy and subjects like history displayed white supremacy and black inferiority (Carrim, 2007). "White learners were taught subjects that led towards higher education and superior skilled and leadership roles in society. Their educational opportunities had unlimited horizons" (Karlsson, 2004). Furthermore, schools serving white learners had more funding per learner than schools serving black learners (Fiske & Ladd, 2005). Unfortunately, decades later, the apartheid legacy still looms large and the poor families still get poor education. Many black parents are still stuck in under resourced schools with unqualified and underqualified teachers (Van Der Berg, 2005; Fleisch, 2008; Msila, 2011; Spaull, 2015; Villette, 2016).

All these inequalities were part of the huge apartheid policy plan to uphold what Hendrik Verwoerd, apartheid architect and the then Minister of Native Affairs, declared in 1953, "There is no space for him (the Native child) in the European community above certain forms of labour".

The Afrikaner leaders of the National Party (NP) (which won the elections in 1948), continued the agenda of the British Colonial Government. Pam Christie (1988:37) quotes George Grey the British Governor of the Cape in 1855 who pointed out:

> If we leave the natives beyond our border ignorant barbarians, they will remain a race of troublesome marauders. We should try to make them a part of ourselves, with a common faith and common interests, useful servants, consumers of our goods, contributors to our revenue. Therefore, I propose that we make unremitting efforts to raise the natives in Christianity and civilisation…

The colonial intent was clear in this postulation. The British sought to colonise the mind of the indigenous people hence "make them a part of ourselves" through education and religion. Later, the Bantu Education Act was to spill over to universities in the 1950s as a Bill was introduced to produce segregated universities that would not only separate Black from White but the African from Indian and Coloured. The universities for Africans were further divided into Xhosa, Sotho and Zulu universities (Tabata, 1980).

Schools and universities' curricula taught the formal curriculum but what was more critical was the hidden curriculum, which among others, demonstrated that people are not and should not be equal in society. Sexism, superiority of Western knowledges, language policies, and dominant Western cultures are some of the examples that entrenched supremacy in the hidden curriculum. Currently, the attempts to Africanise and decolonise the university curricula are endeavours to address the barbaric attempts from apartheid and Western-oriented curricula at universities. This academic barbarism results from the consequences of the curriculum that has led to epistemicides, culturecides, linguicides and historicides amongst others (Ndlovu-Gatsheni, 2018). The unequal curriculum at institutions of higher learning has entrenched inequality and academic barbarism that stunts the development of Africans.

The challenge to decolonialism today is that zombie ideas are perpetuated through zombie leadership. Smyth (2017) states that zombie leadership is a set of dead debunked ideas supreme in universities, and have been accompanied by weird rituals and practices for so long; and he says that this bizarre behaviour is a version of witchcraft. Western hegemonies have been shown to be dangerous and misleading. Based on colonial notions of domination, they marginalise other knowledges and debar Africans from expressing their own knowledges as central. For this reason, Ndlovu-Gatsheni (2018) expresses the need to deprovincialise Europe, as Africa is decolonised. This is a need to dispel the myth and the witchcraft of colonialism as Africa's knowledge is brought to the centre as well. Some knowledges in the curricula of education institutions in Africa are spurious, nebulous and segregating in nature and these are based on zombie ideas that form the essence of academic barbarism.

O'Sullivan (2016) writes about ways in which institutions of learning continue with barbaric academic practices. The role of post-apartheid education institutions is to ensure a system of education that not only humanises but that which champions social justice principles. Schools should not be based on competition that upholds the ideology of barbarism. Academic barbarism brutalises people as it alienates them from their cultures. It entrenches dehumanisation and renders the institutions of learning irrelevant. The South African education ministry's calls to refocus on languages of education, humanising instruction and introducing history curricula in all grades are all commendable in that they seek to address the barbarism entrenched in our system over decades of apartheid domination (DBE, 2018).

This chapter focuses on a few aspects that look at the decolonisation of education in schools:

o   Contexts of Post-apartheid Education
o   Why Decolonisation?
o   Pedagogy Fit for Purpose: Mphahlele on Humanism in Education
o   Ecologies of Knowledge: Eschewing the Dominant Culture
o   Preparing Teachers for Liberatory Teaching
o   Conclusion

Contexts of Post-apartheid Education

We should never minimise the triumph of post-apartheid education over the draconian apartheid system, which as seen above, offered several systems of education including white education system and Bantu Education. However, later, this brought several paradoxes, which include parents moving away from historically black schools in the townships. Many have argued that this exodus has left many historically black schools with a decrepit system of education with underperforming learners and failing schools (Msila, 2004). The apartheid legacy still pervades decades after the fall of apartheid. Numerous learners from historically black schools are unlikely to reach matric and when they do, they are more likely to have lower grades (Spaull, 2015). Therefore, schools have a huge role in pushing for equity as they close the achievement gaps among all schools. Whilst access might have improved in South Africa, schools must strive for quality, socially just and relevant education. Several arguments have highlighted how South African education is characterised by two systems of education. Van der Berg, Taylor, Gustafson, Spaull and Armstrong (2011) posit:

> Within South Africa, the quality of education varies widely. Several authors characterise the South African school system as effectively consisting of two differently functioning sub-systems (Fleisch, 2008; Van der Berg, 2008; Taylor & Yu, 2009). The majority of children are located in the historically disadvantaged system, which still serves mainly black and coloured children. Learners in these schools typically demonstrate low proficiency in reading, writing and numeracy. The second sub-system consists mostly of schools that historically served white children and produces educational achievement closer to norms of developed countries.

Education success appears to be determined by wealth or socio-economic status of the families where the learners come from. This system is still undergirded by epistemic violence and vestiges of colonial principles and beliefs. The South African education system needs the decolonisation to engender equality, relevance and to affirm the identity of the African children. Arguably, various features of the present education still reflect the vestiges of the epistemic violence that characterised mission and apartheid education. Supporting learning materials used such as textbooks, the curricula, teaching methodology are some of the aspects that signify the need for a decolonised system of education.

The debates of decolonising education in South Africa have largely been concentrated on higher education institutions. Yet, it is in primary schools and high schools where the journey for a decolonised curriculum should begin. The struggles of the Fallists Movements in 2015 should have opened up the debates for schools as well. The curriculum in South African schools has remained largely Western with inadequate traces of a decolonised curriculum that varies from school to school and from educator to educator. The calls to decolonise basic education is a call to free and meaningful African education ensuring that it instils knowledges that would compete equally with other (Western) knowledges.

The present contexts seek us to reframe and reinvent the practice and roles of the school. Decolonisation needs to move us from barbarity to freedom, from brainwashing classrooms to enriching critical thinking sites, from stunted growth to intellectual freedom and expression. The gift of decolonised education is immense for our learners and the future in that it will ensure that the learners move beyond the realm of bondage of history to liberatory education that ensure the magnification but not the romanticisation of the African continent.

Why Decolonisation?

There are usually practical questions posed as to how institutions (including schools) can decolonise – where do they start? Who should be involved? What if institutions do not decolonise? What will they benefit if they do? Others even argue for a common understanding of terms. Decolonising and decolonisation are terms that have been explicated and defined by various education role-players and experts. Writing about the state of the First nations people in Canada McGregor (2012) describes the concept decolonising as:

A critical response to imperialism and colonialism:
- Working to advance the interests of indigenous peoples by transforming what is important in settler societies.
- Involving more than changes to formal political power, requires long-term changes to all structures in society (i.e. Education)

Decolonising the schooling system refers to the dismantling of colonial and apartheid systems, systems that were responsible for the oppressive and marginalising divisions discussed above. The colonial and apartheid legacies still loom large in society. Despicable conditions evident in historically black schools reflect decades of marginalising and alienating education. The calls for decolonisation of schools are calls to empower learners, teachers and parents to enable them to resuscitate the school system to serve all equally. Role-players should negate the coloniality of power as they give voice to learners and teachers who might otherwise be alienated by their schools and the inflexible education system. Apartheid education regarded learners as tabula rasas (blank slates).

Furthermore, on the one hand Fundamental Pedagogics literature portrayed the child in and out of school as a pardoned sinner, immature, helpless and dependent (Viljoen & Pienaar, 1972: Killian & Viljoen, 1974; Engelbrecht & Lubbe, 1979; Steyn et al., 1988). On the other hand, the teacher was regarded as an adult and a responsible person who was supposed to impart knowledge on the blank slate personified by the learner.

Yet, decolonisation demonstrates that learners always bring knowledge to the classroom for learners bring values, experiences and histories. Ruddock (2018) argues that when we decolonise education we promote the idea that what is in the centre is changing, "We compel learners to consider other potential centres; we require those who have benefitted from having their own paradigms centralised to occupy the marginal spaces too" (Ruddock, 2018). In decolonial classrooms learners expand their knowledge as the spaces give them an opportunity to experience the ecologies of knowledge.

The ongoing debates on decolonisation of education in South Africa have enabled the society to pose new questions about the role of education. The decolonial debates have enabled communities to rethink what education stands for as they search for education that is fit for purpose. Furthermore, decolonisation has made it possible for all education's role-players to examine education within the context of transformation. Learners and teachers have now legitimised their right to struggle and negotiate for social justice and equity within a system that appears hostile to equality. The society is also gradually learning about the need to apply a culturally relevant pedagogy. Over decades, we have witnessed pedagogical violence that excluded learner involvement. Numerous challenges that public schools face are historical and they include poverty, families' socio-economic factors, language, literacy and technology issues, weak school governance and non-existent parental involvement. In addition to these, schools continue to present curricula that are irrelevant and pedagogy that marginalises learners. It has also been apparent that we cannot decolonise the curriculum without Africanising it first. Africanising education transforms Western models as it injects the rules of Africa conscious pedagogy. Africanisation is the antidote to a curriculum of stupidification for it opposes epithets of oppression and what Macedo (1993) refers to as pedagogy of lies.

Decolonised classrooms accommodate the Freirean agenda in teacher education. Among these are critical literacy and situated pedagogy. Relevant, Africanised curricula will ensure that through critical literacy, all learning areas will develop reading, thinking and writing. Shor (1987:24) argues, "Critical literacy invites teachers and students to problematize all subjects of study that is to understand existing knowledge as a historical product deeply invested with the values of those who developed such knowledge."

A decolonised programme would seek to use situated pedagogy whose goal is to make certain that teachers situate learning in the learners' cultures. Shor (1987:24) contends that these cultures include "their literacy, their themes, their present cognitive and affective levels, their aspirations, their daily lives" (Shor, 1987:24). Mignolo (2007) points out that the decolonial project opposes colonialism and delinks from Eurocentrism as it seeks to reclaim the expression of non-Western cosmologies. It is in this context that decolonised classrooms should enable learners and their teachers to be able to examine the prescribed reading materials' subliminal messages of bias. The learners' engagement with the learning material (texts) should also enable them to be perceptive so that they can contest social injustice and oppression of the marginalised communities.

Mendoza and Garza (2010:40) posit:
> Critical literacy goes beyond critically analysing and understanding texts. It is a process that works with the written language in order to bring to light social injustices and inequities that take place in the world. Besides reading the written word, this approach to literacy focuses on leading

Pedagogy Fit for Purpose: Mphahlele on Humanism in Education

The need for an African identity in universities in Africa was a vision for many prominent African intellectuals. The South African illustrious academic Ezekiel Mphahlele, wrote about the need for an African Humanism. Mphahlele established the Funda Centre in Soweto on his return from exile. The curriculum he drew up for Funda Centre can teach our current experts ways in which they can decolonise the curriculum. Mphahlele spoke of this concept, African Humanism that refers to communality and the concepts conjured traditional African philosophy. To emphasise this concept Mphahlele (2002) contended:
> The African begins with the community and then determined what the individual's place and role should be in relation to the community […] Man finds fulfilment not as a separate individual but within a family and community.

Perhaps Mphahlele was the first academic in South Africa to draw a practical curriculum for Africans, his attention was on African Consciousness and emphasised the need for a curriculum that revives consciousness. Naidoo (1984) says about Mphahlele and African Consciousness:

> Es'kia Mphahlele believed that the regeneration of African consciousness is essential to real African development and progress. African consciousness arises from the norms and values inherent in the traditional way of life. These values were marginalised under colonialism and apartheid when African people were forces to adopt Western norms and values. As a result, they developed a divided consciousness and became spiritually and psychologically weak. In order to regain the pride, dignity, strength, and independence of the African spirits, it is necessary to return to the traditional values. As African people have lost the context that gave rise to these values, regeneration of the African consciousness now depends on the formal articulation of traditional values. And this is what Es'kia Mphahlele has provided in his philosophy of African Humanism. In his articles he sets out the tenets of African Humanism and in his stories and novels, he illustrates the struggle to maintain African values. A study of his writings, therefore, will lead to an understanding of humanism that is essentially African.

Funda Centre offered what Mphahlele termed 'integrated studies' that cut across disciplinary boundaries. The themes of the lectures included the following:

- Know Your Country: South Africa
- Know Your Continent: Africa
- Know Your Environment
- Family Life
- Black Consciousness
- Know Your Civics
- Growing Up in South Africa
- The Arts and Their Social Environment
- The Ascent of Man

Mphahlele understood the anomalies of Bantu Education and worked hard to theorise what needed to be done to retain the dignity of the black learner. His themes of education above are in sync with the ideals of decolonisation. The idea of infusing Black Consciousness philosophy is important in bringing back the dignity of the black learner who was traumatised by Bantu Education. Black Consciousness is necessary to sensitise both black and white learners of the need to see the potential of a free society where black learners and white learners experience equality. There can be no social justice, no African Renaissance if black learners suffer the inferiority complex planted by Bantu Education whose objectives still loom large in African societies today. Black Consciousness should also be reflected in subjects such as history because history as portrayed in today's literature reflects blacks in a past that is barbaric and backward. History needs to demonstrate the existence of black heroes as well (Rodney, 1973; Biko, 1987; Asante, 1995). Asante (1995) argues that hegemonic Eurocentric education stifles what should be taught in schools and this can exist as long as whites maintain that blacks have never contributed to world civilisation.

On history and education, Biko (1987:29) writes:
> [...] the colonialists were not satisfied merely with holding a people in their grip and emptying the Native's brain of all form and content, they turned to the past of the oppressed people and distorted, disfigured and destroyed it. No longer was reference made to African culture, it became barbarism [...] The history of African society was reduced to tribal battles and internecine wars [...] No wonder the African child learns to hate his heritage in his days at school. So negative is the image presented to him that he tends to find solace only in close identification with the white society.

Several cases such as this one alienated the black child from education because they were represented in bad light, hence many might have desired the positive portrayal and privilege of whiteness.

In his plan, Mphahlele was more concerned with a system that would encompass various disciplines and involving human issues rather than disciplinary questions. Mphahlele had a conception of education that spelled out the purpose of education and can be seen to be in line with the ideals of decolonisation of education. He wrote at length about the concept of African Humanism, which is a philosophy to edify Africans. This needs to be part of education where Africans are taught to create bonds "where national political life is torn and poisoned by the manipulation of language and ethnic interests" (Mphahlele, 1974:36). The themes he set about for a decolonial African education were an endeavour to infuse this humanism into education. He perceived education as critical in changing people's lives – which humanism should be revolutionary and deal with the challenges of power, education and poverty. He also argues that humanism needs to bring a productive revolution where African values should translate into educational and economic planning. He also perceived education as a process critical in building identities. Through family, community, societal values the learner would be able to rid herself of alienation and embrace 'a vision of life'. Furthermore, Mphahlele sees life as a dialogue of two selves; the indigenous consciousness and the consciousness derived from the West. All those who have been colonised have these two selves. Education ought to harmonise the two and these should be harmonised through their 'organic vision of life'. The two selves are apt to fight, quarrel, despise each other, hug each other, concede each other's roles (Mphahlele, 1974:281).

Under the themes of understanding one's country and continent, family life and growing up in South Africa, Mphahlele was tackling a number of issues, what decolonised education in schools need today is strong communities with empowered parents. Empowered parents would uphold the teaching of culture as it enhances the school curriculum. Parents are also critical in creating learners' resilience and success. When empowered parents are involved, they will be able to make their children take charge of their learning. Learners will also glean much from family in building their country and continent. It is from strong families that children can learn about subjects such as gender-based violence and how to avert it. The violence witnessed in schools can be addressed constructively if parents and communities worked closely with schools to nurture the learners. The tenets of Mphahlele's African Humanism have the potential to liberate all role players in education as they reinforce the ideals of decolonisation.

African Humanism also embraces the ideals that seek to oppose ills such as patriarchy. Teaching and learning in schools should reflect feminist values as well for when these are present, they would lead to progressive democratic teaching. Feminist education in this sense means, "We enter into a dialogue with our students, meeting them as human beings, and learning with them in community" (Schniedewind, 1987:179). Various other Mphahlele-themes are critical, such as race and culture, the building of a single nation in South Africa and the question of national consciousness.

Higher education institutions cannot change society without the consciously thinking of a curriculum that would free the society from epistemic bondage and academic barbarism. Epistemic bondage means that the people cannot think because they do not have culture, they do not have history, no language and no knowledge. The curriculum reflects Western epistemologies, thus marginalising African knowledges. Curriculum under epistemic bondage also supports barbarism, which undervalues African knowledges and undermines the project of Pan-Africanism. As a result, irrelevant curricula continue to produce students who are disoriented and alienated from their ontological base. The example of language in South Africa currently is one example that shows how indigenous languages have been marginalised and students made to believe that it is the colonial languages such as French, English, Portuguese and English that dominate the education landscape in Africa. Epistemic bondage paralyses thinking, hence we talk of rethinking the curriculum, which is the fundamental issue when it comes to curriculum reforms at higher education institutions. The transformation of curriculum requires leadership that understands transformation otherwise the transformation of curriculum can be stalled. Leadership that does not understand the new paths of change will be just immersed in zombie leadership where leaders support outmoded ideas and by implication academic barbarism.

Ecologies of Knowledge: Eschewing the Dominant Culture

Transformed curricula require people who understand the need for epistemic freedom, which means that knowledge should be open in what is referred to as ecologies of knowledge. The Europeanisation of curriculum was intent on side lining Africa's knowledges and disregard indigenisation. Curriculum that does not take this into cognisance will be missing the mandate of the university under decolonisation of universities in Africa. When leaders lead curriculum transformation, they cannot divorce it from pedagogy. Usually in institutions of higher learning faculty tends to recycle old study materials and as such one will still find material that was prepared years before still in use albeit so irrelevant especially now, in times of transformation. Again, this is the unfairness, the academic barbarity of institutions of higher learning. There are several aspects that we need to look at as we address the episteme of learning in our institutions of higher learning especially in the attempt to build African institutions. The curriculum should respond to the debates on language, a debate that has become almost a taboo in higher education institutions seeking to transform. Throughout Africa, conscientious academics have been posing questions on how to bring indigenous languages to the fore. Some African philosophers have argued that without language African thinkers cannot be able to accurately move for their case thinking in exoglossic languages outside their own cultures. Linked to languages is culture; when Western or European knowledges were introduced, they destroyed the cultures of Africans through the domination of non-indigenous languages. It is difficult to think of a transformed curriculum without thinking about language. However, it should be clear that translating higher education's materials is not addressing the language dilemma. Simply replacing languages is also not addressing the language dilemma. Decolonisation is not about retaliation, but it is about consciously bringing Africa to the fore, it is about changing the consciousness, enriching the people with skills of reclaiming the education institutions.

The calls to use indigenous languages in education is a critical call towards decolonisation and African Renaissance. Cheik Anta Diop argued decades ago that it would be the African languages that should lead in the bringing of a rebirth in Africa. Mboup (2010) posits that, for Diop, history and language represent two among the three key components of cultural identity. Therefore, the Department of Basic Education acted in line with decolonisation principles when history was announced that it would be taught in various grades. Mboup (2010:2) explains:

> Historical conscience is crucial for the consolidation of national conscience and nation building, particularly in the case of a pluri-cultural and multi-lingual nation in the making. Among others, historical conscience refers to the feeling of belonging to the same community from a historical and socio-political point of view, and above all, from the consciousness of commonly shared aspirations, interests and value systems: in Diop's words (Ibid.:212), it is about that which distinguishes a cohesive *people* from the heterogeneous, inorganic *population* of a market.

Language, like history, will instil a sense of identity and national consciousness. McGregor (2012) argues that history is vital in a decolonised system because it allows learners to:

o   resist images and portrayals they see in the media, museums and other sources or stereotypes;
o   identify ways indigenous peoples demonstrate agency; and
o   questions myths and oversimplified narratives about colonisation ... and Eurocentric powers.

Preparing Teachers for Liberatory Teaching

The decolonisation and conscientisation of teachers is critical for decolonised pedagogies. "Educators today are tasked with developing lifelong learners who can survive and thrive in a global knowledge economy" (Blaschke, 2012). Yet what South Africa needs to avoid in the eve of a decolonised education system is a 1998-*de ja vu* where numerous teachers felt left out when the outcomes-based education was introduced in South African schools. Many found themselves deskilled, having been trained under a teacher training programmes that emphasised the banking model where the teacher was always a superior. Decolonised system will also be a huge leap from Western-oriented teacher training programmes. Decolonised classrooms will demand educators who are free to and knowledgeable to teach indigenous knowledges alongside other knowledges.

Liberatory teaching within the ambit of decolonised education means teaching for a purpose; it is a means to make meaning out of education as one teases out elements relevant for the learners' environment and it is critical teachers who employ critical consciousness who will be able to embrace ideals of liberatory teaching. It will be difficult for untransformed teachers to teach in liberatory ways. Decolonised classrooms will endeavor to use critical consciousness to combat ills of society. It should teach learners about ways of sharing power, critical nature of relevance and ways of shedding oppression. Johnson-Hunter and Risku (2003:101) point out:

> The application of a liberatory theory provides other rationale for critical consciousness. In *Teaching to Transgress*, hooks (1994) asserted that critical consciousness can help to combat the White supremacist, capitalist patriarchy (p. 48). In *The Peaceable Classroom*, O'Reilley (1993) stated that if students gain critical consciousness, they will rethink their preconceived ideas about war and violence. Thus, critical consciousness fosters the reduction of the oppression of ethnicity, gender, class, and violence.

In the calls for transformed, meaningful and relevant curricula all over the world is the expectation of teaching that would prepare learners for a changing society that requires a set of new different skills. In his work, Paulo Freire describes critical pedagogy, which is a system of education that changes the world learners live in, and critical pedagogy ensures that education does not alienate. Decolonisation, as explored in this presentation is one method that strives to enhance the social transformation as well as teacher and learner experience and problem posing, and dialogue are critical in this regard. Analysing Paulo Freire's work, Shor (1987:23) captures the role of dialogue teaching concisely:

> A dialogic class begins with problem posing discussion and sends powerful signals to learners that their participation is expected and needed. It will not be easy to learn the arts of dialogue because education now offers so little critical discussion and so few constructive peer exchanges. Dialogue calls for a teacher's art of intervention and art of restraint, so that the verbal density of a trained intellectual does not silence the verbal styles of unscholastic learners.

All learners need an education system that would help bring changes in society. Cappy (2016) describes the need for education to transform society and create a more socially just world. In fact, the calls for a decolonised system of education in South Africa seek to respond to this call for education for transformation.

The decolonial debates have unmasked a number of aspects that were concealed. As we discuss new curricula, transformative pedagogies and novel methods in a decolonial milieu, we all need to think about the need to rethink the university into the future. The transformative pedagogies can never be realised if we cannot focus on how we perceive thinking itself. In fact, decolonisation will be unreachable without thinking about thinking and how we examine systems that would rehumanise and bring life and social justice to education. Ronald Barnett and Soren Bengtsen (2017) discuss of a need for universities to refocus on epistemologies as they adjust their emphasis on pathways from a dissolution of knowledge to the emergence of new thinking. In addition, as demonstrated above in this presentation Barnett and Bengtsen highlight that there is a relationship between the university and knowledge. These authors also offer the idea of an ecological university, which they present as an optimistic university, which might offer a different way of thinking. This ecological optimistic university responds to at least seven ecosystems; knowledge, the economy, social institutions, learning, individual persons, culture, and the natural environment (Barnett & Bengtsen, 2017). The learning institutions that have undergone rethinking exist not only for local ontologies, but they seek inclusion of various epistemologies; it seeks to reflect the ecosystems of the world. The "new university has to be different from its entrepreneur counterparts". Furthermore, Barnett and Bengtsen (2017:10) contend:

> [...] knowledge can only be retained for the university – as a defining concept – if it is rethought. Accordingly, thinking itself and a new way of thinking the university at that has itself to come forward for consideration; and a thinking into the future and for the future.
>
> It may just be that the idea of the ecological university both furnishes a new way of understanding the university and of calling forth a new epistemology for the university that can serve it through the 21st century.

In Africa, the rethinking of the universities can be traced back to the colonial legacy. The university in Africa continues to rethink its role that has long been diluted by colonial and apartheid hegemonies. This has huge implications for basic education. Rethinking thinking in Africa means dismantling epistemic violence and Eurocentrism (Heleta, 2016). Furthermore, Heleta points out that, although direct colonial rule might have disappeared, colonialism pervades in various guises. Furthermore, universities need to completely reframe the curriculum and the pedagogy discussed above. Thus leading to the reconstruction of the curriculum. "This in no way means that decolonisation will lead to localization, isolation or only Africanisation of the curriculum. Africa will not be the only 'focus of the curriculum in the ethnocentric-particularist manner of [the current] Eurocentric approaches'" (Heleta, 2016:5). Rethinking of the curriculum means thinking broadly about the planetary nature of the curriculum. It means rethinking ways in which African knowledges can compete equally with the knowledges of the world.

Transforming the curriculum does not mean tinkering with the current curricula; it does not mean microwaving what we already have. Decolonisation of the curriculum means an overhaul of the curriculum as we have it today. Decolonisation should overhaul the education system and this means changing how we teach and how we learn. The present curricula as it tend to emphasise elitism as well as examinations, frequently disregarding knowledge. The learners have internalised this as well. Understanding decolonised curricula requires people who are able to grasp knowledge of their disciplines. Decolonised curricula are more rigorous and more determined to liberate the learner and the teacher. The classes need to be more liberating and more critical and conscientious. We need to understand the role of the teacher and the role of the learner, teaching strategies utilised. There is a difference between the traditional approaches and the new decolonial or transformative approaches. Reading the texts should be investigated as the learner and the teacher's experiences are enhanced. In South Africa's context, decolonisation will redeem the learners as they take charge of their learning.

Concluding Comments: Confronting Barbarism

The decolonisation of education debates in South African basic education is long overdue for learners and their educators, and South African schools should have long started to interrogate the dominant Western epistemologies. A decolonised system of education will be able to address the epistemic violence of the past engendered by colonial and apartheid education systems. A decolonised system of education implies a humanising education system espoused by Mphahlele above, a system that would liberate individual learners and edify groups of learners to depend on one another for knowledge generation as well as sustainable living. It is only through a compelling foundation of a decolonised basic education system that would produce learners who are ready for engaging liberatory higher education institutions.

However, South Africa has a burden of history, and without addressing the teacher consciousness and learner commitment, the initiatives to introduce a decolonised system will easily falter. Communities should play a critical role in transforming the system of education from closed colonised systems to a dismantled system of Western-oriented education. The re-education of educators will be central to the attainment of a decolonised system for if teachers do not meaningfully embrace transformation initiatives, the plan to decolonise will only be a pipe dream. Universities, community-based structures and political organisations should be among the institutions that take a lead in the fruition for a just, decolonised system of basic education.

Finally, we should know that decolonial pedagogy means the real renaissance to African schools. The application of African philosophies should magnify access to education and open more opportunities for indigent families. South Africa continues to need an education system that would bring unity and a magnified future. A decolonised system of education should also bring epistemological freedom that would see South Africa working in unity with other African states. African intellectuals like Nyerere (1970) perceive education as a keyword to development and is more important than anything else (Vilby, 2007). The importance of education should continue in South Africa's basic education as we introduce Infomartion and Communication Technology (ICT). But ICT should also be used within the decolonisation agenda and social justice principles. Zembylas (2009:23) contends that critical theory of ICT in education is needed and that is "a theorization that, on the one hand, develops 'criticality' about the uses of ICT as tools of social injustice and domination, and on the other hand, rejects the simplistic assumptions of digital divide. Implements that are used in a decolonised system of education should lead to true interdependence, intellectual freedom and applicability in our society". Julius Nyerere (1970) refers to the latter as education for self-reliance, and it should be this mammoth prize of self-reliance that a decolonised education system should move towards.

This chapter is adapted from a paper delivered as a keynote address at the Third Annual Basic Education Sector Lekgotla, 21 January 2019. Birchwood Hotel, Benoni, South Africa.

References

Asante, M.K. 1995. *The Afrocentric Idea in Education*. In: F.L. Hord & J.S. Lee (eds.), *I Am Because We Are*. Amherst: University of Massachusetts Press.

Barnett, R. & Bengtsen, S. 2017. Universities and Epistemology: From a Dissolution of Knowledge to the Emergence of a New Thinking. *Education Sciences*, 7(1):38. https://doi.org/10.3390/educsci7010038

Biko, S. 1987. *I Write What I like*. London: Heinemann.

Blaschke, L.M. 2012. *Heutagogy and Lifelong Learning: A Review of Heutagogical Practice*.

Cappy, C.L. 2016. Shifting the Future? Teachers as Agents of Social Change in South African Secondary Schools. *Education as Change*, 20(3):119-140. https://doi.org/10.17159/1947-9417/2016/1314

Carrim, N.H. 2007. *Human Rights and the Construction of Identities in South African Education*. Unpublished Doctoral Dissertation. Johannesburg: Wits University.

Christie, P. 1988. *The Right to Learn: The Struggle for Education in South Africa*. Braamfontein: Sached/Ravan.

Department of Basic Education (DBE). 2018. *Basic Education*. [Online]. Available: https://www.education.gov.za

Engelbrecht, S.W.B. & Lubbe, A.N.P. 1979. *History of Education and Theory of Education*. Goodwood: Via Africa.

Fiske, E.B. & Ladd, H.F. 2005. *Racial Equality in Education: How far Has South Africa Come?* Working Paper Series SAN05-03. January 2005, Terry Sanford Institute of Public Policy.

Fleisch, B. 2008. *Primary Education in Crisis: South African Schoolchildren Underachieve in Reading and Mathematics*. Cape Town: Juta.

Heleta, S. 2016. Decolonisation of Higher Education: Dismantling Epistemic Violence and Eurocentrism in South Africa. *Transformation in Higher Education*, 1(1):1-8. https://doi.org/10.4102/the.v1i1.9

Johnson-Hunter, P. & Risku, M.T. 2003. Paulo Freire's Liberatory Education and the Problem of Service Learning. *Journal of Hispanic Higher Education*, 2(1):98-108.

Kallaway, P. 1988. *From Bantu Education to People's Education in South Africa*. Cape Town: UCT.

Karlsson, J. 2004. Schooling Space: Where South Africans Learnt to Position Themselves Within the Hierachy of Apartheid Society. *Pedagogy, Culture and Society*, 12(3):327-346. https://doi.org/10.1080/14681360400200206

Kilian, C.J.G. & Viljoen, T. A. 1974. *Fundamental Pedagogics and Fundamental Structures*. Durban: Butterworths.

Landman W.A. 1981. *An Introductory Reader in Fundamental Pedagogics for the Teacher and the Student*. Cape Town: Juta.

Macedo, D. 1993. Literacy for Stupidification: The Pedagogy of Big Lies. *Harvard Educational Review*, 63(2):183-207.

Mazrui, A. 1996. *The African Renaissance: A Triple Legacy of Skills, Values and gender*. Keynote Address at the 5th General Conference of the African Academy of Sciences, held in Hammamet, Tunisia, 22-27 April 1996

Mboup, S.B. 2010. *An African Cultural Renaissance Perspective on Constitutionalism, Democracy, Peace, Justice and Shared Values: Challenges & Stakes for Statehood and Nation-building*. African Union: Study on Constitutionalism & Shared Values. pp. 1-32.

McGregor, H.E. 2012. *Decolonizing Pedagogies Teacher Reference Booklet for the Aboriginal Focus Schools*. Vancouver School Board.

Mendoza, M.S. & Garza, A. 2010. Critical Literacy: Changing the World through the Word. *McNair Scholars Research Journal*, 6(1): 39-44.

Mignolo, W. 2007. Delinking: The Rhetoric of Modernity, The Logic of Coloniality and the Grammar of Decoloniality. *Cultural Studies*, 21(3):449-514.

Mphahlele, E.1974. *The African Image*. New York: Praeger Publishers.

Mphahlele, E. 2002. The Fabric of African Culture and Religious beliefs. In: E. Mphahlele (ed.), *Es'kia: Education, African Humanism & Culture, Social Consciousness, Literary Appreciation*. Cape Town: Kwela.

Msila, V. 2005. The Education Exodus: The Flight from Township Schools. *Africa Education Review*, 2(2):173-188. https://doi.org/10.1080/18146620508566299

Msila, V. 2011. School Choice – As if Black African Learners matter: Black African Learners' Views on Chooisng Schools in South Africa. *Mevlana International Journal of Education*, 1(1):1-14.

Naidoo, M. 1984. *Eskia Mphahlele: Father Come Home*. Johannesburg: Ravan Press. [Online]. Available: https://bit.ly/2PAcFdm

Ndlovu-Gatsheni, S.J. 2018. *Epistemic Freedom in Africa: Deprovincialisation and Decolonisation*. London: Routledge. https://doi.org/10.4324/9780429492204

Nyerere, J.K. 1970. *Nyerere: Freedom and Unity/Uhuru na Umoja*. Dar es Salaam: Oxford.

O'Sullivan, M. 2016. *Academic barbarism, Universities and Inequality*. London: Palgrave. https://doi.org/10.1057/9781137547613

Rodney, W. 1973. *How Europe Underdeveloped Africa*. London: Bogle-L'Ouverture Publications.

Ruddock, P. 2018. *Decolonising Education in South Africa*. [Online]. Available: https://bit.ly/30DVOg6

Schniedewind, N. 1987. Feminist Values: Guidelines for Teaching Methodology in Women's Studies. In: I. Shor (ed.), *Freire for the Classroom: A Sourcebook for Liberatory Teaching*. Portsmouth: Heinemann.

Shor, I. 1987. Educating the Educators: A Freirean Approach to the crisis in Teacher Education. In: I. Shor (ed.), *Freire for the Classroom: A Sourcebook for Liberatory Teaching*. Portsmouth: Boyton/Cook.

Shor, I. 1999. What is Critical Literacy? *Journal of Pedagogy, Pluralism, and Practice*, 1(4). Article 2. [Online]. Available: https://bit.ly/3a3kbXD

Smyth, J. 2017. *The Toxic University: Zombie Leadership, Academic Rock Stars and Neoliberal ideology*. London: Palgrave. https://doi.org/10.1057/978-1-137-54968-6

Spaull, N. 2015. Schooling in South Africa: How Low-Quality Education Becomes a Poverty Trap. *South African Child Gauge 2015*. pp. 34-41.

Steyn, P.D.G., Bisschoff, T.C., Behr, A.L. & Vos, A. J. 1988. *Education 3: The Philosophical Foundations of Education*. Cape Town: Maskew Miller Longman.

Tabata, I.B. 1980. *Education for Barbarism*. London: Unity Movement of South Africa.

This is Africa. 2017. *Ngugi Wa Thiongo Calls for Preservation and Inclusion of African Languages In Learning Institutions*. [Online]. Available: https://bit.ly/33lkg1P

Van der Berg, S. 2005. *Apartheid's Eduring Legacy: Inequalities in Education*. Paper to Oxford University? University of Stellenbosch Conference on The South African Economic Policy Under Democracy: A 10-Year Review, Stellenbosch, 27-28 October 2005.

Van der Berg, S., Taylor, S., Gustafson, M., Spaull, N. & Armstrong, P. 2011. *Improving Education Quality in South Africa. Report for the National Planning Commission*. Department of Economics, Stellenbosch University. Stellenbosch: University of Stellenbosch.

Vilby, K. 2007. *Independent? Tanzania's Challenges since Uhuru: A Second Generation Nation in a Globalised World*. Dar es Salaam: E & D Vision Publishing Ltd.

Villette, F. 2016. The Effects of Apartheid's Unequal Education System Can Still be Felt Today. *Cape Times*, 15 June.

Viljoen, T.A. & Pienaar, J.J. 1972. *Fundamental Pedagogics*. Durban: Butterworths.

Wa Thiongo, N. 1993. *Moving the Centre: The Struggle for Cultural Freedoms*. New York: James Currey.

Zembylas, M. 2009. ICT for Education, Development and Social Justice: Some Theoretical Issues. In: C. Vrasidas, M. Zembylas & G.V. Glass (eds.), *ICT for Education, Development, and Social Justice*. Arizona: IAP.

Chapter Two

Indigenising Mathematics in Schools: Why Ethnomathematics Matters

Monicca T. Bhuda
Thabo I. Pudi

Ethnomathematics Changing the Culture of Teaching

The existence of ethnomathematics is a testimony that mathematics is not only from the Western epistemology. Katz (1994) argues that numerous mathematical ideas "grew out of the needs of various cultures around the world, it is vitally important that students in Western nations be exposed to the fact that mathematics is a universal phenomenon". Mathematics grew out of the needs of the various kinds of people around the world over centuries. Additionally, Katz (1994:26) explains:

> The mathematical ideas to be considered developed out of specific needs in the cultures involved and although the ideas were not developed by people we would call 'mathematicians', all of these concepts were explored further, either in the original civilization or in later ones, far beyond the immediate context of the original problem. Students also learn in this way, by beginning with the consideration of a specific problem and then following the ideas further to try to answer new questions […] It is vitally important that modern curricula, particularly at the secondary level, the level at which most of the ideas here are first introduced, incorporate materials like the ones presented in order to broaden our students' understanding not only of mathematics but of the world in which we live.

Eurocentrism has denied ethnomathematics its rightful place among other knowledges as learners in many African schools are underachieving in mathematics. Gerdes (1994) also contends that the current African education is elitist and tends to favour foreign knowledges. African classrooms are not using what Zaslavsky (1973) referred to as sociomathematics, which may be considered a forerunner of ethnomathematics. Gerdes (1994) traces the history of mathematical activity in Africa and postulates that women were the first mathematicians, as they had to keep their cycle using the lunar calendar. Gerdes cites Zaslavsky who traced mathematics back to Ishango (the present day Zaire). Zaslavsky presented a bone dated between 9 000 and 6 500 BC that was used by the Ishango people to tally as it had notches as well as tallying marks. There were also several small mathematical instruments used by the San in South Africa around 3 500 BC. Gerdes also cites Bogoshi and others research which was reported in 1987 after they had discovered an older mathematical artefact. Gerdes (1994:348) quotes Bogoshi:

> A small piece of the fibula of a baboon, marked with 29 clearly defined notches, may rank as the oldest mathematical artefact known. Discovered in the early seventies during an excavation of Border Cave in the Lebombo Mountains between South Africa and Swaziland, the bone has been dated to approximately 35 000 BC. They note that the bone "resembles calendar sticks still in use today by Bushmen clans in Namibia".

The passion for mathematics can be traced in indigenous games around Africa long before the advent of the Western hegemony. African traditional games across the Continent demonstrate that indigenous people have used mathematics from time immemorial. Experts have questioned the reason why schools in Africa in particular do not use indigenous mathematics to enhance performance in mathematics. Forbes (2018) claims that there is alarming underperformance in mathematics worldwide and conscientious teachers and parents have searched for better pedagogical practices. Mathematics has the potential to marginalise many students who do not find their culture reflected in that learning area.

Furthermore, in an age of social justice education and inclusion, ethnomathematics is ideal because it expresses a relationship between mathematics and culture (Forbes, 2018). In line with social justice principles, the teaching of ethnomathematics introduces the idea of culturally sensitive teaching strategies. Around the world, research has shown how indigenous learners are failing mathematics because of alienating nature in classrooms. Forbes (2018:16) argues, "For example, the low achievement of indigenous (native, Aboriginal) students in comparison to their non-native counterparts within Canada and other countries such as Australia, America, and New Zealand is associated with a disconnection between indigenous and Western ways of knowing". Tylenda (2015) cites Bremigan who also emphasises that ethnomathematics enables teachers to relate mathematical knowledge with their learners; furthermore, in classrooms the teachers can help learners make connections between mathematics and the world that surrounds them. This then means that when teachers are professionally developed to incorporate various cultures into mathematics education, they will be encouraged to engage their learners in effective and meaningful relevant mathematical instruction (Tylenda, 2015). Francois (2009) states that initially ethnomathematics was reserved for the nonliterate people. However, today some Western classrooms have found it necessary to respond to cultural diversity occurring in every classroom (Francois, 2009). Ethnomathematics has been necessitated by the existence of classrooms that embrace ethnical, linguistic, gender, social and cultural diversity (Francois, 2009).

Sunzuma and Maharaj (2019) point out that geometry and culture are interrelated, and this makes school geometry linked to environment as well as culture in which it is taught. In fact, Sunzuma and Maharaj claim that teachers should not avoid geometry and that learners perform badly in mathematics because teachers have a lack of content knowledge. This chapter examines why ethnomathematics is crucial for (South) African schools today. Some of the subtopics that will be discussed are, Ethnomathematics – A Methodology for Decolonisation; Critical Indigenous Theory; Teaching Ethnomathematics; Challenges of Integrating Ethnomathematics; and The future of Ethnomathematics in South African Schools.

Ethnomathematics – A Methodology for Decolonisation

Colonial education marginalised African methodologies in all learning areas with no recognition of the fecundity of the traditional or indigenous cultures. Teacher education programmes ought to realise the potency of ethnomathematics in an attempt to decolonise mathematics. Schools around the world have become so heterogeneous as families migrate continuously. Shirley (2001:85) opines, "Intracontinental migration brings newcomers to African schools, east Asians and Latinos, in schools where sometimes as many as twenty languages are spoken by the students". Like other countries of the world, South African schools are fast reflecting the diversity found in various African societies as families from numerous African states gravitate towards South Africa for economic reasons. Learners in numerous South African schools can speak up to 15 African languages. This means a richness of culture and history that has a potential to enhance teaching methodologies of learning areas, including mathematics. Such classrooms lead to diverse environments that is enhanced by a variety of values and cross-cultural communication. In such classrooms, teachers need to be open-minded and understand that mathematics is not the property of the West (Shirley, 2001). In ethnomathematics classrooms, the following are critical:

- Multiculturalism,
- communication,
- connections, and
- innovative teaching strategies such as traditional games.

Shirley (2001) highlights the first three and we have observed the last one on traditional games in South Africa. Below the focus is on each of the factors above.

Multiculturalism and Ethnomathematics Classrooms

Shirley (2001) argues that multiculturalism has become critical in diverse classrooms. Shirley adds that mathematics textbooks around the world use multicultural themes in expositions, examples, and regular exercises. The history of mathematics has magnified its scope to include mathematics from non-European sources. All these are aspects that teacher education programmes need to include. Multiculturalism is an effective concept to describe education that incorporates histories, cultures, texts, and practices. Ethnomathematics gleans from these various qualities. Multiculturalism can be perceived as a form of transformation in education, an education that seeks to include rather than exclude. Furthermore, the multicultural idea behind ethnomathematics alludes to equity and social justice in the teaching and learning of mathematics. School mathematics is likely to show more fragmentation in education as it specifically supports Western-oriented mathematics.

Gay (2004) asserts that a multicultural education boosts academic success and prepares learners for roles as productive citizens. Teachers in effective, diverse classrooms should use multicultural content to teach reading, mathematics, science, and social science (Gay, 2004). Furthermore, Gay (2004:33) argues:

> For example, teachers could demonstrate mathematical concepts, such as less than/greater than, percentages, ratios, and probabilities using ethnic demographics. Younger children could consider the ethnic and racial distributions in their own classrooms, discussing which group's representation is greater than, less than, or equal to another's. Older students could collect statistics about ethnic distributions on a larger scale and use them to make more sophisticated calculations, such as converting numbers to percentages and displaying ethnic demographics on graphs.

The circumstances in these multicultural classrooms will enable the teachers to stimulate learners to use critical analyses during lessons as they appreciate different cultures. Gay also adds that in developing a curriculum for multicultural classrooms, two categories of curriculum development are critical, and these are reality/representation and relevance.

Communication in Ethnomathematics Classrooms

Shirley (2001) contends that there is much necessity for learners to communicate mathematics thinking vividly in multicultural classrooms. Shirley (2001:86) cites the National Council of the Teachers of Mathematics (NCTM), which argues that programmes should enable learners to "communicate their mathematical thinking coherently and clearly to peers, teachers, and others". Furthermore, Shirley avers that teachers should encourage the participation of all learners and underscore the importance of every learners' contribution to the learning process. Analysing what others say is critical in ethnomathematics classrooms. Widada, Herawaty, Yanti and Izzawati (2018) state that learning mathematics needs the leaners to communicate effectively and this includes verbal as well as written communication. Looking closely at Widada et al.'s model of learning mathematics, these authors point out that "learning with an ethnomathematics-based realistic mathematical approach has been able to improve mathematical abilities, including mathematics communication" (Widada et al., 2018:881). In enhancing communication, the learners in multicultural classrooms will communicate or interact with one another. The learners can start with the local environment as a beginning of learning because local culture makes it easy for learners to engage in horizontal mathematising (Widada et al., 2018). Widada et al. (2018) also point out that realistic learning model based on ethnomathematics helps learners in abstraction, idealisation, and generalisation.

Connections drawn in Ethnomathematics Classrooms

Making connections in ethnomathematics refers to finding links within mathematics, between mathematics and other subject areas, looking at mathematics as a learning area that is part of the learners' everyday experience (Shirley, 2001). Le Roux (2002) emphasises the need for teachers to be culturally competent communicators. Effective ethnomathematics teaching will make teachers to be sensitive to several aspects, which include intercultural knowledge and mutual enrichment between culturally diverse learners. Ethnomathematics teachers ought to have the knowledge of culture to be effective in classrooms so that they could be able to make connections between mathematics with culture.

Anderson-Pence (2016) declares that teachers should always help learners make connections between different factors of mathematical thinking. This then means that opportunities presented for learners' learning play a critical role in advancing mathematical competence (Anderson-Pence, 2013). Mathematics should find these connections otherwise it will be divorced from real life – this interferes with meaningful problem solving. Naresh (2015) also maintains the need for a mathematics curriculum to empower learners through the promotion of meaningful connections designed between ethnomathematics theory and practice and demonstrate how this curriculum can help address the key areas of a critical ethnomathematics curriculum. Naresh (2015) also mentions several important connections in ethnomathematics classrooms and these include connections between culture, context and mathematics; mathematical tasks and local or global contexts; as well as contexts between everyday mathematics and academic mathematics.

Games as Innovation in Ethnomathematics Classrooms

Nkopodi and Mosimege (2009) state that it is important to include games when learning about mathematics, especially ethnomathematics. Nkopodi and Mosimege also maintain that learners find it easy to communicate in mathematics classrooms and this may work well in multicultural classrooms as well. Ethnomathematics and its rich methodologies are found in the community ceremonies and rituals, in story-telling, proverbs, folktales, recitation, demonstration, sport, reasoning, riddles, praise, songs, word games, puzzles, tongue-twisters, dance, music, and other education-centered activities (Ngara, 2007).

Games provide an opportunity for teachers to give learners a platform to present common games they play at home, bring them into the classroom, allow learners to play them then later introduce a topic that has concepts and relate them to those found in the games. In that fashion, learners will be able to understand the content in lessons since it will speak to their cultural background. According to Bruner (1990), constructivists encourage children to constantly use prior knowledge to understand new and complex experiences and information, which they scaffold into unique knowledge structures.

Before Rome, when there was no Greece and Europe was still in the stone age 4 500 years ago, Africans were practicing mathematics and making it part of their daily lives. For instance, countries in Southern Africa have mathematics that is imbedded in peoples' cultural practices. Such mathematics is in textile technologies, beadwork, rock art, mural art, and indigenous games. In South Africa, according to Grine, Henshilwood and Sealy (2000), the oldest ethnomathematical artefact is the red ochre which is engraved with geometric designs at Blombos outside Cape

Town, South Africa, dating between 80 000 and 100 000 years. The discovery at Blombos shows that the Sothern Africans were the first to invent the concept of symbolic behaviour, symbolic thought, and symbolic logic. Ethnomathematics can be further seen from the beadwork and mural art of the Ndebele, which is expressed, as symmetrical geometry. The Ndebele people started using symmetrical geometry as a way of communication after they lost the war to the Dutch speaking Boers in 1849-1883, and it is known that this was an instruction from the gods of the cosmos to use the geometric shapes as a form of communication. Since the 19th century, symmetrical geometry has been used for cultural significance in the Ndebele culture and used for communication, spiritual purposes, and symbolism.

Ethnomathematics amongst the Ndebele continues to be visible in their indigenous games. These indigenous games are common in other cultural groups of South Africa and they are identified with different names. Indigenous games like *diketo, morabaraba,* and *moruba* have an ability to teach people social skills and mathematics. It is estimated that the history of indigenous games in South Africa dates back to before the 19th century and the history of all games practiced in different ethnic groups differs with time. Indigenous people of South Africa have been migrating on the continent for decades and were separated from their initial cultural groups over time due to unavoidable external factors like weather conditions and colonialism, which makes it difficult to trace when they started practicing indigenous games. Over the years, indigenous games in South Africa have been used as tools of solving problems, counting, and tracking time by the old and young. Therefore, indigenous games have a potential to create a spontaneous interaction amongst learners as they communicate their activities to fellow participants. Interestingly, these games is that they are not restricted to a specific cultural group, which suggests that they can be used in a multicultural setting (Nkopodi & Mosimege, 2009).

Critical Indigenous Theory and Ethnomathematics

In an era of decolonisation there is more awareness about theories that challenge the Western ways of knowing and conducting research to position the indigenous people who have been denied power. Critical indigenous studies also have a potential to offer accounts of the "contemporary worlds of the indigenous people that centre our ways of knowing and theorizing" (Moreton-Robinson, 2009). Critical indigenous theorists use challenging and innovative writing and apply questions that concern our communities (Moreton-Robinson, 2009). Martinez (2015) cites

Brayboy who writes about critical Indigenous Knowledge Systems (IKS) and anti-colonial principles focused on the needs of communities. Indigenous values and knowledges guide the indigenous research paradigm. Martinez (2015:63) highlights Brayboy's key principles of critical indigenous research (CIRM). These principles are:

1. CIRM is rooted in Indigenous Knowledge Systems, is anti-colonial and is distinctively focused on the needs of communities.
2. CIRM is rooted in relationships, responsibility, respect, reciprocity and accountability.
3. Research must be a process of fostering relationships between researchers, communities and the topic of inquiry.
4. CIRM recognises the role of particular components that make it viable for communities.

Critical indigenous research, like Critical Indigenous Theory, alludes to communities and the focus is on community needs. Some have posed questions as to what the concept indigenous knowledge refers to. Lanzano (2013) states that this is contested and usually presents more contradictions than answers. Lanzano (2013:4) also points that the introduction of the concept indigenous knowledge was linked to "traditional and local knowledge. Anthropologists who were trying to ensure that there is recognition of cultural difference first used it". There has in many instances the subordination of indigenous knowledge to Western knowledge. Critical Indigenous Theory seeks to address such anomalies. Ermine, Sinclair and Jefferey (2004:29) state:

> However, the continuing attempts to formulate research that is respectful to Indigenous Peoples still conform to the fundamental Eurocentric orientation of fitting Indigenous knowledge into Western frameworks and interests [...] Research conducted into Indigenous spaces, as a legitimized process of academic freedom, is seen as problematic process of ethics for Indigenous Peoples because of the latent biases, inherent misconceptions, and outstanding issues of power and control.

As pointed out above, D'Ambrosio (2001) posits that ethnomathematics expresses the relationship between culture and mathematics. D'Ambrosio (2001) goes on to separate the definition of *ethno* and *mathematics* when he points out that the term ethno describes "all of the ingredients that make up the cultural identity of a group: language, codes, values, jargon, beliefs, food and dress, habits, and physical traits". Mathematics expresses a "broad view of mathematics which includes ci hering, arithmetic, classifying, ordering, inferring, and modeling". Many educators may be unfamiliar with the term, yet a basic understanding of it allows teachers to expand their mathematical perceptions and more effectively instruct their students. D'Ambrosio (1985) posits that ethnomathematics is the mathematics practiced among identifiable cultural groups such as national-tribe societies, labour groups and professional classes.

According to Naidoo (2010), for a long time in South Africa, mathematics has been considered as abstract, the result of a Western curriculum structuring that separated Ethnomathematics as a discipline from individuals' regular day-to-day existences. This approach to the classification of mathematics and ethnomathematical knowledge has had negative effects on how indigenous South African students learn and relate with mathematics in the school curricular. It is argued that the social cognition and intelligent behaviour of Africans lies in capturing shared routines and participatory learning, rather than in completing school-based instruments (Nsamenang, 2006). South Africa's National Curriculum Statement of 2005 and the current Curriculum Assessment Policy Statement (CAPS) fails to spell out comprehensive strategies for the proper integration of multi-cultural mathematics in mathematics lessons in schools. This status quo has contributed to the negative perceptions amongst educators and students thereby resulting in cosmetic changes to the integration process.

Furthermore, rural and economically disadvantaged communities fail to see the link between school mathematics and their reality. Rural communities have well-knit and solid cultural activities which possess intricate and diverse mathematical concepts, and as such, these cultural activities should be part of the curriculum in order to accommodate learners who are well rooted in the diverse cultures of South Africa. The guidelines of the National Council of Teachers of Mathematics (NCTM, 1991) highlighted why it was important to build integration between the daily life of a learner's culture and concepts taught in mathematics lessons. This approach has been seen by Rosa and Orey (2006:34) as effective as they affirmed "when practical or culturally-based problems are examined in a proper social context, the practical mathematics of social groups is not trivial because they reflect themes that are profoundly linked to the daily lives of students". Rosa and Orey (2011) further argue that culturally relevant mathematics curriculum should concentrate on the role of mathematics in a socio-cultural context that involves the ideas and concepts connected with ethnomathematics, utilising the ethnomathematical point of view for tackling contextualised problems that learners encounter in the learning process.

Naresh (2015:451) declares, "Ethnomathematics need to be used to advocate the ideals of culturally relevant Mathematics education". Ethnomathematics should be included in the mathematics curriculum as its approaches are intended to make school mathematics more relevant and meaningful to the learners' environment and cultural persuasions at large. In this point of view, if mathematics is considered as a cultural construct, then it becomes a product of cultural growth. It is indeed necessary to incorporate a culturally relevant curriculum in the existing mathematics curriculum. This point of view is an important component of making education culturally relevant and even goes further to provide decolonised content in the curriculum that has recently been a rallying point in higher education discourses across South Africa. Such an approach proposes that teachers should contextualise mathematics learning by relating mathematical content to learners' culture and real-life experiences/situations.

Teaching Ethnomathematics

Teaching mathematics will be a challenge to teachers who were taught that it is only (Western) mathematics that matters. Apart from training in the application of ethnomathematics, they would also need a paradigm shift. To teach about the connection between culture and mathematics – teachers need to believe in it. This means that teachers should be able to mediate learning in diverse classrooms. All teachers who teach children from indigenous, indigent backgrounds should be able to understand the lack of social capital, their home life, their mother tongue, and culture to be able to understand how these learners can be effective in Mathematics classrooms. In this chapter, we have highlighted how Ndebele children can glean from their culture whose decorations and art are geometric. Sieman et al. (2012) underscore the need to appreciate the mathematics of non-Western peoples and how this has led to transformational geometry. All teachers should understand the role of various cultures to mathematics as they seek culturally responsive pedagogy. Meticulous educators will be able to teach mathematics in context and this can enhance the quality of learners understanding. Mullan (2015) lists four crucial factors that can be incorporated in ethnomathematics in the classrooms:

- Create an indigenous perspective for lessons.
- Integrate mathematics into a history lesson on culture.
- Demonstrate mathematics from different cultures to show learners cultural differences in teaching and learning mathematics.
- Demonstrate various cultural counting and number systems (e.g. Egyptian hieroglyphics number system).

Effective teachers will be able to rouse the interest of learners in mathematics as they demonstrate how it reflects culture thus raising awareness of its connectedness to the learners' lived reality. Teachers who use ethnomathematics can lower the learners' fear of mathematics. Yet, it is not always easy for teachers to incorporate ethnomathematics in their classrooms for several reasons. Sunzuma and Maharaj (2019) discovered in their study that there were major challenges that teachers encountered as they tried to teach geometry elements using ethnomathematics. The challenge teachers encountered included the following: lack of knowledge on ethnomathematics, approaches and how to integrate these approaches into the teaching of geometry; teachers' views of geometry taught in schools; teachers' competence in teaching geometry; teaching and professional experience; as well as resistance by teachers (Sunzuma & Maharaj, 2019:1). Therefore, as we contemplate the introduction of ethnomathematics subject advisors from districts should strategise ways in which mathematics teachers' pedagogy can be developed to be able to include ethnomathematics. This will require many to learn to unlearn their traditional ways of viewing mathematics as an unbending Western learning area. The infusion of ethnomathematics would help numerous teachers to be inclusive and learner-centred. They will also be able to appreciate learners' differences.

To overcome the challenges similar to the above, teachers should embrace critical pedagogy expatiated in several chapters in this volume. There is also a need to understand the nomenclature because this might bring ideas on how to utilise ethnomathematics in a progressive pedagogy in classrooms. Orey and Risa (2007) cite Gerdes who lists a number of concepts that express the nature of ethnomathematics and what they refer to as school mathematics. The concepts are: indigenous mathematics, socio mathematics, informal mathematics, spontaneous mathematics, oral mathematics and oppressed mathematics, hidden or frozen mathematics (Orey & Rosa, 2007). These authors state that Gerdes points out that all of these concepts are united under the huge concept – D'Ambrosio's ethomathematics. Some of these concepts from various experts can help teachers understand the essence of ethnomathematics because they are themselves self-explanatory. They show the decolonial visage of the nature of ethnomathematics. Furthermore, teachers need to understand that school mathematics in ethnomathematics loses its purity. Ethnomathematics is a combination of mathematics, cultural anthropology and mathematical modeling (Orey & Rosa, 2007).

Teachers should always keep in mind the potential of ethnomathematics in raising the learners' self-worth, creativity, and enhancing cultural dignity (D'Ambrosio, 1990). Orey and Rosa (2006) state that educational processes should not hold learners in old ways of thinking such as idealising only Western knowledge systems. Orey and Rosa (2006:66) maintain that the process of introducing ethnomathematics is likely to succeed if ethnomathematics:

- looks forward not backward; that is ethnomathematics as an expression of contemporary thought, is not just a recording of historical ideas and practices; and
- assumes a sophisticated knowledge system because it is not just mathematical skills and drills.

Yet, Orey and Rosa (2006) are aware of some of the challenges of ethnomathematics curriculum and these include absence of university ethnomathematics course, for teachers and the danger of ethnomathematical being taught as 'folkloristic and primitivist' thus different from school mathematics.

South African Policies and the Integration of Indigenous Knowledge in Mathematics Lessons in the Foundation Phase

The CAPS curriculum (DoE, 2011) aims at ensuring that learners acquire and apply knowledge and skills in ways that are meaningful in their own lives. In this regard, the curriculum promotes the idea of grounding knowledge in local contexts and supports the indigenous approaches to be integrated in the school curriculum. This policy is training to build the fact that there are many ways of knowing. This policy highlights that learners must be exposed to the history of mathematics and indigenous knowledge from other times and cultures. Indigenous Knowledge Systemshave their origin in different worldviews. The curriculum should accommodate different cultures in which indigenous knowledge were developed.

The IKS policy 2004 ensures that the national education strategy is synergistic with nurturing of indigenous knowledge. In the development of new Curriculum statements, there have been a strong drive towards recognising and affirming a critical role of indigenous knowledge. The IKS policy emphasises the relevance of having learner-centred curriculum because such a curriculum gives value to learners, previous knowledge, exposures and considers child as the center of interest, which is the most natural approach. The drafted Indigenous Knowledge Systems Bill of 2016 promotes public awareness and understanding of indigenous knowledge for the wider application and development in South Africa. The arts and culture policy 2002 highlights that in the foundation phase, the arts and culture learning area should be integrated in all three programmes – numeracy, literacy and life skills. This policy promotes public awareness and understanding of indigenous knowledge for the wider application and development.

Challenges of Integrating Indigenous Knowledge in the Mathematics Curriculum

Naidoo (2010) states that policy makers have failed to develop a curriculum that clearly include IKS concepts that can be used in different schools. According to Grange (2012), calls for the integration of indigenous knowledge in school curricula are not peculiar to South Africa but also in all countries where knowledge systems were subjugated and displaced by colonial authorities. These calls have been made for education to include the different knowledge systems, and that the curricula to be designed in a way that acknowledge knowledge perspectives and languages of Indigenous peoples (Khupe, Keane & Cameron, 2012).

There are challenges of including different or competing knowledge systems in the curricula. One of the challenges is that there are hardly any noticeable practical steps taken by the Department of Basic Education regarding IKS integration in the school curricula, implementation has been left up to the teachers (Moyo, 2011). The visible absence of indigenous knowledge-related assessment undermines the position of indigenous knowledge as an underpinning principle of the curriculum (Gundry & Cameron, 2008).

Furthermore, Lebakeng (2014) argues that the South African teachers have been inundated with frequent curriculum changes, and this has caused problems coping with all of them. "The valuing and inclusion of IK [indigenous knowledge] is probably one of the 'smaller' curriculum changes that teachers can afford to ignore, especially when exams over the years have not singled it out as important" (Lebakeng, 2014). These challenges outlined here diminish the role of indigenous knowledge in learning in the classroom. The failure of integration of indigenous knowledge in the curriculum can be apportioned to the use of English as one of the only two languages of instruction other than Afrikaans. According to De Klerk (2006), "The medium of instruction, English, has been a contributory factor also, with only 0.4% and 1.0% of the population of Limpopo and Mpumalanga respectively being able to communicate in English". The colonial and apartheid systems enforced monolingualism and a type of bilingualism, which favoured English and Afrikaans, while African languages were denied space to operate in official domains (Ndimande-Hlongwa & Ndebele, 2017:67).

South African legislation and education policy does not endorse which of the 11 official languages ought to be used as a language of instruction. The language policy statement leaves the decision to choose the language of instruction to school governing bodies, which are contained by a parent majority and additionally the school principal. As of now, most schools in which many learners are not L1 English or L1 Afrikaans speaking, choose to use their First Language in foundation phase and after that progress to English as the language of instruction in the fourth grade. This approach, however, though not overly mandatory, has been encouraged by the provincial departments of education. A few schools, nevertheless, have gone 'Straight-For-English' as the language of instruction from the first grade. The Curriculum and Assessment Policy Statements (CAPS) additionally endorses that in some schools, English ought to be the language of instruction, while in other schools Afrikaans is considered the language of instruction.

In spite of this, the fact that most of the learners in the school do not use English as their home language (DoE, 2011), the language policy still has to be upheld and this jeopardises learner concept formation from an early age. Subsequently, most schools use English medium as the language of instruction and this further alienates students from their mother tongue from as early as Grade 1. In schools, learners with an African home language have essentially continued to perform at worse than to those who have English as their home language.

In higher education institutions where teachers are trained, they receive their education and training based on Eurocentric approaches that trivialise their cultures and knowledge. The learners taught by these teachers are unfamiliar with the Western approaches of teaching and learning since they are from African cultural background. This fact is clearly illustrated by Gerdes (2009) who cites that the Kpelle people of Liberia who attended Western-oriented schools where they were "taught things that have no meaning within their culture. As such, it was difficult to comprehend the Mathematics taught". In most cases, this can result in the development of negative attitudes towards the subject, because it has no relevancy to learners' environmental experiences. Moloi (2016) elaborates further that the challenge that is faced by Mathematics teachers is that the culture of the teachers differs from that of learners.

Masola (2010) concurs with Moloi (2016) by pointing out that most of these teachers have been instructed to use mathematics textbooks, which are written in the European languages, style and illustrations. It is argued that some of the examples given in school textbooks are difficult to understand because the context in which they are composed is new to both the educator and the learner (Masola, 2010). Some of these Mathematics educators neglect to think of the systems that can help learners to comprehend mathematics concepts, principles and build critical thinking and consequently we have the high failure rate in mathematics in South African schools.

It is one of these reasons that mathematics teachers should attend and understand the culture of their learners so that their teaching will be embedded in the culture of their learners as a means of enhancing the teaching and learning of mathematics. Therefore, there is a need for mathematics of Africa, which is embedded in culture to be part of the content in mathematics books (Lebakeng, 2014). This means that also having textbooks written in African languages will ensure that mathematics is firmly grounded within their environment of the learners (Gerdes, 2009). Furthermore, Masola (2010) suggests that teachers should capitalise on the background of learners for performance to be enhanced; children meet mathematical concepts every day and operate in rich mathematical contexts even before they set their eyes on a Mathematics worksheet.

The Future of Ethnomathematics in South African Schools

The introduction of ethnomathematics is one strategy that should be seen not only addressing decolonisation but also an attempt to redress past imbalances in South African education. The uneven unequal education disadvantaged blacks who were generally the underperformers in mathematics and science. Macrae (1994) traces the crisis in mathematics from apartheid legacy. "The legacy of apartheid for mathematical education includes the subordination of ethnocentric considerations to Eurocentric traditions and the exclusion of the majority of the population from access to and participation in the mathematics-related professions" (Macrae, 1994:271). In fact, right from its inception, apartheid education was meant to illustrate that black people would not have the same education as their white counterparts. The largely Eurocentric nature of education alienated many learners who would have benefited in studying through a system that also embraced the local content.

Macrae (1994) points out that underperformance in mathematics is evident in all levels of the South African society from primary school to higher education. Annually, South Africans see how grade 12 learners struggle in mathematics and the huge challenges are in historically black schools. Numerous schools still have underqualified and unqualified mathematics teachers. There are very few black people in mathematics related professions and this is a manifestation of underperformance of learners at school. More than two decades after apartheid's demise, blacks are still few in the mathematics related professions.

Macrae (1994) also writes about how learners who fail mathematics become alienated to the subject and this means that the society loses from such an anomaly. The apartheid effect in South Africa is making it difficult to implement ethnomathematics to uphold a positive pedagogy for apartheid deskilled many black learners. Macrae (1994:278) contends:

> In proposing social approaches to numeracy, Castle (1992) warns that in South Africa a mathematical agenda has now been set by race and culture, where Eurocentric mathematics is deemed valuable and superior and 'the mathematics generated in African cultures is considered inferior or negligible' (p. 14). Unfortunately, although questions about connections between aspects of numeracy and prevailing social conditions are easy to formulate, they are difficult to answer.

Ethnomathematics in South Africa could play a role in democratising mathematics. Among these are to consider the use of indigenous languages in the teaching of mathematics. Furthermore, more focus should be on content of mathematics. Brodie (2016) argues that experts should consider curriculum processes such as critical thinking, problem solving, and the issue of identity. The introduction of ethnomathematics is a positive move to transform mathematics where learners are able to critique mathematics for example "how algorithms structure our lives in ways in which reproduce inequality" (Brodie, 2016). The alienating manner in which mathematics has been presented to many people has made them not see its potential to transform the society.

South Africa's history of divisive, racial and, oppressive education may glean from the methodologies of pedagogies that seek to include those who were excluded in the past. However, several researchers have been opposed to the introduction of ethnomathematics for several reasons (Rowland & Carson, 2002; Horsthemke & Shafer, 2006). Domite and Pais (2009) point out that Horsthemke and Shafer maintain people should not politicise science, for mathematics like science, have very little to do with social justice. Laws and principles govern these. Rowlands and Carson as cited by Domite and Pais (2009:1475) claim that "rationality may be the preserve of an oppressive cultural system but that does not necessarily mean that rationality is in itself oppressive". Furthermore, the paradox of ethnomathematics raised by Horsthemke and Shafer (2006) is that the manner in which ethnomathematics applied into South African schools contributes to the exclusion of learners rather than inclusion. They find that African learners or blacks may be excluded from studying school mathematics as their backgrounds are magnified in classrooms. Vithal and Skovsmose (1997) also maintain that ethnomathematics cannot work with the realities in South Africa. They state that the concept is itself problematic although it has achieved the purpose of establishing an understanding of mathematics and mathematics education as culturally and socially negotiated. Vithal and Skovsmose (1997) also question the debate on culture when it comes to ethnomathematics. The idea of infusing culture in mathematics is not necessarily leading to harmony in the classroom. Furthermore, in South Africa with its strong history of apartheid, concepts of culture, ethnicity, and race are enmeshed with potent divisive connotations (Vithal & Skovsmose, 1997).

Yet Domite and Pais (2009) point out that people should not merely regard ethnomathematics with ethnicity; they concur with ethnomathematics critics that ethnomathematics should not be only an emphasis on local knowledge and the valorisation of the learners' background. Domite and Pais (1997) point out that the challenge may be the school itself; schools as we have them today may not be ready for ethnomathematical methodologies. Domite and Pais (2009:1481) opine:

> Preparing students to become participants in a society is also preparing them to assume critical points of view about society, different ways of thinking, acting and doing mathematics. Using the words of D'Ambrosio, we need to emancipate students by learning academic mathematics, but also by reinforcing its roots. If we analyse the role of school in modern societies, this is obviously a paradox.

Therefore, despite the insightful criticism against ethnomathematics, one cannot disavow the usefulness of ethnomathematics despite these contradictions and paradoxes. As we phase in ethnomathematics, we need to introduce new paradigms in schools where learners and their teachers will learn to embrace innovations in education as they change their view of schools and curricula. As pointed out above, there is some evidence from research, which specify that including cultural content within the curriculum will benefit learners because such cultural aspects contribute in the recognition of mathematics as part of daily life, enhancing the ability to make meaningful connections, and deepening the understanding of mathematics (Bishop, 1988).

In this regard, Chieus (2004) states that "the pedagogical work towards an ethnomathematics perspective allows for a broader analysis of the school context in which the pedagogical practices transcend the classroom environment because these practices embrace the sociocultural context of the students". Damazio (2004) concurs with this perspective and suggests that the pedagogical elements necessary to develop the mathematics curriculum which are found in the school community. Therefore, the field of ethnomathematics provides some possibilities for educational initiatives that help to reach this goal.

It is assumed that an ethnomathematically-integrated curriculum motivates learners to recognise mathematics as part of their culture and "enhances students' ability to make meaningful mathematical connections by deepening their understanding of all forms of mathematics" (Rosa & Orey, 2011:32). The objective of developing an ethnomathematical curriculum model for classrooms is to assist students to become aware of how people mathematise and think mathematically in their cultures, to use this awareness to learn about formal mathematics, and to increase their ability to mathematise in any context in the future (Rosa & Orey, 2006). This ethnomathematical curriculum leads to the development of a sequence of instructional cultural activities that enables students to become aware of potential practices in mathematics in their culture so that they are able to understand the nature, development, and origins of academic mathematics (Rosa & Orey, 2007).

At the global level, it has become increasingly imperative that indigenous knowledge take centre stage in key development trajectories. Both the World Bank and United Nations have intimated the importance of indigenous knowledge in development issues in local communities for the enhancement of sustainable development. In South Africa, there are diverse indigenous cultures which are embraced differently. Including such cultures in the curriculum should be the priority of policy makers. The current curriculum policy needs to be carefully assessed and examined on whether it accommodates the diverse ethnomathematical cultures of South Africa. This will assist in developing critical ideas on how to improve future school curriculum policy statements. There is a call for the South African curriculum to accommodate learners who are from indigenous background (Gay, 2000). Such a curriculum will allow learners to value and appreciate their own indigenous mathematical knowledge, which will permit them to understand and experience these cultural activities from a mathematical point of view.

Conclusion

This chapter demonstrates how ethnomathematics can help bring historically marginalised learning areas in classrooms. The current education demands the inclusion of all learners as well as their reality in classrooms. Ethnomathematics will not only address decolonisation and indigenisation; it also includes diversity and social justice. Ethnomathematics is critical because it infuses cultural aspects, which are sometimes manifested by mathematical artefacts of various groups. The discussion has also revealed how the use of concepts are related to the learners' cultural and daily experiences thus making it easy for the learners to elaborate meaningful connections and deepen their understanding of mathematics (Rosa & Orey, 2011). Evident in the research cited above, is that ethnomathematics can enhance understanding for African learners who struggle in mathematics classrooms. The Ndebele art geometric shapes can help Ndebele learners in understanding geometric concepts and angles. Ethnomathematics enables the learners to develop their intellectual, social, emotional and political learning as they use cultural referents (Rosa, 2011).

The role of ethnomathematics is huge when one examines decolonisation. For many centuries mathematics, like other sciences has been presented as a neutral subject; Western values have taught us that the facts in mathematics cannot be bent. Yet ethnomathematics demonstrates that mathematics is not value free and is influenced by cultures. Indigenisation of learning areas such as ethnomathematics opposes the Eurocentric view of mathematics in traditional classrooms as reflected by Western hegemony. Culture influences mathematics as does language. Ethnomathematics shows that cultural factors and the environment are bound to influence that way teachers teach and how learners learn mathematics.

Teachers who teach ethnomathematics should be prepared to see their subject as a decolonising approach that seeks to centre marginalised aspects of curriculum. Teachers in initial teacher education programmes as well as in-service teachers should learn about the methodologies of ethnomathematics and experiment ways that would liberate the mathematics learners.

References

Anderson-Pence, K.L. 2013. Ethnomathematics: The Role of Culture in the Teaching and learning of Mathematics. *Utah Mathematics Teacher*, 6:52-61.

Bishop, A.J. 1988. *Mathematical Enculturation: A Cultural Perspective on Mathematics Education*. Dordrecht: Kluwer Academic Publishers.

Brodie, K. 2016. How to 'Decolonise' Maths in South Africa. *BusinessTech*, 14 October. [Online]. Available: https://bit.ly/3hoyucj

Bruner, J.S. 1990. *Acts of Meaning*. Cambridge: Harvard University Press.

Chieus, G.J. 2004. Reflections on Teaching Practice. In J.P.M. Ribeiro, M.C.S. Domite & R. Ferreira (eds.), *Role, Value and Meaning*. Sao Paulo: ZOUK.

Damazio, A. 2004. *Conceptual Specifications of Mathematical Activities of Coal Extraction*. Natal. RN Brazil: UFRN.

D'Ambrosio, U. 1985. Ethnomathematics and its Place in the History and Pedagogy of Mathematics. *For the Learning of Mathematics*, 5(1):44-48.

D'Ambrosio, U. 1990. *Ethnomatematica* [Ethnomathematics]. Sao Paulo: Editora Atica.

De Klerk, V. 2006. Code Switching, Borrowing and Mixing in a Corpus of Xhosa English. The International Journal of Bilingual Education and Bilingualism, 9 (5):597-14. http://doi.org/10.2167/beb382.0

Domite, M. & Pais, A.S. 2009. Understanding Ethnomathematics from its Criticisms and Contradictions. Proceedings of CERME 6, 28 January-1 February. Lyon, France.

Department of Education (DoE). 2011. *Report on the National Senior Certificate Examination Results*. Pretoria: Government Printers.

Ermine, W., Sinclair, R. & Jeffrey, B. 2004. *The Ethics of Research Involving Indigenous Peoples*. Saskatoon: Indigenous People's Health Research Centre.

Forbes, W.A. 2018. Using Ethnomathematics Principles in the Classroom: A Handbook for Mathematics Educators. Unpublished Masters Dissertation. Ontario: Brock University.

Francois, K. 2009. The Role of Ethnomathematics Within Mathematics Education. Proceedings of CERME 6, 28 January-1February 2009, Lyon, France. [Online]. Available: https://bit.ly/3llxrMh

Gay, G. 2000. *Culturally Responsive Teaching: Theory, Practice and Research*. New York: Teachers College Press.

Gay, G. 2004.The Importance of Multicultural Education. *Educational Leadership*, 61(4):30-35.

Gerdes, P. 1994. On Mathematics in History of Sub-Saharan Africa. *Historia Mathenathia*, 21:345-376. https://doi.org/10.1006/hmat.1994.1029

Grange, L.L. 2012. *Ubuntu* as an Architectonic Capability. *Indilinga: African Journal of Indigenous Knowledge Systems*, 11(2):39-145.

Gundry, D. & Cameron, A. 2008. *The Conceptual Complexity of IKS in the Physical Sciences Curriculum*. In: M.V. Polaki, T. Mokuku & T. Nyabanyaba (eds.), Paper Presented at the 16th Annual Southern African Association for Research in Mathematics Science and Technology Education Conference Maseru, Lesotho. 14-18 January 2008.

Horsthemke, K. & Schafer, M. 2006. *Does 'African' Mathematics Facilitate Access to Mathematics? Towards an Ongoing Critical Analysis of Ethnomathematics in a South African Context*. Third International Conference on Ethnomathematics: Cultural Connections and Mathematical Manipulations. Auckland, New Zealand. 12-16 February 2006.

Katz, V.J. 1994. Ethnomathematics in the Classroom. *For the Learning of Mathematics*, 14(2):26-30.

Khupe, C., Keane, M. & Cameron, A. 2012. *A Phenomenographic Analysis of High School Students' Conceptions of 'Respect'*. Implications for Science Teaching and Learning. Conference XV Symposium of the International Organisation for Science Teaching and Learning, October 2012.

Lanzano, C. 2013. What Kind of Knowledge is Indigenous Knowledge? Critical Insight from a Case Study in Burkina Faso. *Transcience*, 4(2):3-18.

Lebakeng, T. 2014. Towards Salvaging the Social Sciences and Humanities through Indigenisation in South Africa. *The Independent Journal of Teaching and Learning*, 9(1):17-29.

Le Roux, J. 2002. Effective Educators are Culturally Competent Communicators. *Intercultural Education*, 13(1):37-48. https://doi.org/10.1080/14675980120112922

Macrae, M. 1997. A Legacy of Apartheid: The Case of Mathematical Education in South Africa. *International Journal of Educational Development*, 14(3):271-287. https://doi.org/10.1016/0738-0593(94)90041-8

Martinez, C. 2015. *Tecno-Sovereignty: An Indigenous Theory and Praxis of Media Articulated Through Art, Technology and Learning*. Unpublished Doctoral Dissertation. Phoenix: Arizona State University.

Masola, A. 2010. Classrooms in South Africa are Failing our Children. *Mail & Guardian*. [Online]. Available: https://bit.ly/3hnbAC8

Mkabela, Q. 2005. Using the Afrocentric Method in Researching Indigenous African Culture. *The Qualitative Report*, 10(1):178-189.

Moloi, K.C. 2016. An African Narrative: The Journey of an Indigenous Social Researcher in South Africa. In: D.M. Mertens, F. Cram & B. Chilisa (eds.), *Indigenous Pathways into Social Research: Voices of a New Generation*. New York: Routledge.

Moreton-Robinson, A. 2009. Introduction. *Cultural Studies Review*, 15(2):11-12.

Mullan, A. 2015. *Ethnomathematics: Using Ethnomathematics in the Classroom*. [Online]. Available: https://ema300assignment2weekly

Naidoo, P.D. 2010. *Teachers' Interpretation and Implementation of the Policy on Indigenous Knowledge in the Science National Curriculum Statement*. Unpublished Doctoral Thesis. Edgewood: University of KwaZulu-Natal.

Naresh, N. 2015. The Role of a Critical Ethnomathematics Curriculum in Transforming and Empowering Learners. *Revista Latinoamericana de Etnomatemática*, 8(2):450-471.

Ndimande-Hlongwa, N. & Ndebele, H. 2017. Embracing African languages as Indispensable Resources Through the Promotion of Multilingualism. *The Journal of Language Learning, Per Linguam*, 33(1):67-82. https://doi.org/10.5785/33-1-692

Ngara, C. 2007. African Ways of Knowing and Pedagogy Revisited. *Journal of Contemporary Issues in Education*, 2(2):7-20. https://doi.org/10.20355/C5301M

Nkopodi, N. & Mosimege, M. 2009. Incorporating the Indigenous Game of Morabaraba in the Learning of Mathematics. *South African Journal of Education*, 29:377-392. https://doi.org/10.15700/saje.v29n3a273

Nsamenang, A.B. 2006. Human Ontogenesis: An Indigenous African View on Development and Intelligence. *International Journal of Psychology*, 41(4):293-297. https://doi.org/10.1080/00207590544000077

Orey, D.C. & Rosa, M. 2006. Ethnomathematics: Cultural Assertions and Challenges Toward Pedagogical Action. *The Journal of Mathematics and Culture*, VI(1):57-78.

Rosa, M. & Orey, D.C. 2011. Ethnomathematics: The Cultural Aspects of Mathematics. *Revista latinoamericana de Etnomatematica*, 4(2):32-54.

Shirley, L. 2001. Ethnomathematics as a Fundamental of Instructional Methodology. *ZDM*, 33(3):85-87. https://doi.org/10.1007/BF02655699

Sieman, D., Beswick, K., Brady, K., Clark, J., Faragher, R. & Warren, E. 2012. *Teaching Mathematics: Foundations to Middle Years*. Melbourne: Oxford.

Sunzuma, G. & Maharaj, A. 2019. Teacher-related Challenges Affecting the Integration of Ethnomathematics Approaches into the Teaching of Geometry. *Eurasia Journal of Mathematics, Science and technology Education*, 15(9). https://doi.org/10.29333/ejmste/108457

Tylenda, M. 2015. Ethnomathematics in the Classroom. Unpublished Senior Honours Thesis. Indiana: Ball State University.

Vithal, R. & Skovmose, O. 1997. The End of Innocence: A Critique of 'Ethnomathematics'. *Educational Studies in Mathematics*, 34: 131-157. https://doi.org/10.1023/A:1002971922833

Widada, W., Herawaty, D., Yanti, D. & Izzawati, D. 2018. The Students' Mathematical Communication Ability in Learning Ethomathematics-Oriented Realistic Mathematics. *International Journal of Science and Research*, 7(9):8881-8884.

Zaslavsky, C. 1973. *Africa Counts*. Boston: Prindle, Weber & Schmidt.

Chapter Three

Decolonising Science: Challenging the South African Classroom through Indigenous Knowledge Systems

Phillip M. Ramadikela
Thabo Pudi
Hamza Mokiwa

From the Past to the Present: Demystifying Science

The search for a decolonised system of education has opened a myriad of debates in learning institutions. In South Africa, the Department of Basic Education is intent on decolonising the entire education system. Decolonising education refers to the accommodation of historically marginalised knowledges in preference of Western knowledges. Colonisation and apartheid in South Africa have over decades ensured that education for black people was always inferior to white education. Arguably, the inequalities evident in education today emanate from the history of segregation. Historically, black education suffered the consequences of the legacy of apartheid and colonialism. Bantu Education for blacks was meant to ensure that black people supplied labour for the South African economy. Christie (1988:12) quotes various apartheid leaders' perceptions of black education:

> When I have control over native education, I will reform it so that natives will be taught from childhood that equality with Europeans is not for them.
>
> H.F Verwoerd, 1953

> We should not give the Natives any academic education. If we do, who is going to do manual labour in the community?
>
> J.N. Le Roux, 1945

None of these two leaders would have supported science education for black children. In fact, the Eiselen Commission on Native Education in 1949 recommended the intensification of reforms in black (Bantu) education. This Commission was appointed by government to investigate aspects of native education. Among others, the Eiselen Commission pointed out that Bantu Education is different from education and it was established to ensure that it fits into the doctrine of white supremacy. "The African must understand that European civilisation in its broadest sense is closed to him, and his learning of culture must be confined to the primitive culture of his life in the reserves" (Federation of South African Women, 2013:2).

Today, in historically black schools, teachers are still faced with the challenge of demystifying science and in a time of decolonisation debates, explore ways of injecting African indigenous knowledges as well. As cited by Msila in the Preface, Macedo (1993) discusses the *Pedagogy of Big Lies*, which points out that poor children cannot succeed in school because of their socio-economic status. Yet when people speak of decolonisation, they seek to see schools as correctors of socio-economic equality and social injustices (Bude, 1985). Historically, black children in historically black schools have not fared well in Mathematics and Science and this is no wonder when one looks at the objectives of apartheid education highlighted above. In the past unqualified and underqualified teachers taught these subjects due to a shortage of qualifies teachers in these learning areas. In historically black schools today, many teachers may believe in the pedagogy of big lies; that learning areas such as Mathematics and Science are not for poor children because of their low social capital.

The objectives of this chapter are to explore how a decolonised system has a potential of demystifying science, thus making it relevant to the learners' life world. The chapter seeks to investigate the role that can be played by Indigenous Knowledge Systems and linked to this is language, which is usually seen as a purveyor of culture. The use of the learners' knowledge from home can be beneficial for not only Science but also all knowledge in schools. Naidoo and Vithal (2014) point out that, in South Africa, Indigenous Knowledge Systems (IKS) play a critical role in Natural, Physical and Life Sciences and they are part of the Department of Basic Education's policy. Furthermore, these authors claim that the inclusion of IKS provides motivation and self-esteem, cultural responsiveness and relevance, increased peer interaction, as well as positive learning experiences. Van Wyk (2002:311) perceives a new space for IKS in South African schools today as he avers:

> IKS therefore posits a critical choice of frameworks (Odora-Hoppers, 2000:8) to assist educators to become aware of the cultural space (Prakash & Esteva, 1998:30) of learners and how they may be able to bridge the distance that separates them from their learners. Science and technology educators could develop a new consciousness or awareness of the value of integrating their learners' way of seeing and way of being (Odora-Hoppers, 2000:6) with existing paradigms and epistemologies used in science and technology. [...] IKS embodies ultimately a pedagogy that fosters cultural, social and identity criticism to validate the centrality of the learners' experiences [...]

Conscientious educators who want to enhance science education in South African classrooms will try to adopt a correct consciousness that would promote the ideals of IKS-focused education. All African schools need a critical pedagogy that would democratise and humanise education.

Towards IKS Science: A Search for a Humanising Pedagogy

In his seminal work, *Pedagogy of the Oppressed*, Paulo Freire (1970) explores ways of achieving liberatory teaching and learning. Freire writes about a need to avoid the banking model in education and supports a system where the learner is in charge and not following rote learning. Freire seeks to see education as that which empowers. Mackinlay and Barney (2012) cite Smith who argues that decolonisation empowers indigenous people to "reclaim, re-name, re-write and re-right and in a similar vein Fanon asserts that decolonisation is not a formal administrative term, but rather a restructuring of subjects of history into agents of history". Science classrooms that promote IKS will have to lean towards critical pedagogy that will need to be embraced by both teachers and their learners. Paulo Freire used the term *conscientizacao*, a Portuguese term that was later translated into English as *conscientisation*. Conscientisation is a refusal to domestication – the learners take charge of their own learning. Macedo (2017) sees conscientisation as an antidote to banking education. For many years, due to their supposed difficulty, learners have been using the banking model to study science as well as mathematics. These subjects were mystified for both teachers and their learners. The search for a decolonised science curriculum may be a search for conscientisation where IKS will be utilised to reveal the learners' active reality. Science needs to conscientise the learners, thus showing them how they can effect changes in their environment. The actual practice of teaching Science needs to reflect the embrace of conscientisation. Conscientisation also promotes humanising pedagogy, which regards every learner an agent of change. Unfortunately, for many poor learners in historically black schools dehumanising education pervades. Macedo (2012) writes:

> The banking model of education is largely supported by instrumental literacy for the poor, in the form of a competency- based approach, and the highest form of instrumental literacy for the rich, acquired through higher education in the form of professional specialization. However, despite their apparent differences, the two approaches share one common feature: they both prevent the development of critical thinking that enables one to 'read the world' critically and to understand the reasons and linkages behind the facts and behind what may appear seemingly obvious but remain ill understood.

The banking model of education cannot address pedagogy based on indigenous knowledges. In his entire work, Paulo Freire perceived the role of effective education as transformative and able to bring social change. Teachers who are not prepared for this will not be able to change the society. In *Pedagogy of the Heart*, Freire (1998) points out that, for education to be transformative, it needs to have scientific and professional development. The dialogue required in IKS inspired education will furnish this, as education will accommodate all voices as knowledge is shared in classrooms that are opposed to teacher-centred classrooms where the teacher is the sole expert.

Shirley (2017) speaks of indigenous social justice pedagogy (ISJP) which has a huge role in Indigenous nation building. For a country such as South Africa where there are efforts to redress past imbalances brought about by colonialism and apartheid, social justice pedagogy is crucial in this regard; it is relevant because it supports deep social transformation. Shirley (2017:165) posits:

> Social justice pedagogy is rooted in the educational frameworks of multicultural education and critical pedagogy (Cammarsta, 2011; Chapman & Hobbel, 2009). Multicultural education includes multiple dimensions that aims to support the practical component of providing equitable learning opportunities for all students through the curriculum affirming diverse student identities and experiences (Grant & Sleeter, 2007). Critical pedagogy critique the dominant knowledge within curriculum, critically examines inequities in society…

Indigenous social justice pedagogy is an endeavour to rethink schooling for indigenous learners. The main objective of this pedagogy is to reframe curriculum and the aim is to preserve indigenous epistemologies (Shirley, 2017). This pedagogy is a human rights-based model and is built upon the principle of humanising pedagogy that liberates. There is collaboration with indigenous peoples in education setting by addressing the nearness between critical pedagogy and race including the cultural and political aspects of indigeneity (Falcon & Jacob, 2011). In numerous countries, schools have become diverse and teachers have to cope with the uncertainty as they teach in schools of increased cultural and ethnic diversity (Wiltse, Johnson & Yang, 2014).

African Experiences – Brief Literature Review

Literature around Africa demonstrates that the time for decolonisation of not only science but also all learning areas has arrived. The impact of Western knowledge is evident in the entire Africa and the pace to transform varies from country to country. There are many similar challenges when it comes to the introduction of IKS in schools. Among these are teacher apathy as teachers show negative predisposition to indigenous knowledges. The literature below shows how several hindrances delay the introduction of IKS in African classrooms. Despite the challenges though, there is evidence of many schools who are trying against the odds to include the local content in education.

Researchers around Africa have explored the use of Indigenous Knowledge Systems in classrooms. In one study by Erinosho (2013) it was found out that in Nigerian secondary schools teaching methods that include indigenous scientific knowledge are beneficial for reinforcing learning. Furthermore, Erinosho points out that learners understanding of the scientific concepts and were excited in their interaction with local resources. Erinosho (2013:1141) also points out:

> The benefit of contextualizing school science within indigenous scientific knowledge might be in the dynamics of the instructional environment that is more open, flexible, and interactive. Teaching science with such resources helped students to see the relevance and applicability of the subject content. For instance, the local cloth weaving (asooke) provided practical resource to simplify the concepts of tension, gravitational force, and circular motion also had a chance to see inaction practical use of lever system, incomplete burning, flames and tensile strength at the blacksmith site.

Ugwu and Diovu (2016) discovered that schools that integrate indigenous knowledge and Western knowledges in teaching Chemistry would achieve success. Ugwu and Diovu point out that indigenous knowledge and practices combined with effective teaching and learning lead to improved academic achievement. Writing about Kenya, Owuor (2008) argues that sustainable development can be attained in Africa when indigenous knowledges are infused in school curricula. She states that IKS will address knowledge deficiencies as it challenges the dominance of Western knowledge in Kenya's school system. Furthermore, Owuor (2008) declares that IKS has become central in global discourse as a strategy to social, economic, and political challenge in African countries. Communities need to be more involved in decision making in education to uphold sustainable development. "Part of what is stressed in these is the incorporation of cultural heritage and values as the grounding for education, perpetuated through indigenous language" (Owour, 2008:34). Owuor maintains that, in Kenya, the cultivation of individual's responsibilities to their communities becomes a critical objective of the teaching and learning process in indigenous education.

Tsindoli, Ongeti and Chang'ach (2018) present an example of IKS when they point out that schools can derive knowledge from the Luhya tradition in Kenya, which has a variety in traditional decorations, weaving, constructions, games, and storytelling. These writers also add that indigenous mathematical knowledge can be infused in the Mathematics curriculum for effective understanding. Ng'asike (2019) posits that IKS can address issues of relevance in education. He adds that the nomadic Turkana who live in the Northwest of Kenya, their children underperform in schools. Ng'asike attributes this underperformance to inappropriate instruction materials used because these do not reflect the pastoralist children's local indigenous culture and environment.

Zimbabwe and Malawi, like many other African states, also tend to follow Western-oriented education where IKS is marginalised and negated. Hapanyengwi-Chemhuru and Makuvaza (2017) claim that in Zimbabwe just like in Malawi, education tends to be too colonial and still marginalises indigenous education; there are also few attempts to indigenise education. According to these writers, education still imitates European education or Western knowledges. More research in these countries need to be conducted to ensure that the introduction of IKS is not superficial. Hapenyengwi-Chemhura and Makuvaza (2017:93-93) assert:

> In other words, there is need to go beyond technology related knowledge. What the Malawian experience shows is that the curriculum developers are ignorant of what is or what to include under IKSs. In the Malawian example, which is similar to the Zimbabwean experiences, the teachers perpetuate negative perceptions of IKSs by focusing on the negative aspects of taboos instead of engaging their positive aspects such as why they were in place in the first place. Kayira (2013:7) criticises the privileged position of western knowledge in Malawian schools pointing out "presently, Eurocentric science has the power and influence in the school science curriculum but is largely irrelevant to Malawian villagers."

Therefore, whilst education policies in various African countries support the introduction of indigenous knowledges, there appears to be not much done to attain this goal. Yet, some experts in various countries point out that teachers also make it difficult for the acceptance of indigenous knowledge in classrooms because they are unwilling to integrate IKS in their classrooms (Shizha, 2008). Teachers' reluctance impact negatively on the learners' engagement with science. Shizha (2008) explicates that many learners in Zimbabwe are not competent in school science due to pedagogical methodologies and practices that alienate learners from their experiential knowledge.

Outside Africa, there has been intensified attempts by certain governments to indigenise the education system when it comes to science education. The Australian parliament supports the inclusion of indigenous knowledges and 2017 was the year they marked the 50th anniversary of the 1967 referendum on Indigenous Affairs Policy (Carroll, 2017). Furthermore, Carroll (2017) highlights the 2013 report entitled, *Indigenous Engagement with Science: Towards Deeper Understandings*, which underscored that "there are significant opportunities for government and industry to engage with indigenous people in a way that will maximise the potential for increased productivity across a wide range of scientific activity".

Wohling (2009) points out that, in recent decades, indigenous knowledge has been recognised as contributor to natural resource management. Wohling also adds another dimension to the debate by pointing out that people should not accept indigenous knowledge uncritically thus blind to the shortcomings. This author also emphasises that the Australians do not debate limitations of IKS especially with regard to natural resource management. Researchers and government should not be prescriptive because the voices of indigenous people tend to be lost; thus, many indigenous people find themselves not being able to contradict, question or disagree with researchers (Wohling, 2009).

Yet, Hill, Grant, George, Robinson, Jackson and Abel (2012) contend that indigenous peoples in Australia have used several decentralised approaches to environmental management where they integrate indigenous knowledge and Western science to promote cultural diversity in the upholding of social-ecological system. Robbins (2018) also mentions one example of how ecologists in Australia are learning from indigenous people as land managers have collaborated with the native people to control fires. Robbins (2018) cites Gammage who states that long before colonisation in Australia, the natives managed the landscape with "fire and no fire" and this is what was referred to as "fire stick farming". Gammage lists five stages of indigenous use of fire: controlling wildfire fuel; maintaining diversity; balancing species; ensuring abundance; and locating resources conveniently. The early settlers acknowledged the skill of indigenous used to control fire.

Writing about New Zealand, Harmsworth (2002) points out that the concept Maori Sustainable Development is a term reflecting the aspirations of contemporary Maori. This is Maori IKS, which describes Maori values, cultural identity, and purpose. The knowledge retains and emphasises the use of Maori knowledge. The Maori, like many other nations around the world, are trying to combat colonisation vestiges and cultural domination. Maori aspirations have been enhanced in New Zealand by focus on one or more of the following: improved Maori well-being and standards of health; increased human and social capacity; strength of cultural identity; sustainable management of natural resources; and culturally appropriate strategies for economic growth (Harmsworth, 2002).

Van Driessche (2013) discusses how some of the above is retained by New Zealand schools to preserve the Maori culture. In New Zealand, not only is Indigenous Knowledge Systems of the Maori taught to Maori schools – there has been initiatives to teach Maori IKS to non-Maori learners as well (Ministry of Education, 2007). The Maori continue to utilise their knowledge systems, their values in their curriculum. They use their education system to promote cultural values and indigenous knowledge to sustain it in their youth (Van Driessche, 2013).

IKS in Science Classrooms: Aiming at Critical Pedagogy

In one meeting we attended, a mathematics professor explained that it is unthinkable to speak of decolonising the 'hard sciences' such as Mathematics and Science. He went on to say that the formulae remained the same and that these sciences are not like history or any field in the humanities. Yet when we talk about decolonising a learning area such as mathematics, it refers to the transformation of teaching methodology – ensuring that mathematics is accessed by all and not meant only for 'top-students'. In fact, Mathematics and Science in schools has been reserved for certain elite students and schools have used this for creaming purposes. Top learners are made distinct from the rest because they excel in Mathematics and Science. The decolonisation of science education would open doors and enable all learners to access education irrespective of their social background. Musitha and Mafukata (2018) posit that decolonising basic education is perceived as a catalyst to create human capital that will promote economic development to end poverty. Furthermore, the quest for decolonised education system is the search for sustainable society. Uleanya, Rugbeer and Olaniran (2019) assert that restructuring the educational system to suit the needs of society will raise a sustainable developed society. Therefore, it is critical for the educational system to be fashioned or reinvented before the society can experience new and sustainable development. Additionally, Tikly (2019) points out that if education is to play a transformative role, it ought to be re-oriented and harnessed to wider processes of economic, cultural, and political transformation in the interest of social justice. Conscientised science teachers should always try to address the transformative agenda. As pointed out above education needs to produce fecund learners instead of perpetuating cultural and linguistic epistemicide (Tikly, 2019).

IKS refers to the ways or practices that indigenous people have always been exposed to as part of their everyday living. It includes knowledges that were marginalised hence not found in any reading material or textbooks. Keane (2015) refers to IKS as that which includes "a local community's traditional technology; social, economic and philosophical learning grounded in spirituality skills and ways of being in nature". Khupe (2014) describes IKS as an integrated pattern of human knowledge, beliefs, and behaviour. Furthermore, Khupe adds that language; ideas, beliefs, customs, taboos, rituals, ceremonies, folk stories, artefacts, and techniques are all part of IKS. Indigenous Knowledge Systems are values passed from generation to generation; they are the reason for the survival of the community under the guidance of elders and leaders. IKS have over decades proven to society that communities in Africa and various abodes of indigenous people that people had their own practiced sciences.

Over the years, there has been negative notions in describing Indigenous Knowledge Systems as Western scientists tend to regard IKS as not adequately scientific. Shizha (2008) states that there are varied meanings as IKS is based on cultural, social, political, and ideological definitions. "The fashionable perspective about indigenous knowledge has been that of uncodified knowledge that is often generally considered not compatible with positivists methods and not compatible with modern Western science" (Shizha, 2008:80). Mazzocchi (2006) emphatically states that Western science and traditional knowledge although different forms of knowledge, can glean much from each other. This is a fact that education planners, communities, teachers, and all education's role players should understand. Wisdom in traditional societies has been passed from generation to generation and the fact that much of these were not written does not make them empty knowledges.

Mazzocchi (2006) explains that European colonisation has nullified and lampooned traditional knowledges and replaced these with Western educational and cultural systems. Yet, there is now the realisation that IKS is an important part of humankind's cultural heritage and this knowledge is critical for our future. There needs to be constant dialogue between IKS and Western knowledges, and in decolonisation terms we may refer to this coexistence as forging a planetary system where historically marginalised knowledges are also brought to the centre to inform education. In science, there are many complex issues that need to be attended and the combination of IKS and Western knowledge are pertinent in addressing these complexities (Mazzochi, 2006). The Western tradition of thinking generates certain approaches in dealing with complexities but it is also equally crucial to learn how IKS explain such complexity (Mazzochi, 2006).

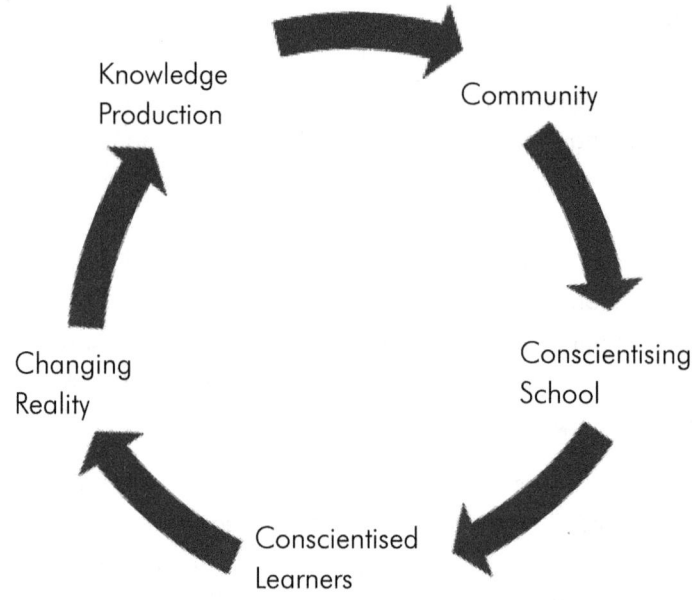

Figure 3.1   IKS Transmission in a Science Classroom (Ramadikela et al., 2019)

In Figure 3.1, we illustrate how IKS can be transferred from the community to schools and demonstrate how the knowledge can enable learners to understand their reality as they make sense of science. At the centre is the use of both African epistemologies as well as Western epistemologies. The problem with colonised education system is that it excluded or marginalised other knowledges. For example, we read above how apartheid education marginalised the African knowledges of black people under Bantu Education.

Teacher Expertise and Indigenous Knowledge Systems (IKS)

Carter (2011:314) cites Anderson who states that science education needs to change the learners' ways of leaning has to be changed as well as how teachers teach. It is clear from the discussions above that teachers utilising IKS in classrooms need some preparation and first they may need to unlearn the notions of IKS as inferior and Western science as credible and scientific. Teacher professional development programmes would need to introduce pre-service and in-service teachers to the paradigm of multicultural science learning and teaching environments (Mhakure & Mushaikwa, 2014). These authors also point out that teacher education research should enhance schooling in marginalised and diverse communities. New teaching models should serve diverse communities. Mhakure and Mushaikwa (2014:156) argue that science teachers should form teacher identities by facilitating teaching and learning activities, "such as reflecting on practice and empowering decision making through action research, thus leading to the creation of a positive and personally meaningful teacher identity, since this empowers teachers". This means that science teachers for today's classrooms must prepare to teach in diverse environments.

Teachers in traditional science might take time to embrace IKS in their science classrooms. Hewson (2014) contends that the teaching of science in South Africa is a disappointing failure. She states that there is a disconnect between two systems of knowing the Western and IKS. Figure 3.1 above demonstrates the synergistic approach that science teachers should strive for. Hewson (2014) also cites Hernandez et al. who suggests science teachers need a model of culturally responsive teaching that involves content integration, knowledge construction, prejudice reduction, social justice, and academic development. Working on teacher beliefs is critical for science teachers. In their study on science teachers, seeking identities Mhakure and Mushaikwa (2014) discovered the following as critical emerging themes about teacher beliefs about indigenous knowledge and Western science:

- Got freed from bondage of thinking that only Western Science has all the solutions to human problems.
- Some science concepts can be taught from indigenous knowledge. There is science in indigenous knowledge.
- Belief in multicultural sciences.
- Science is invasive, therefore it must be taught within learners' social-cultural context.
- Science is a human enterprise and it is contextual.
- Science has limitations just like indigenous knowledge.
- Successful integration of indigenous knowledge and Western science should focus on in-service teacher training – a change of mindset with regard to indigenous knowledge.

Teachers who attempt to use IKS must have the above beliefs to be successful indigenous knowledge advocates and IKS teachers.

Conclusion

The era to decolonise education and infuse IKS in the curriculum has arrived. It is so critical that education authorities in Africa and everywhere where there are historically, marginalised indigenous people should embrace transformative models of education that would promote not only social change but social justice as well. IKS are among these transformative models. Education that only has Eurocentric models can never be adequate to initiate social change. Furthermore, education that involves all citizens will address social justice and dignity as it humanise the former oppressed or marginalised. Models explored from various countries above demonstrate the need for innovative IKS inspired models would be enriched by the integration with western science. What teachers need to take into cognisance though is that when they approach indigenous knowledges, they must think of indigenous social justice pedagogy. As Freire (1970) points out, education is a political act and when one thinks of transformation and social change, it has to be to what extent indigenous knowledges in classrooms can change the society.

References

Brayboy, B. & McCarthy, T.L. 2010. *Indigenous Knowledges and Social Justice Pedagogy*.

Bude, U. 1985. *Primary Schools, Local Community and Development in Africa*. Baden-Baden: Nomos Verlagsgessellschaft.

Carter, L. 2011. The Challenges of Science Education and Indigenous Knowledge. *Counterpoints*, 379:312-329.

Carroll, J. 2017. Indigenous Knowledge: Adding Value to Science and Innovation. *Parliament of Australia*. [Online]. Available: https://bit.ly/2AtaDrq

Christie, P. 1988. *The Right to Learn*. Braamfontein: Sached Trust/Ravan Press.

Federation of South African Women 1954-1963. 2013. *Educating for Ignorance: The South African Congress of Democrats*. Historical Research Archive. Johannesburg: The University of Witwatersrand.

Erinosho, S.Y. 2013. Integrating Indigenous Science with School Science for Enhanced Learning: A Nigerian Example. *International Journal for Cross-Disciplinary Subjects in Education*, 4(2). https://doi.org/10.20533/ijcdse.2042.6364.2013.0160

Falcon, S.M. & Jacob, M.M. 2011. Human Rights Pedagogies in the Classroom: Social Justice, US Indigenous Communities, and CSL Projects. *Sociologists Without Borders*, 6(2):23-50.

Federation of South African Women 1954-1963. Educating for Ignorance. Johannesburg: Historical Papers Research Archives.

Freire, P. 1970. *Pedagogy of the Oppressed*. New York: Continuum.

Freire, P. 1998. *Pedagogy of the Heart*. New York: Continuum.

Hapanyengwi-Chemhuru, O. & Makuvaza, N. 2017. Re-thinking Education in Postcolonial Africa: Educating Munhu/Umuntu in Zimbabwe. In: E. Shizha & N. Makuvaza (eds.), *Re-thinking Postcolonial Education in Sub-Saharan Africa in the 21st Century*. Rotterdam: Sense Publishers. https://doi.org/10.1007/978-94-6300-962-1_6

Harmsworth, G.R. 2002. *Maori Environmental Performance Indicators for Wetland Condition and Trend. Coordinated Monitoring of New Zealand Wetlands, Phase 2, Goal 2*. Auckland: Ministry for the Environment SMF Project.

Hewson, M.G. 2914. Embracing Indigenous Knowledge in Science and Medical Teaching. *Cultural Studies of Science Education*, 10:119-131. https://doi.org/10.1007/978-94-017-9300-1_9

Hill, R., Grant, C., George, M., Robinson, C.J., Jackson, S. & Abel, N. 2012. A Typology of Indigenous Engagement in Australian Environmental management: Implications for Knowledge Integration and Social-Ecological System Sustainability. *Ecology and Society*, 17(1):23. https://doi.org/10.5751/ES-04587-170123

Keane, M. 2015. Why Indigenous Knowledge has a Place in the School Science Curriculum? *The Conversation*. [Online]. Available: https://bit.ly/2B0A43C

Khupe, C. 2014. Indigenous Knowledge and School Science: Possibilities for Integration. Unpublished Doctoral Thesis. Johannesburg: Wits University.

Macedo, D. 1997. An Anti-Method Pedagogy. In P. Freire., J.W. Fraser., D. Macedo., T. McKinnon & W.T. Stokes (eds.), *Mentoring the Mentor: A Critical Dialogue with Paulo Freire*. New York: Peter Lang.

Macedo, D. 2012. Conscientization as an Antidote to banking Education. *Rizoma Freireano*, 23.

Mackinlay, E. & Barney, K. 2012. *Unknown and Unknowing Possibilities: Transformative Learning, Social Justice and Decolonising Pedagogy in Indigenous Australian Studies.*

Mazzochi, F. 2006. Western Science and Traditional Knowledge. *European Molecular Biology Organisation*, 7(5):463-466. https://doi.org/10.1038/sj.embor.7400693

Mhakure, D. & Mushaikwa, N. 2014. Science Teachers' Indigenous Knowledge Identities. *Mediterranean Journal of Social Sciences*, 5(20):1554-1563. https://doi.org/10.5901/mjss.2014.v5n20p1554

Musitha, M. & Mafukata, M.A. Crisis of Decolonising Education: Curriculum Implementation in Limpopo Province of South Africa. *Africa's Public Service Delivery & Performance Review*, 6(1) [Online]. Available: https://bit.ly/3hodjXM https://doi.org/10.4102/apsdpr.v6i1.179

Naidoo, P.D. & Vithal, R. 2014. Teacher Approaches to Introducing Indigenous Knowledge in School Science Classrooms. *African Journal of Research in Mathematics, Science and Technology Education*, 18(3):253-263. https://doi.org/10.1080/10288457.2014.956407

Ng'asike, J.T. 2019. Indigenous Knowledge Practices for Sustainable Lifelong Education in Pastoralist Communities of Kenya. *International Review of Education*, 65:19-46. https://doi.org/10.1007/s11159-019-09767-4

Owuor, J.A. 2008. Integrating African Indigenous Knowledge in Kenya's Formal Education System: The Potential for Sustainable Development. https://doi.org/10.20355/C5Z594

Robbins, J. 2018. Native Knowledge: What Ecologists Are Learning from Indigenous People. *Yale Environment 360*. [Online]. Available: https://bit.ly/2AWvdAl

Shirley, V.J. 2017. *Indigenous Social Justice Pedagogy: Teaching into the Risks and Cultivating the Heart.*

Shizha, E. 2008. Indigenous? What indigenous Knowledge? Beliefs and Attitudes of Rural Primary School Teachers Towards Indigenous Knowledge in the Science Curriculum in Zimbabwe. *The Australian Journal of Indigenous Education*, 37:80-90. https://doi.org/10.1017/S1326011100016124

Tikly, L. 2019. Education for Sustainable Development in Africa: A Critique of Regional Agendas. *Asia Pacific Education Review*, 20(2):223-237. https://doi.org/10.1007/s12564-019-09600-5

Tsindoli, S., Ongeti, K. & Chang'ah, J.K. 2018. Integration of Existing Indigenous Knowledge within Mathematics Curriculum for Primary Schools in Kenya. *International Academic Journal of Social Sciences and Education*, 2(1):74-87.

Ugwu, A.N. & Diovut, C.I. 2016. Integration of Indigenous Knowledge and Practices into Chemistry Teaching and Students' Academic Achievement. *International Journal of Academic Research and Reflection*, 4(4):22.

Uleanya, C., Rugbeer, Y. & Olaniran, O. 2019. Decolonisation of Education: Exploring a New Praxis for Sustainable Development. *African Identities*, 17(2):94-107. https://doi.org/10.1080/14725843.2019.1659752

Van Driessche, R.E. 2013. Indigenous Knowledge: A Look at the Maori in a Modern Day Education System. Unpublished Bachelor of Arts Dissertation. La Crosse: University of Wisconsin- La Crosse.

Van Wyk, J. 2002. Indigenous Knowledge Systems: Implications for Natural Science and technology Teaching and Learning. *South African Journal of Education*, 22(4):305-312.

Wiltse, L., Johnston, I & Yang, K. 2014. Pushing Comfort Zones: Promoting Social Justice Through the Teaching of Aboriginal Canadian Literature. *Changing English*, 21(3):264-277. https://doi.org/10.1080/1358684X.2014.929287

Wohling, M. 2009. The Problem of Scale in Indigenous Knowledge a Perspective from Northern Australia. *Ecology and Society*, 14(1). [Online]. Available: [https://bit.ly/2YqVpep] https://doi.org/10.5751/ES-02574-140101

Chapter Four

Inclusive Education without Resources: A Policy Approach for Sub-Saharan Africa

Maxwell P Opoku

J-F

Introduction

Inclusive education as an overarching philosophical framework offers a comprehensive approach for all students to have equal access to learning (Ashman, 2015). Simply put, inclusive education as a framework argues that learning opportunities should be made available to all students irrespective of their backgrounds, abilities, and locations (Armstrong, Armstrong & Spandagou, 2011; Ashman, 2015; Slee, 2001). Discrimination in any form is regarded as human rights violation and as such, it is essential for systems to embrace policies that would enable all children to learn together in regular schools located in their environments (UNICEF, 2007; WHO, 2011). Particularly, it has been argued that the special schooling system is counterproductive and does not prepare children with disabilities to partake in income generation activities (Armstrong, 2005; Miles & Singal, 2010). For example, special schools mainly train children with disabilities to acquire basic living skills, which is not tailored or directed towards the job market (Miles & Singal, 2010). If society is interested in alleviating poverty among persons with disabilities, then the best place to teach them is environments where they would acquire relevant skills to participate in economic activities.

In this, inclusive education explicitly provides opportunities to explore all-inclusive approaches to learning and to develop non-discriminating school and curriculum practices to support all students, and especially students with disabilities both within and outside of the classroom (Armstrong et al., 2011; Ashman, 2015;

Slee, 2001). This all-inclusive understanding is essential in sub-Saharan African (SSA) countries (i.e. Ghana, South Africa and Tanzania), as they lack funds, have shortages of specialist services, and more importantly, there are very few special schools and professional/clinical support facilities. However, the question – to what extent can inclusive education as an overarching framework come to support students without external resources – has not been addressed clearly and thus requires urgent exploring. More specifically, the challenge for inclusive education in SSA countries: To what extent can curriculum, personal experiences, and learning environments be adapted, changed and improved to cater for the needs of students with disabilities with little or no resources? The fundamental question that this chapter aims to tackle is, to what extent can students with disabilities be supported at all levels of schooling (i.e. systems, student, and curriculum) without external resources? Perhaps, a starting place to explore this concept is to understand how inclusive education is defined in terms of policies and operational practices within SSA countries, and then to examine how inclusive education is contextualised to assist students with disabilities within the SSA context.

Ghana's Inclusive Education policy is described in terms of "… ensuring access and learning for all children: especially those disadvantaged from linguistic, ethnic, gender, geographic or religious minority, from an economically impoverished background as well as children with special needs including those with disabilities…" (Republic of Ghana, 2015:7). The principle concept of 'ensuring' and 'access' appear to be intricately reliant on external resources (i.e. funds and facilities) – the how, when and where are not clear, and move the focus away from capitalising on the student's strengths, abilities, and competencies. Further, the notion of 'providing' something implicitly seems to be embedded in resources. Importantly, there are no operational standard built-in to know how or whether 'ensuring' is effective or ineffective, which again inadvertently is related to resources and measurement? Importantly, very little attention is given to building or developing student strengths and abilities (J-F et al., 2017).

In South Africa, the Education White Paper defines inclusive education as:
> [...] acknowledging that all children and youth can learn and that all children and youth need support. Enabling education structures, systems and learning methodologies to meet the needs of all learners [...] Acknowledging and respecting differences in learners, whether due to age, gender, ethnicity, language, class, disability, HIV or other infectious diseases [...]
>
> Department of Education, 2001:6

However, it is not clear to what extent inclusive education is possible without a system-based resource enabling structure/s? Further, the concept of 'acknowledging' and 'enabling', once again are implicitly linked to resources in terms of identifying and supporting students which to a great extent, are still dependent on funds and specialist services. It appears that even to kickstart support (i.e. acknowledging) a systems-level resource-driven top-down model is necessary in South Africa. Inclusive education or, for that matter, supporting students with disabilities appear to be a top-down resource embedded model, moving away from recognising children's strengths, self-reliant capabilities, and agencies they bring to learning and their own development (J-F et al., 2017).

In Tanzania, inclusive education is the community's willingness to meet the learning needs of all students. In recent National Inclusive Education Strategy, inclusive education was defined as "an approach which transforms education system, including its structure, policies, practices and human resources, to accommodate all learners in the mainstream education by addressing and responding to learners' diverse needs" (United Republic of Tanzania, 2017). Tanzania places inclusive education within the context of 'community' wherein the expansion of access to equitable education to all learners is the responsibility of the community, including those with special needs as well as those who are marginalised (United Republic of Tanzania, 2017:20). It is unclear what 'community' and 'willingness' mean or imply, especially in terms of service provision, accountability, and the role of delivery in terms of supporting students with disability. The very notion of community is a far-reaching construct and convoluted with the pragmatics of who does what, when, and how, but does it recognise the needs of learners without external resources? However, though it is essential to locate and localise *community* so that it becomes responsible and held accountable in how they come to support students and foster their strengths (J-F et al., 2017).

The above-mentioned definitions are full of complexities and seem to be top-down concepts with little or no clarity around the pragmatics surrounding the implementation of an inclusive education framework in terms of service provision, support mechanisms and measurement. Further, to a great extent, the notion of an ongoing supply of resources seem to be the driving force for inclusive education agenda in SSA countries (Kalyanpur, 2014; Meekosha, 2011). It appears that the very implementation of inclusive education as a paradigm in SSA countries seems to be positioned on the availability of resources and facilities (i.e. well developed curricula, organisational arrangements, specialist staff, technical assistance, specialised material, and assistive learning devices) (Anthony, 2011;

Opoku et al., 2015; 2016; Stubbs, 2008). In SSA countries, schools and teachers seem to have the expectancy that inclusive education is only possible when resources are available (Stubbs, 2008). A number of studies confirm that teachers in SSA countries report that resources (i.e. funding, facilities and aids) are fundamental to support learning and that without such resources they would not be able to help students with disabilities (Arrah & Swain, 2014; Opoku et al., 2015; 2017a; 2017b).

The SSA countries seem to have inadvertently adopted a "upply stream endowment model", this term is coined to mean that support is only possible when there is a continual flow of resources from an infinite source. In SSA countries, this supply stream endowment model expectancy appears to be evident at all levels: from a system based process level to teacher pedagogical training and to the pragmatics of providing everyday support in the classroom (Kalyanpur, 2014). It also appears that this "supply stream endowment model", unfortunately, seems also to have created a real and unnecessary problem that top-down supply of resources is both necessary and imperative for teachers to be effective (Kalyanpur, 2014). But SSA countries have limited resources and have other social and economic challenges such as poverty, high levels of unemployment, corruption, and illiteracy, just to name a few. More importantly, they have failed to value the strengths, assets and self-reliant abilities that students bring with them (Eleweke & Rodda, 2002; J-F et al., 2017; Kalyanpur, 2014).

The SSA context requires a different approach to practising inclusive education and supporting students with disabilities away from supply stream endowment model to more cost-minimising, sustainable, strengths-based, and student self-reliant practices (Sharma, Forlin, Marella & Jitoko, 2017; J-F et al., 2017; Stubbs, 2008). Thus, it is essential to re-conceptualise inclusive education in terms of making it conducive to SSA countries through how it assists students with disabilities where resources are scarce. Equally, it is essential to locate the concept of disabilities in the inclusive education paradigm within the SSA context.

Disability as Part of Inclusive Education in SSA Countries

Largely, it appears that this supply stream endowment model has also come to define how students with disabilities are supported in SSA countries (Grech, 2015; Meekosha, 2011). Assisting students with disabilities is even more complicated as SSA countries have a very antagonistic view and language around disabilities (Engelbrecht, 2004; Kebaneilwe, 2016; Lamptey, De-Lawrence, Minnes &

McColl, 2015; Setume, 2016). For example, the very view of disability is defined as a deformity, and an impairment in functional physiological abilities and cognitive incapacities throughout one's life course (Ndlovu, 2016; Powell, 2006). Put another way, any classification of identification of a concern as a disability or spectrum therein is deemed a lifelong incapacity (Setume, 2016). This notion of disability is further reinforced by how SSA countries have come to interpret disability through: a socio-cultural perspective; a medicalised view to cure disability; and that disability is an economic liability.

Socio-cultural perspectives with regard to disabilities take the view that disability is a punishment for the sins of parents, and that disability is caused by a supernatural force as a penance for the atonement of errors of parents and ancestors (Agbenyega, 2003; Avoke, 2002; Opoku, Mprah, Mckenzie, Sakah & Badu, 2017c). These views are still prevalent and active today, and SSA countries more commonly interpret disability as a curse from gods, to the extent that the families (i.e. extended and biological), relatives, and friends choose not associate with children with disabilities or their immediate siblings and families, and sever long-held support and kinship ties (Avoke, 2002; Engelbrecht, 2006; Opoku et al., 2017b; Opoku et al., 2018). Such views have a negative impact on the child as they grow up learning that it is because of them that their families are ousted out of their immediate communities, and sometimes, even their own immediate families abandon them (Agbenyega, 2003; Avoke, 2002; Kebaneilwe, 2015; Opoku et al., 2017c). This further alienates, not only the children with disabilities, but also puts them away from receiving the much needed community support, help, and care.

In terms of implications within an educational context, the socio-cultural perspective highlights the significant level of discrimination and marginalisation of students with disabilities at the family and community level (Gregorius, 2016; Singal, Mahama Salifu, Iddrisu, Casely-Hayford & Lundebye, 2015). The very notion that students with disabilities are seen as a 'curse' is likely to lead to rejection by peers, an unwelcomeness in learning environments, and ostracisation by the local community, wherein they are likely to experience significant restrictions in accessing schools (Avoke, 2001; Kassah, 2008; Opoku et al., 2018). Students with disabilities are expected to remain at the end of the societal spectrum and pay the penance for the sins of parents (Baffoe, 2013). At a student level, such views disempower them and they are likely to be marginalised both within and outside of school.

Unfortunately, many teachers endorse and share these negative views about disability (Mprah, Dwomoh, Opoku, Owusu & Ampratwum, 2016; Opoku et al., 2015; Setume, 2016). It is reported that teachers are reluctant to include students with disabilities in their classrooms, and do little to challenge these negative views, which is more likely to contribute to the marginalisation of students with disabilities which keeps them from having a real possibility of learning (Mprah et al., 2016; Opoku et al., 2015; 2017c). Furthermore, it has been reported that teachers resist the inclusion of students with disabilities in the classroom, and are hesitant to teach students with disabilities as this would slow teaching and learning activities for others (Arrah & Swain, 2015; Mprah et al., 2016; Ocloo & Subbey, 2008; Opoku et al., 2015; 2017a). It is well documented that teachers in SSA countries actively exclude students with disabilities from learning and even encourage them to drop out of school (Agbenyega, 2007; Ocloo & Subbey, 2008; Opoku et al., 2015). To have a comprehensive and equitable approach to learning, SSA countries must root out all ill-informed views at all levels of society.

The Medicalised premise around disability in SSA countries is intricately linked to the notion of impaired bodies (Avoke, 2002; Grech, 2015; Meekosha, 2011; Ndlovu, 2016). This model places the problem within the individual as an infection (i.e. virus) needing to be cured, so that the original condition of functioning without deficits and defects is restored (Kassah, Kassah & Phillips, 2018; Meekosha & Soldatic, 2011). Put another way, disability is seen as a sickness and illness that needs to be treated and fully cured (Geldoff, 2016). And, to some extent, this medicalised notion got traction due to international communities trying to assist SSA countries by providing pharmacological support to alleviate symptomologies, pain, and co-morbid concerns associated with disabilities, but they seems to have been mistakenly interpreted to be a cure for disability itself (Kassah, 1998; 2001). SSA countries have somehow misunderstood the role of pharmacological support and assistive technology, to the extent that they have been lobbying international aid communities to develop strategies on a cure principle in supporting students with disabilities (Kalyanpur, 2014; Ndlovu, 2016; Setume, 2016). Further, communities receiving assistive technology and pharmacological support argue that if the right equipment and/or the right medication is prescribed, that disability can be cured once and for all, and regrettably, to some extent that SSA countries have accepted the medicalised view of cure (Geoldoff, 2016).

In terms of implications within an educational context, the medicalised premise around disability has severe negative consequences. Primarily, it leads to the notion that pharmacological support, assistive technology, and specialist facilities are the only way to support (i.e. cure) students with disabilities (Engelbrecht, 2004; Lamptey et al., 2015). To the extent that it has been reported that teachers argue regular schools are not avenue for students with disabilities, and they direct students with disabilities to special schools (Mprah et al., 2016; Opoku et al., 2015; 2017a). Such views can lead to a segregated system of education and encourage discrimination and exclusion of students with disabilities from learning places and communities (Armstrong, 2005; Avoke, 2001; Barton, 1997; Powell, 2006).

Even before accessing or exploring educational opportunities, most families and parents are pre-occupied for years searching for a cure, and go from one specialist to another in search of remedy for the right prescription and the correct medication, which is not only likely to delay the student's involvement in learning, but can lead to significant negative view of themselves that they cannot be cured and likely to interrupt their schooling and result in gaps in knowledge (Avoke, 2001; 2002). Unfortunately, when all diagnosis and pharmacological support fails to cure, it further reinforces the socio-cultural view that disability is a curse from gods (Kebaneilwe, 2016; Setume, 2016). Thus, there is an urgent need to educate families, parents, and teachers in understanding the role of pharmacological support, assistive technology, and specialist facilities, and to counter the view that disability needs to be cured.

The economic liability is grounded in the notion that students with disabilities are a liability to the society (Opoku et al., 2017b). Consequently, society views students with disabilities as lifelong economic dependents who will never contribute meaningfully to the growth and development of the community (Kassah et al., 2018; Kassah, 2008). In addition, given the agriculture and resource-driven SSA cultures, the view is that all investment must yield their due profits and rewards in due course, and the communal family-knit economical model demand that children are expected to support parents as they grow older, as well as actively contribute towards the economic welfare of the whole family (Devereux & Getu, 2013). Thus, when children with disabilities are unable to contribute or support families, they are seen as a liability and incapable of making valuable contribution to family and the wider community (Kassah, 2008).

In terms of implications within an educational context, the economic liability positions students with disabilities as a burden on the schooling system (Stubbs, 2008). Within this notion, a student with disabilities is deemed as an ongoing expenditure and a drain on school resources and facilities, as limited as they are

(Downing, Eichinger & Williams, 1997; Elewoke & Rodda, 2002). In the SSA context, teachers and school systems seem to take the view that students with disabilities are a real economic burden on the rest of the students, and perhaps this is partly due to the socio-cultural opinions discussed earlier (Agbenyega, 2007; Eleweke & Rodda, 2002; Ocloo & Subbey, 2008). This also brings into question as to the kinds of students who would be referred to and supported by audiologists, psychologists, speech pathologists, communication support workers, and interpreters to support students with disabilities (Eleweke & Rodda, 2002; Engelbrecht, 2006; Srivastava, De Boer & Pijl, 2015). This notion of liability primarily positions students with disabilities as an inactive member of the society and actuarial liabilities, and as an impractical investment with little guarantee of any returns (Opoku et al., 2017b, 2017c). Such views perpetuate the cycle of pushing students with disabilities further out into the margins (Engelbrecht, Oswald, Kitching & Eloff, 2005).

Human Right Approach and Decolonising Education

A re-thinking of inclusive education and how to support students with disabilities in the SSA countries without resources needs to be urgently addressed with practical and realistic solutions. Further, the socio-cultural perspective, the medicalised view to cure disability, and disability as an economic liability must be challenged alongside the supply stream endowment model. Of the many, the Human Rights Framework is useful as it provides the central premise that education is a fundamental right for every child and that each child must be given a chance to participate and explore opportunities available in societies (UNICEF, 2007; WHO, 2011). The Human Rights Framework provides critical ingredients in challenging economic liability view, the socio-cultural perspectives, and the medicalised notion of cure to disability (Lindsay, 2003; Mittler, 2000; Peters, 2004; UNICEF, 2007). The Human Rights Framework first proposes that localised resources must be mobilised to capitalise on what is available and to maximise their use and potentials (Kalyanpur, 2014; Stubbs, 2008). Second, it argues that individual strengths must be developed and built upon, wherein positions students in a positive light with capabilities and possibilities that need to be discovered and established, so that they are self-reliant and resourceful (WHO, 2011). Third, it takes the view that supporting students with 'disability' is everyone's business and responsibility, and that it should begin by changing the attitudes prevalent in the society (UNICEF, 2007; WHO, 2011).

Utilising Localised Resources

Utilising localised resources must start with equipping classroom teachers with skills in how to support students with disabilities (Lomofsky & Lazarus, 2001; Sharma et al., 2017). In almost every SSA country, teacher-training institutions have courses in special education to equip pre-service teachers with skills needed to adopt inclusive education approach and principles (Dalton, Mckenzie & Kahinde, 2012; Engelbrecht, 2006). However, it appears that many teachers are unable to transform the knowledge they have acquired to provide practical support for students with disabilities without the 'supply stream endowment' model (Agbenyega, 2007; Eleweke & Rodda, 2002; Ocloo & Subbey, 2008). This is because teacher-training primarily rotates around using supportive materials and technological resources to support students with disabilities rather than using localised materials and tools that are within the immediate reach (Stubbs, 2008).

More focused and specialised training is required to inform and educate teachers to use and capitalise resources within their own means, such as: time, space, natural surroundings (e.g. vegetation, animals, soil, minerals and water), natural resources (e.g. rivers, mountains and landscape) and the community (e.g. peers, other teachers and elders in the community). This kind of training will enable teachers to make the best of what is available within their own means and scope. This is what we refer to as 'immersive teaching' where teaching and learning activities are intertwined with materials available in the local communities.

For instance, in countries such as Ghana, Sierra Leone, Tanzania, and Uganda, most people are engaged in farming, and as such, it would be worthwhile to link learning to activities to the most common practices in the community. Additionally, Central Uganda, where the hospitality industry is booming, teachers could be urged to collaborate with industry partners to offer students practical experience, training, and apprenticeship beyond the classroom. Further, when a student with a disability identifies an area of interest, efforts should be directed towards supporting them to specialise and advance their interest. The priority here is to develop the capacity of teachers to utilising localised resources and to empower students with disabilities (Ashman, 2015). It is important to add here that not everyone will be in classroom for academic purposes. Therefore, there is the need for entrepreneurship and skills training geared towards equipping students with disabilities the skills to participate in economic activities.

Develop Individual Strengths and Assets

Fostering students' strengths within their learning is likely to improve both their engagement and will capitalise on their strengths and assets (Sternberg, 2000; Sternberg & Grigorenko, 2000). The primary focus of teaching and learning should be to develop students' strengths and assets especially when it comes to supporting students with disabilities (Ashman, 2015). The decisive priority is to support students to capitalise on acquiring skills, using their own strengths and assets. In an inclusive classroom, students with disabilities need teachers' support to explore their talents and work toward specialising in what they are able and capable of doing (Setume, 2016; Stone-MacDonald, 2012). Students learn best when it is based on interests, strengths and assets, which teachers need to capitalise in an effort towards practising inclusive education (Ashman, 2015). Knowing student's background, their experiences and allowing each student to uniquely participate in learning is likely to enrich their interest in learning. What's more, teachers using and building on students' interests and curiosity are likely to build their confidence and give a voice to students to share what they are good at and how they see their strengths being used in their learning (Sternberg, 2000; Sternberg & Grigorenko, 2000).

Changing Attitudes and Building an Inclusive Society

Pre-service teacher preparation must position teachers as agents of change (Setume, 2016; Swanepoel, 2009; Watson, 2012). This is more important and necessary in the SSA context as teachers have high social status in their local communities, and teachers play an integral part as knowledge experts, interpreters, translators, and generally dominate in almost every society (Setume, 2016; Stone-MacDonald, 2012). Further, teachers are likely to become policymakers and decision makers so they should be empowered to address and tackle issues of discrimination, inequality, and challenge the various myths and negative stereotypes in the society (Opoku et al., 2017b; 2017c; Swanepoel, 2009). Teachers should be the drivers of inclusive education and must be given a real voice in policy development and around the pragmatics of its delivery (Sharma et al., 2017).

In developing a comprehensive SSA system of education, the first step is to work towards changing attitudes of teachers towards individuals with disabilities. No declaration or pronouncements can change the minds of people if concerted efforts are not put in place to address the negative and misinformed views about disability. Thus, pre-service teacher education must be educated to challenge and address all negative aspects and understandings about disabilities (Johansson, 2014; Singal, 2006). Pre-service teacher education in SSA must focus on equipping and developing strong links between theory, practice and culture so that teachers can understand and explore the inter-connectedness of educational methods, classroom practices and cultural values (Singal, 2006).

One of the missing links in teacher education programmes within SSA is the role of cultural views around disabilities, in other words, it is not dealt with in practice. SSA communities have practised a different form of inclusive practices, and it is essential to building inclusive education on empowering teachers to be agents of change (Berghs, 2017). Teacher education must move away from traditional methods that disadvantaged students with disabilities and embrace innovative ways of teaching practices (Agbenyega & Deku, 2011). It is high time SSA countries take action in making teachers resourceful social agents of positive change and give them a platform and a voice to positively engage in the implementation of inclusive education (Stone-MacDonald, 2012; Swanepoel, 2009; Watson, 2012). The governments should develop a system where teachers advocate for the rights of their students with disabilities and educate themselves to care and share useful strategies.

Conclusion

It appears that SSA countries have inadvertently exercised a different form of inclusive education and practices that are not culturally driven, and it is essential to build inclusive education on empowering teachers to be agents of change alongside empowering student with disabilities. This chapter has explored barriers to inclusive education in SSA countries and has shown how schools, systems and teachers are unable to adequately serve and support students with disabilities because of the supply endowment model alongside the socio-cultural views, medicalised cure principle and the economic liability notion around disabilities.

The chapter has made the case that supporting students with disabilities should be re-conceptualised away from the supply endowment model to capitalising and using local resources, means, and materials. This is not to say that resources in terms of external funds are not necessary or that funding is not needed, but this chapter makes the case that systems, personnel, curriculum, and pedagogy must not be solely dependent on funding. Perhaps the issue in SSA countries is not be over dependent on the supply endowment model. To address this notion of dependency, this chapter has highlighted the need for change in teacher attitudes, build a system of capitalizing on resources and to empower students with disabilities. Consequently, teacher-training programmes in SSA countries must revised their training programmes and must prepare teachers to be real agents of change at all levels of schooling and in the community.

References

Agbenyega, J. 2003. *The Power of Labelling Discourse in the Construction of Disability in Ghana*. Paper presented at the Australian Association for Research in Education Conference, Newcastle Association of Active Educational Researchers (AARE).

Agbenyega, J. 2007. Examining Teachers' Concerns and Attitudes to Inclusive Education in Ghana. *International Journal of Whole Schooling*, 3(1):41-56.

Agbenyega, J.S. & Deku, P. 2011. Building New Identities in Teacher Preparation for Inclusive Education in Ghana. *Current Issues in Education*, 14(1):4-37. https://doi.org/10.14221/ajte.2012v37n5.2

Anthony, J. 2011. Conceptualising disability in Ghana: implications for EFA and inclusive education. *International Journal of Inclusive Education*, 15(10):1073-1086. https://doi.org/10.1080/13603116.2011.555062

Armstrong, D. 2005. Reinventing 'inclusion': New Labour and the Cultural Politics of Special Education. *Oxford Review of Education*, 31(1):135-151. https://doi.org/10.1080/0305498042000337237

Armstrong, D., Armstrong, A.C. & Spandagou, I. 2011. Inclusion: by choice or by chance? *International Journal of Inclusive Education*, 15(1):29-39. https://doi.org/10.1080/13603116.2010.496192

Arrah, S. & Swain, K. 2014. Teachers' Perceptions of Students with Special Education Needs in Cameroon Secondary Schools. *International Journal of Special Education*, 29(3):101-110.

Ashman, A. 2015. *Education for Inclusion and Diversity*. Melbourne, Victoria: Pearson Australia.

Avoke, M. 2001. Some Historical Perspectives in the Development of Special Education in Ghana. *European Journal of Special Needs Education*, 16(1):29-40. https://doi.org/10.1080/08856250150501789

Avoke, M. 2002. Models of Disability in the Labelling and Attitudinal Discourse in Ghana. *Disability & Society*, 17(7):769-777. https://doi.org/10.1080/0968759022000039064

Baffoe, M. 2013. Stigma, Discrimination & Marginalization: Gateways to Oppression of Persons with Disabilities in Ghana, West Africa. *Journal of Educational and Social Research*, 3(1):187-198.

Barton, L. 1997. Inclusive Education: Romantic, Subversive or Realistic? *International Journal of Inclusive Education*, 1(3):231-242. https://doi.org/10.1080/1360311970010301

Berghs, M. 2017. Practices and Discourses of *Ubuntu*: Implications for an African Model of Disability? *African Journal of Disability*, 6(1):1-8. https://doi.org/10.4102/ajod.v6i0.292

Dalton, E.M., Mckenzie, J.A. & Kahonde, C. 2012. The Implementation of Inclusive Education in South Africa: Reflections Arising from a Workshop for Teachers and Therapists to Introduce Universal Design for Learning. *African Journal of Disability*, 1(1):1-7. https://doi.org/10.4102/ajod.v1i1.13

Department of Education South Africa. 2001. *Education White Paper 6: Special Needs Education*. Pretoria: Department of Education.

Devereux, S. & Getu, M. 2013. *Informal and Formal Social Protection Systems in Sub-Saharan Africa*. Kampala: Organisation for Social Science Research in Eastern and Southern Africa.

Downing, J.E., Eichinger, J. & Williams, L.J. 1997. Inclusive Education for Students with Severe Disabilities: Comparative Views of Principals and Educators at Different Levels of Implementation. *Remedial and Special Education*, 18(3):133-142. https://doi.org/10.1177/074193259701800302

Eleweke, C.J. & Rodda, M. 2002. The Challenge of Enhancing Inclusive Education in Developing Countries. *International Journal of Inclusive Education*, 6(2):113-126. https://doi.org/10.1080/13603110110067190

Engelbrecht, P. 2004. Changing Roles for Educational Psychologists within Inclusive Education in South Africa. *School Psychology International*, 25(1):20-29. https://doi.org/10.1177/0143034304041501

Engelbrecht, P. 2006. The Implementation of Inclusive Education in South Africa after Ten Years of Democracy. *European Journal of Psychology of Education*, 21(3):253-264. https://doi.org/10.1007/BF03173414

Engelbrecht, P., Oswald, M., Swart, E., Kitching, A. & Eloff, I. 2005. Parents' Experiences of their Rights in the Implementation of Inclusive Education in South Africa. *School Psychology International*, 26(4):459-477. https://doi.org/10.1177/0143034305059021

Evans, J. & Lunt, I. 2002. Inclusive Education: Are there Limits? *European Journal of Special Needs Education*, 17(1):1-14. https://doi.org/10.1080/08856250110098980

Geldof, M. 2016. Health-Seeking by Caregivers of Children with a Disability in Two Communities in the Ashanti Region, Ghana. *Knowledge Management for Development Journal*, 11(2):141-151.

Grech, S. 2015. Decolonising Eurocentric Disability Studies: Why Colonialism Matters in the Disability and Global South Debate. *Social Identities*, 21(1):6-21. https://doi.org/10.1080/13504630.2014.995347

Gregorius, S. 2016. Exploring Narratives of Education: Disabled Young People's Experiences of Educational Institutions in Ghana. *Disability & Society*, 31(3):322-338. https://doi.org/10.1080/09687599.2016.1167672

J-F., Pullen, D., Swabey, K., Carroll, A., Heath, A., Lombard, S., Yael, I-C, O'Grady, P. & Garate, M.P. (eds.). 2017. *Lifespan Development in an Educational Context*. Queensland: Wiley.

Johansson, T.S. 2014. A Critical and Contextual Approach to Inclusive Education: Perspectives from an Indian Context. *International Journal of Inclusive Education*, 18(12):1219-1236. https://doi.org/10.1080/13603116.2014.885594

Kalyanpur, M. 2014. Distortions and Dichotomies in Inclusive Education for Children with Disabilities in Cambodia in the Context of Globalisation and International Development. *International Journal of Disability, Development and Education*, 61(1):80-94. https://doi.org/10.1080/1034912X.2014.878546

Kassah, A.K. 1998. Community-based Rehabilitation and Stigma Management by Physically Disabled People in Ghana. *Disability and Rehabilitation*, 20(2):66-73. https://doi.org/10.3109/09638289809166056

Kassah, A.K. 2008. Begging as Work: A Study of People with mobility Difficulties in Accra, Ghana. *Disability and Society*, 23(2):163-170. https://doi.org/10.1080/09687590701841208

Kassah, B.L.L., Kassah, A.K. & Phillips, D. 2018. Children with intellectual disabilities and special school education in Ghana. *International Journal of Disability, Development and Education*, 65(3):341-354. https://doi.org/10.1080/1034912X.2017.1374358

Kebaneilwe, M.D. 2016. Disability as a Challenge and Not a Crisis: The Jesus Model. *Journal of Disability and Religion*, 20(1-2):93-102. https://doi.org/10.1080/23312521.2016.1152939

Lamptey, D.L., Villeneuve, M., Minnes, P. & McColl, M. A. 2015. Republic of Ghana's Policy on Inclusive Education and Definitions of Disability. *Journal of Policy and Practice in Intellectual Disabilities*, 12(2):108-111. https://doi.org/10.1111/jppi.12114

Lindsay, G. 2003. Inclusive Education: A Critical Perspective. *British Journal of Special Education*, 30(1):3-12. https://doi.org/10.1111/1467-8527.00275

Lomofsky, L. & Lazarus, S. 2001. South Africa: First Steps in the Development of an Inclusive Education System. *Cambridge Journal of Education*, 31(3):303-317. https://doi.org/10.1080/03057640120086585

Meekosha, H. 2011. Decolonising Disability: Thinking and Acting globally. *Disability & Society*, 26(6):667-682. https://doi.org/10.1080/01436597.2011.614800

Meekosha, H. & Soldatic, K. 2011. Human Rights and the Global South: The Case of Disability. *Third World Quarterly*, 32(8):1383-1397. https://doi.org/10.1080/09687599.2011.602860

Miles, S. & Singal, N. 2010. The Education for All and Inclusive Education Debate: Conflict, Contradiction or Opportunity? *International Journal of Inclusive Education*, 14(1):1-15. https://doi.org/10.1080/13603110802265125

Mittler, P. 2000. *Working Towards Inclusive Education: Social Contexts*. Madison, New York: David Fulton Publishers.

Mprah, K.W., Dwomoh, A.J., Opoku, M.P., Owusu, I. & Ampratwum, J. 2016. Knowledge, Attitude and Preparedness of Teachers Towards Inclusive Education in Ejisu-Juaben Municipality in Ashanti Region of Ghana. *Journal of Disability Management and Special Education*, 6(2):1-15.

Ndlovu, H.L. 2016. African Beliefs Concerning People with Disabilities: Implications for Theological Education. *Journal of Disability & Religion*, 20(1-2):29-39. https://doi.org/10.1080/23312521.2016.1152942

Ocloo, M.A. & Subbey, M. 2008. Perception of Basic Education School Teachers Towards Inclusive Education in the Hohoe District of Ghana. *International Journal of Inclusive Education*, 12(5-6):639-650. https://doi.org/10.1080/13603110802377680

Opoku, M.P., Alupo, B.A., Gyamfi, N., Odame, L., Mprah, W.K., Torgbenu, E.L. & Badu, E. 2018. *The Family and Disability in Ghana: Highlighting Gaps in Achieving Social Inclusion. Disability, CBR & Inclusive Development*, 28(4):41-59. https://doi.org/10.5463/dcid.v28i4.666

Opoku, M.P., Badu, E., Amponteng, M. & Agyei-Okyere, E. 2015. Inclusive Education at the Crossroads in Ashanti and Brong Ahafo Regions in Ghana: Target not Achievable by 2015. *Disability, CBR & Inclusive Development*, 26(1):63-78. https://doi.org/10.5463/dcid.v26i1.401

Opoku, M.P., Mprah, W.K., Badu, E., Mckenzie, J. & Agbenyega, J. 2017a. Decade of Inclusive Education in Ghana: Perspectives of Special Educators. *Journal of Social Inclusion*, 8(1):4-20. https://doi.org/10.36251/josi.114

Opoku, M.P., Mprah, W.K., Dogbe, J.A., Moitui, J.N. & Badu, E. 2017b. Access to Employment in Kenya: The Voices of Persons with Disabilities. *International Journal on Disability and Human Development*, 16(1):77-87. https://doi.org/10.1515/ijdhd-2015-0029

Opoku, M.P., Mprah, W.K., Mckenzie, J., Sakah, B.N. & Badu, E. 2017c. Lives of Persons with Disabilities in Cameroon after CRPD: Voices of Persons with Disabilities in the Buea Municipality in Cameroon. *International Journal on Disability and Human Development*, 16(1):67-75. https://doi.org/10.1515/ijdhd-2016-0009

Peters, S.J. 2004. *Inclusive Education: An EFA Strategy for All Children*. Washington: World Bank.

Higher Education

Chapter Five

The Dislocated Rural Student: Calls for Decolonisation

Berrington Ntombela

Introduction

It is true that students initiated the recent call for decolonisation of education particularly in South Africa (Prinsloo, 2016; Le Grange, 2016). However, in the academic circles, the voices of students seem to have been muted and the debates and the project of decolonisation usurped by academics with a legitimisation claim because such a project is an intellectual exercise that can be best handled by scholars, especially those in the humanities (Prinsloo, 2016). Unfortunately, this usurpation means that the initial call for decolonisation remains misunderstood, misdirected and is running a risk of being killed unaddressed. Part of this chapter is to problematise this usurpation.

Furthermore, this chapter interrogates the multiplicity of academically colonised subjects. It does so by profiling a typical student in a 'rural' university and shows how the university dubbed 'rural' dislocates such a student by way of appealing to universal discourses of academia. Although the notion of a rural university appears straightforward when viewed from geographical location, there are nuances that disturb such a label. Nonetheless, it remains that geographical location all by itself cannot absolutely measure the state of rurality of a university; students on the contrary, even though they may not absolutely take the label of rural, have among them those whose lineages and rootedness are absolutely rural. These lineages can be linguistically and rhetorically explained. The profiling is therefore achieved through the analysis of a student's transactional letter written to the researcher in an indigenous language.

The analysis underscores the space occupied by a typical rural student by (re)constructing the context surrounding the student and the community that embodies the student. The chapter argues that it is critical for the university to understand this space and the context community in order to avoid dislocation. This dislocation results from the construction of rurality, which seems to satiate marketing imperatives called for by commodification of education.

Sufficed to mention that the global drive towards urbanisation marginalises the rural. In fact, the paradox is that whilst there is acknowledgement of rurality, the underlying project is to urbanise the rural. Ruralisation is not only viewed as backward but is taken as an unworthy course in which investment is seen as wasted. In this way, students with rural lineages are doubly colonised as their discourses are bastardised in favour of urban ones. This explains why there has never been a project of ruralisation despite the fact that scores of communities particularly in the South African landscape remain rural.

In fact, dominant Western thought continues to view Africa as an expanse of rural landscape whose preservation is for the gaze of the civilised tourist. Therefore, the reconstruction of rurality is hardly for the betterment and humanisation of rural residents than a tourist attraction move meant to commoditise the people and their lived experiences. It is the argument of this chapter, therefore, that decolonisation is essential for students in institutions, especially those located in rural communities.

Students' Call for Decolonisation

The #RhodesMustFall campaign in 2015 at the University of Cape Town will go down in history as an impetus for subsequent demonstrations such as #FeesMustFall which did not only draw national and international attention but was equally revolutionary. These campaigns a success given the fact that the Rhodes statue did fall and fees did fall for a certain category of students. The students who were at the forefront of these campaigns iterated that these were just part of the bigger project of decolonising education in the context of South African higher education. What did students mean by the project of decolonisation?

To answer this question, we need to consider the modus operandi in the successful campaigns mentioned above. In the first instance, the envisaged outcome was the removal of Cecil Rhodes statue. To demonstrate the vulgarity imposed by the statue, protesting students defiled it by smearing it with human excrement. Human excrement represented the highest form of repudiation. When humans defecate, the universal practice is to cover the excrement from both the owner's and the public eye. The message was well registered and the statue came down but not without muffled protests from those who had legitimised its perpetual existence on historical grounds. Mbembe (2015) is on point in asserting that the question should have never been on whether the statue should be removed or not but on why it took so long. Why indeed? Why were the academics blind to it? Did they not read the same message that was so loud and clear to the students? Perhaps the answer lies in the intellectualisation of the obvious so much as to mask the depravity entailed.

Similarly, the calls for free quality education did not go unheeded. The universities, especially those that benefited a particular class of students, argued strongly that this was marking the demise of university education hitherto known. At the heart of #FeesMustFall campaign is the question of access. Previously, it was easy to bar entrance on the grounds of colour; but when the system that legitimated such exclusion fell, fees became the new exclusionary mechanism. Very few students from black communities could afford the exorbitant fees charged by the former white universities. The historically black universities (HBUs) had, at the same time, never been able to catch up with their counterparts in terms of resources and facilities; they were instead retrogressing as numbers swelled whilst facilities shrank. Given these realities, the legitimate course of action for students was to call for the slashing of fees. As mentioned, students explained these campaigns as preliminaries for a larger decolonisation of universities project (Le Grange, 2016).

Although calls for and debates on decolonisation are not new, the pragmatism displayed by students in these campaigns is revolutionary. Their actions are reminiscent of the change of many regimes when many African states gained independence. These campaigns had casualties just as Fanon (1963) contends that decolonisation is chaotic, brutal and unsettling. In decolonisation, there is replacement of the settler, re-establishment of the marginalised and re-ordering. In practice, these are very difficult actions. Cecil John Rhodes' statue, for example, had stood as a constant source of pride to the beneficiaries of his legacy; it was taken for granted that this statue had a unitary text, which could only be read in one way – the philanthropic way. That there were casualties of his legacy was never thought to exist, yet the whole population of black South Africans was constantly reminded of shame and humiliation posed by the statue (Mbembe, 2016). The only way to reverse the aspirations of Cecil Rhodes' colonial escapade was to remove the representation of his vision. No amount of argument or debate could have swiftly accomplished what their actions did. Their actions triggered a series of debates around the decolonisation of universities, but these so far remain only as debates and the reason for that should be obvious.

The petition that led to the removal of the Rhodes statue at the University of Cape Town read: "We demand that the statue of Cecil John Rhodes be removed from the campus of the University of Cape Town, as the first step towards the decolonisation of the university as a whole" (Mamdani, 2016:68). The removal of the statue was a physical act, but decolonisation would demand something more than a physical act. The students must have read the silent text represented by the statue (even though academics were silent on the same text). The text spoke of an underlying tradition that the university embodied which academics perpetuated. The calls for decolonisation by students were not an easy bone to chew. Andreotti, Stein, Ahenakew and Hunt (2015:25) argue about the "recognition of ontological hegemony and metaphysical entrapment" that maps the university into a state of beyond reform. What they mean is that there is no escaping the university system, which is anyway heading for a crash. This would partly explain why the removal of a statue only called for a council vote, whilst decolonisation generated debates among academics as to what it really means.

Fanon's critique of decolonisation as captured by Mbembe (2016) stemmed from the adulteration of the masses by the African middle class that had bought into the colonial system and sought to perpetuate its hegemony to the annihilation of fellow Africans. In other words, this kind of decolonisation was based on the new form of colonialism where the new masters had perfected the system of exploitation, as it seemed to have worked for the old masters. Wa Thiongo, on the other hand (Mbembe, 2016), envisaged the centering of Africans and their languages as viable instruments of intellectual pursuit which had been bastardised by the Western system of thought.

Tuck and Yang (2012) convincingly argue that, perhaps, the biggest challenge or hindrance to decolonisation lies in its metaphorisation. Decolonisation is as brutal, unsettling and revolutionary as colonisation. If countries, ideologies, cosmologies, ontologies and epistemologies were violently disrupted by the act of colonisation, it should be naturally expected that the reversal (decolonisation) would bear similar repercussions. It is this fact that prevents decolonisation because the beneficiaries of colonisation would not think of parting with their benefits of power, privilege, lands, etc. The easiest way out is metaphorisation which ensures that the status quo is maintained; and the colonised must perpetually fight their way up in order to catch up with the privileged and canonised people who have never been at the receiving end of colonisation and therefore have settled on the normalcy of their privileged position. Therefore, the rhetoric of the decolonisation of education exemplifies this metaphorisation as the onus is placed on the colonised to participate in dismantling the shackles of colonisation through colonial instruments. These colonial instruments include continual citations of say pedagogies that do not begin with a description of colonisation so that the reverse would be made possible. The reverse, for instance would entail the adoption of the local but universalisation that grounds the university system glorifies the global, which in fact is a foreign local made universal by the hegemony of the Western epistemology.

To illustrate further, Mbembe (2016) asserts that the human being in the present era has entered the anthropocene epoch where humans are no longer the centre of existence but part of all objects in the cosmos. This is exemplified by the current reality of global warming that is regarded as the natural world's response to the interference of human beings in misbalancing the natural order. This has dire implications in the existence of the world and all its inhabitants and may have well triggered apocalyptic extinctions. The world therefore, has never needed human beings more now than human beings need the world. None of these players is important than the other. Interestingly, it is the Western intelligentsia which Mbembe represents that seems to have come to this realisation; Africans have always cosmologically held this view. In fact, the criticism that Mbembe received during his tenure as director of CODESRIA (The Council for the Development of Social Science Research in Africa) was that he reintroduced the sovereignty of Western scholars whilst reducing African scholars into observers (Mamdani, 2016). The human being has always been held on the same par with other objects in an African cosmology. For instance, in Zimbabwe, there is a ritual held as part of clothing the land, i.e. cleansing the land by planting trees that were lost during the bush war of liberation (Feris & Moitui, 2011). In this ritual, songs that address trees as human beings are sung where apologies for all the brutal acts human beings inflicted on trees are given (Feris & Moitui, 2011). The tree is directly addressed as a woman whose womb gives all the amenities provided by the tree (Feris & Moitui, 2011). This behaviour is in harmony with Nguni mythology where living creatures of all kinds are said to have sprung from the Tree of Life (Mutwa, 2003).

Another dilemma faced by indigenous studies lecturers at university is the pedagogical approach that promotes Indigenous Knowledge Systems and worldviews whilst at the same time maintaining rigour in the Western tradition of knowledge construction (Nakata, Nakata, Keech & Bolt, 2012). The goal is to remain true to the decolonisation of indigenous studies whilst acknowledging the intricacies of Western epistemologies. Nakata et al. (2012) in this regard admit that ultimately it remains with the student to decide the manner in which they would want to respond to the indigenous studies in terms of whether "they resist, oppose, defend, convert, patronise, tolerate, or thoughtfully engage the content of their courses to the best of their ability" (Nakata et al., 2012:136). In this instance, it is clear that decolonisation is metaphorised.

Muted Student Voices in Decolonisation Debates

Prinsloo (2016), supporting Mbembe (2015), contends that the issues of decolonisation are intellectual matters and must be dealt with by intellectuals. What they imply is that the student campaigns that were part of decolonisation were handled unintellectually. Indeed, Fanon (1963) would argue that decolonisation is not an intellectual exercise. It is just as unintellectual as colonialism. However, that does not mean that students who initiated calls for decolonisation did not act out of their intellect. In fact, they possessed pragmatic intellect that the traditional academy puts into abeyance under the pretence of agreeing to disagree. Had the students relied on that logic, the statue might still be mocking them.

Furthermore, the project of decolonisation has been unpacked, defined and redefined by scholars following the intellectual tradition. In fact, some plainly confess that they are adding to the debates on decolonisation (Le Grange, 2016; Prinsloo, 2016). Unfortunately, such contributions may only remain contributions and not amount to actions in the same momentum that saw the removal of Rhodes' statue and slashing of fees for deserving students. This is because the intellectual tradition has its own bureaucracies in the form of administrators and academics, as Prinsloo (2016) acknowledges the role played by #RhodesMustFall Campaign in opening up issues of decolonising universities and thereafter appeals that academics and university management must take students' concerns seriously.

In addition, the many facets of decolonisation that academics have debated include, decolonising knowledge (Mbembe, 2015), decolonising the curriculum (Le Grange, 2016), decolonising methodology (Keane & Khupe, 2017) and so forth. What these facets seem to have achieved is to metaphorise decolonisation

(Tack & Yang, 2012). Tack and Yang (2012) argue that decolonisation is easily reduced into a metaphor when it no longer addresses the plight of the colonised by reversing their situation to what it ought to have been. Using the case of indigenous Americans, they contend that decolonisation in their case entails that they get their land back, which was usurped by Europeans during the colonial expansion. When the Native Americans lost their territories, the colonialism that was responsible for it was never a metaphor but was real action and process. Decolonisation therefore would follow a similar mode of operation.

It therefore remains paradoxical that the custodians of knowledge, curriculum and methodology. would come up with means that would not favour their positions. The student who cries foul play is not given a platform because the game is played with the instruments of the academy to which a student is only an infantile novice. The student is not deemed to possess the expertise and intellect to grapple with the intricacies of decolonisation; his and her voice consequently remains muted. As Tack and Yang (2012) argue, metaphorisation of decolonisation serves to assuage the guilt of the coloniser who is not ready to give up the privileges gained through colonisation. In the same vein, the academics and university administrators consider themselves direct beneficiaries of the traditions of the academy and have it as their duty to induct students into the same traditions, which explains why calls for decolonisation did not come from their circles. Students, on the other, hand continue to be spoken about in forms that sometimes reduce them into hooligans and ungrateful spoiled brats. This metaphorisation is therefore used to allay the guilt that academics and administrators have in perpetuating the oppression of students. For example, exorbitant fees are justified because they support research and salaries of university employees – the question of exclusion becomes irrelevant.

Similarly, metaphorisation helps academics and scholars work out knowledge, curriculum, methodologies, and epistemologies in ways that totally exclude student input. Using their scholarly traditions, they would appeal to dominant discourses for epistemic balance meant to safeguard the established global lineages sometimes at the detriment of the local. It is for this reason that students normally take the pragmatic route. However, it is not always the easy route to take especially for rural students.

Profiling of Rural Students and Rural Universities

Pillay and Ngcobo (2010) in their study about stressors and support for first year students in an HBU cite, inter alia, socioeconomic factors and fear of failure experienced by these students. These factors seem to characterise rural students whose educational background has been stereotyped as wanting. Their research was conducted in the same institution as this study. They argued that, among other stressors, were residential issues exacerbated by the location of the institution that is far from a metropolitan area where students can easily access housing. Other stressors include death of family members especially in the context of HIV and AIDS pandemic. Hussain, Guppy, Robertson and Temple (2013), although researching the physical and mental health of students in a rural university, had similar findings to Pillay and Ngcobo (2010). Like many studies, Hussein et al. (2013) focused on the negative experiences of rural students. This could be understood in the light of a disjuncture between university life and rural life. University life seems to favour and seeks to mimic urban culture and regard rurality as backward. In fact, Byun, Meece and Irvin (2012a) assert that rurality has been approached from a rural disadvantage perspective where emphasis is placed on "lower socioeconomic status, lower parental expectations, and poorer high school preparation" (Byun et al., 2012a:2). Notwithstanding these disadvantages, Byun et al. (2012a) admit that rurality has advantages of strong social resources, high family, school, and religious connections.

Similarly, Byun et al. (2012a) concur with Pillay and Ngcobo (2010) in that rural students have socio-economic problems and poor academic preparation. Byun, Irvin & Meece (2012b) further report that generally, rural students face unique challenges compared to urban students. These problems range from alienation, attrition, to higher levels of stress. Rural students also have challenges of adjusting to urban life that they find in the university. The question arises of whether the same challenges persist for students attending a rural university. It sounds like a rhetorical question but even though a university is said to be rural, it is rural only in terms of its locale but the culture is an urban one and differs profoundly from rural communities' culture.

Malebana (2014) in his research about the intentions of rural university students in Limpopo Province to start a business, reports that whilst the percentage of individuals with entrepreneurial intentions had generally decreased, there were few entrepreneurial activities in rural areas compared to urban settings; the majority of his respondents intended to start a business in the future. He however admitted that, although the intentions are good indications, they might not be immediately used to infer to the probability of starting a business. Part of the variables that may make such an inference inaccurate is the rural setting with its own communal dynamics at times at odds with an urban setting. For instance, many rural settings still hold traditional notions of hospitality. According to Derrida (2000:5):

> [a]bsolute hospitality requires that I open up my home and that I give not only to the foreigner but to the absolute, unknown, anonymous other, and that I give place to them, that I let them come, that I let them arrive, and take place in the place that I offer them, without asking of them ... reciprocity.

Clearly, this would have a bearing in the entrepreneurial activity as traditionally defined. The urban setting on the other hand would seek to maximise profit from the foreign. In fact, tourists are the normal target for profit making where they are sold things at inflated prices.

Limanond, Butsingkorn and Chermkhunthod (2011) define a rural university as one located far away from distractions such as shopping malls, theatres, nightclubs, etc. In relation to the research they conducted about travelling patterns of students in a rural university, they contend that the transport system in a rural area is typically poor, inaccessible and has lower network coverage (Limanond et al., 2011). This however comes as an advantage in that students in such a situation tend to spend their time over weekends and weekdays doing group activities. This maximises student interaction with each other – a trait that is common in rural communities. Therefore, Limanod et al. (2011) concluded that in the rural setting where their research was conducted, transportation among university students is characterised by high social interdependency which is in stark contrast with Danaf, Abou-Zeid and Kaysi's (2014) research conducted at the American University of Beirut located in an urban setting where they found that time is a determining factor on the mode transport which makes most students use own cars. In fact, Danaf et al. (2014) propose that strategies for improving public transportation, such as decreasing the amount of time for bus travelling and increasing the efficiency of taxi sharing transportation would encourage wealthier students from American University of Beirut to use more sustainable modes of transport. The point here is to underscore the communal versus individualistic inclinations of rural and urban students respectively.

Paton-Lopez, Lopez-Carallos, Cancel-Tirado and Vazquez (2014) in their research about food insecurity among students in a rural university point out that in comparison to their urban counterparts, rural students are more prone to food insecurity. Their research confirmed that more than half of the sampled students were food insecure, which had a direct effect on their educational attainment, which in turn affected upward social mobility, among other things. When students are faced with such situations, they are more likely to be reduced to beggars.

Alienation of the Rural Student

Klomegah (2006) defines alienation as a feeling of being lost, desire for dependence, confusion with the environment and inability to have any influence on the environment. This happens when a social being is removed from his/her social environment. Klomegah's (2006) study was conducted in the context of international students who come to study in the US. He concluded that in comparison to local students, international ones experience serious alienation in adjusting to college life and further underscores that social contact correlates with feelings of alienation.

Shoho (1996) conducted a study on the alienation of rural middle school students and its implication to gang membership. He observed that although the school population consisted of 80% Hispanic students, they felt more alienated than the Anglos mainly because they felt powerless to influence the system. Indeed, it can be inferred that generally, the educational system has a tendency of favouring a certain people group; say the urban and the wealthy that can identify with the system whilst other groups are left with the burden of adjusting. The university system is no exception. In South Africa, black students already come with a label of disadvantage because of educational, linguistic, and literacy exposure at high school. Shoho (1996) highlights three determinants of alienation, which are powerlessness, normlessness, and isolation. Whilst on the one hand, isolation, according to Shoho (1996), refers to a state of loneliness caused by dissociation with peers, on the other hand, normlessness refers to a state where students feel they do not conform to the norm associated with school such as good grades, good behaviour, feelings of being part of a crowd, etc. This sense of normlessness is likely to make students perceive themselves and believe that they are perceived by others as "different in a negative way" (Shoho, 1996:7). Furthermore, Shoho (1996) regards powerlessness as inability of the student to influence educational choices. According to Shoho (1996), powerless students are likely to take any effort in attaining educational goals as a waste of time.

In an earlier study conducted by Benjamin, Van Iran and Benjamin (1983) on the alienation of Vietnamese students in the United States of America, they assert that Vietnamese students operate in the margins of Vietnamese and American culture – increasing the probability of marginality leading to alienation. Benjamin et al. (1983) regard alienation as the psychosocial phenomenon that prevents an individual from participating in the society. A rural student who is removed from his/her environment is most likely to feel alienated in the university especially when the university system prevents students from contributing to it. Students are most likely to feel that they are not part of the university and the university is not contributing to their feeling of acceptance.

I shall now turn to the letter that the student wrote me whose analysis would highlight many of the arguments raised thus far. The analysis would further accentuate the discourses and experiences of a typical rural student.

Understanding the Discourses of the Rural

The letter (appended at the end of this chapter) is written in isiZulu, one of the eleven South African official languages in South Africa. The choice of the language is important because the course that I was teaching the student was Practical English and therefore every correspondence would be expected to be carried out in English. The presence of English in the student's linguistic repertoire is only represented by few occurrences of code switching involving isiZulu and English: *ngayenza* first semester and second *yasala* (I did it first and second semester but it was left). Certainly, there is no way of avoiding code switching in a bilingual or multilingual situation. Choosing an African language therefore speaks of both resistance to the English language and acknowledgement of our common lineage as the student knew that we shared the same indigenous language. The student therefore felt at ease to address herself in the language that would not impose any barriers. It also implies that given the choice between the language of learning and teaching and the indigenous language, the student is most likely to choose the mother tongue. But this is not novelty because research abounds which indicates that the most successful education is carried out through the mother tongue (UNESCO, 2016; Ntombela, 2017). That education in South Africa continues to be exclusively in English or Afrikaans speaks volumes about the linguistic exclusion of the masses. Unfortunately, many academics do not see anomaly in that situation; instead, some reduce calls for education in indigenous languages to a neurosis (Akpome, 2017).

The letter that the student wrote follows the conventions of informal letters. It is not only the structure but also the diction, which is largely colloquial that characterise informal letters. Structurally, the student's address appeared on top of the right hand corner of the letter, consisting of the subject code: ENQ (for enquiry) followed by the initial and the last name of the student; the telephone contact number in the next line, and the date in the last line. Unlike a typical letter with either postal or residential address, this one has a telephone number implying that the reply would be expected to be given orally over the telephone. This seems to indicate preference for oral over textual transaction. Interestingly, the student does not seem to consider the letter as a written text than an oral transaction when she says *Ukhuluma nomntwana omfundisayo* meaning 'You are talking to the child you are teaching'. The letter therefore assumes a telephonic conversation where the person on the other side of the line must introduce himself or herself in terms of who is speaking or talking. The letter therefore assumes some kind of oral interaction. This already creates a disjuncture with university education that elevates the text and downgrades the oral. For this student, important matters are transacted orally which is why (as explained in the letter) she had first tried to come to my office in person and only resorted into writing a letter when she could not find me. But for the university tradition, matters must be reduced into writing – the very exams that have frustrated this student are textually-oriented.

The salutation simply begins with the title of the addressee meant to indicate acknowledgment of my position. The opening line then addresses me as 'father', perhaps the father in a religious setting as the student proceeds to greet me in the name of the Lord. This means that the student considers me to be occupying the same position as that of a priest. By this opening, the student may have possibly meant to influence my mind so that whatever decision or action I take afterwards, it should be reminiscent of what a priest would do under similar circumstances. In addition, the address 'father' represented the father figure in a family setup. This is confirmed by the fact that the student refers to herself as the child (*umntwana*). She explains that she is the child in the context of learning, i.e. a grown-up child who is already a mother 'Mkhwenyana [a pseudonym]' (...*umntwana osekhulile umama Mkhwenyana*). The church and family are two important institutions in a rural setup. These are some of the advantages that Byun et al. (2012a) referred to. In other words, education is seen as another wing that extends family and religious harmony. These institutions command similar respect. This means that in a rural worldview, the lecturer holds the same position as with the priest and the father at home. These have a moral obligation towards those who are under their tutelage. In other words, just as the priest and the father are obliged not to fail the congregants and children respectively, the lecturer is equally obliged not to fail the students.

After the opening sentence which is a greeting, the student proceeds in the tradition of an oral interaction to introduce herself. She addresses me with my praise name (Mahlobo) and then explains the reason for this exchange. Without any major punctuation to terminate each sentence, the student uses commas. For instance, after introducing herself a full stop would be expected so that the reasons for this transaction begin a new sentence. But as I have indicated, these punctuation obligations belong to a textual transaction and not the oral one, which the student's letter represents. Even the persisting typographical errors are tolerated, as speech has no spelling.

The student then explains that she had been to my office on Tuesday and Wednesday because after writing on Monday, when she calculated correct answers, she could not get anything above 30. Although she admits that she might not be accurate in her calculation, this is already a cause for concern because the course in question is being repeated the fourth time. She had even written a special exam, which is written by students who are left with one or two modules to graduate, but did not pass. This letter is therefore an appeal (*ngiyacela*) that I do something about her situation. The question is why would she make such an appeal to me? The answer perhaps lies in the possibility that the four times she had not passed the course she may have come to believe that the lecturers have something to do with it. For her, the power of passing and failing is in the hands of lecturers, the same way that the priest has the spiritual keys for the believer, and the biological father, the keys of physical nourishment for a child.

For her, a lecturer can easily manipulate a number. The 30 that she thinks she got can be grown into a pass mark by a lecturer. There is no question of her qualitative gain on the course but the whole engagement with the course seems to have been reduced to a statistic. She cannot be blamed for that because that is what gets emphasised in universities – success is quantitatively measured, and numbers assume some magical attainment. This is to the extent that those students who get good scores are likely to be considered by others as lucky instead of brilliant. Therefore, the 30 that this student feels she must have got has no direct relation to her level of performance but simply represents a bad omen.

In the following paragraph, she details her plight. She starts by mentioning that she had received sponsorship by God's grace, which is meant to register that should she not clear the course, she would probably lose sponsorship. She then punctuates her appeal with *baba ngiyazithoba* (father I humble myself). It is almost as if she is a repentant sinner in front of a priest. This humility is triggered by her request that if when I mark, I find that she did not do well, I must give her 50 which is what is standing before her and the course. Fifty, in other words, has assumed some magical figure capable of resolving somebody's life problems. In fact, it seems the student interprets the educational endeavour as some statistical configuration where 30s and 50s represent failure and success respectively.

The details that follow highlight the predicament that the student has gone through because of this course she has been failing. She lost an employment opportunity and she now fears that she will end up being a laughingstock in her neighbourhood. She looks after herself and sometimes her relatives help her out. Her children have piece jobs and the young one just has a job of taxi driving. All this mean that they are still depending on her. As part of accentuating her plight, she appeals to a biblical account where Jesus' disciples had toiled the whole night without catching any fish. She likens her situation with that of the disciples, meaning that I am some sort of Jesus who must deliver her from this fruitless toil. In addition to the stress that this course gives her, she is a single mother who was abandoned by her husband in 1996 having been married in 1993. Although she apologises for divulging this detail, to her, the matter surrounding the course simply adds to the burdens she is carrying. This means her educational experiences subjectively affect every aspect of her being. She now sees this course standing on her way for a better life. It is colluding with her husband who abandoned her after only three years of marriage.

At 29 years of age, she seems to have gone back to school the following year after having been abandoned. She enrolled for Standard 6 and continued until she completed Standard 10 in 2001. She then registered with the University of Zululand in 2002, but in 2005 when there was a strike at the university, she was injured and had to drop out. She was only able to get back almost ten years later in 2014. In the interim, she had been teaching Grade R until the government insisted that only qualified teachers should be employed which is probably why she went back to the university *ukuqoqa imilenze* (to collect legs).

Collecting legs is a university student discourse in isiZulu, which means re-doing all the courses you have failed. The courses are metaphorically referred to as legs because that is what you use for movement. Therefore, when a person collects legs literally, it is a sign that he/she is about to move. Courses are therefore legs inasmuch as they either allow or hinder someone from progressing. Therefore, when a student collects legs, it means the student's degree would be completed and the student would soon graduate. For this student, the legs she set out to collect seem to be misbehaving. Her future seems to be hanging in a balance with uncertainty about this module. She had come back in 2016 just for this module and now she does not feel she made it. She ends that long paragraph with her date of birth to indicate how desperate she is given the ticking time of her age. Coincidentally, she wrote the letter when she was left with seven days to celebrate her 48th birthday. This means that at 48, she was yet to complete her first degree she started 14 years prior. This is one of the many realities that rural students face.

The last paragraph begins with a similar plea: *ngiyazithoba ngiyacela Baba Ntombela* (I humble myself I plead with you Father Ntombela). Her main plea is that when I mark her paper, God must touch my heart because she does not think she wrote well. What may have added to her poor performance is that she wrote bereaved. Her sister who had been ill at a hospital passed away and at the time of writing the letter, they were preparing for her funeral, which was to be held on a Sunday. Pillay and Ngcobo (2010) have already identified bereavement as a common stressor among students in a rural university. God must therefore touch me concerning all her troubles.

Furthermore, her plea was that I should give her 50 so that she passes and would not need to seat for a re-exam because she did not pass the previous re-exam. Re-exams are given to students whose final mark ranges between 40 and 48. They must get not less than 50 to pass the re-exam. She then promises that if I am gracious in my marking, she would come back to express her gratitude. In other words, my attendance to her plea is like another transaction to which she would be indebted. She would therefore need to pay that debt in some form of gratitude. What she is implying is that she understands I will be going out of my way to help her out and therefore would have to be compensated for that.

This is followed by some kind of invocation where she charges me with re-building her homestead which she had so far built all by herself (... *ake uvuse leliyakaya engilikhale ngingedwa* ...). In other words, the 50 she is requesting is as big as her homestead. My generosity in marking would be treated as a work of re-building a rather collapsing house. I am therefore invited to team up with her in building up a collapsing homestead. She then presents me with the list of referrals that would authenticate her story. These are her uncle, her mother's cousin and another Mrs Mpaka who have stood with her through thick and thin. She provides telephone numbers for her uncle Mr Ntenga and Mrs Mpaka. These are the people who would verbally substantiate her story. The presence of these people around her life encapsulates the African concept of *Ubuntu* where her personhood is confirmed by other persons around her. The quest therefore is not to develop an absolute individual but an absolute community. She therefore views me as part of the community around her life.

In a university tradition, testimonials and commendations can only be accepted when in writing, but in this case, as with typical rural settings; the oral testimonials are just as authentic. These people have helped her so much that she is even afraid (*Sengiyabesaba*), as if she is indebted. Her grandfather who is a neighbour to her former husband's home is a pensioner and he sometimes helps her when she does not have food. This further confirms food insecurity among rural students as reported by Paton-Lopez et al. (2014). The letter concludes with an explicit promise that the gratitude she spoke about in the preceding paragraph is a monetary one. That is, she expected that I would notify her how things went and then as soon as she gets employed she would come to thank me, but that must remain between me and her, and God would be her witness if she does not live up to her promise. This would easily be interpreted as bribery or 'marks monetary transaction'. Whilst it might as well border in that, the whole educational experience she has gone through has been a monetary transaction. She had paid tuition fees and miscellaneous fees and this would simply add to that list. Another possibility though is that this is the practice she has grown to know at a university. Stories of marks manufactured in this and other unscrupulous means are not uncommon. But in this case, it is clear that desperation seems to have driven the student right to the end of her tether. She does not believe she has any options left except appealing for the lecturer's mercy which she also feels cannot go unrewarded.

Conclusion

This chapter is based in an HBU in South Africa. Almost all HBUs in South Africa are rural because they were formed to service the black population that had been pushed out of the metropolis to make way for the white population and most importantly to cater for black students in homelands. The rurality of these institutions has been in terms of both geographical location and resources. Educational investment was placed in the institutions that serviced white students and HBUs perpetually lagged behind. When democracy broke into the lives of South Africans, access that was previously denied was given to many black South Africans. When these South Africans experienced the education that was previously closed to them, they were hit with insults and mockery staged by the legacies of the apartheid regime both ideologically and artistically. As they could take it no longer, protests broke out in various former 'whites only' campuses demanding for the decolonisation of institutions. Among the successes of these campaigns were the dismantling of the Cecil Rhodes statue at the University of Cape Town and the announcement of free higher education for deserving students. These two examples are perfect illustrations of decolonisation. Notwithstanding such a successful start, academics and scholars who through their various intellectual traditions interpreted and reinterpreted calls for decolonisation to the extent that it seems to have lost its simplicity and urgency usurped the rest of the project of decolonisation. However, these movements and campaigns do not seem to have catered for a typical rural student or university. With rural universities aspiring to be something similar to their urban counterparts, the rural student is bound to be alienated. To understand this alienation and dislocation, we needed to revisit the discourse of a rural student accessed through the analysis of a transactional letter written in an indigenous language.

This whole transaction interestingly blurs the lines between an educational diction and that of religious and family one. The Dr Ntombela to whom the letter is addressed is both regarded as a father figure in a family setup and at the same time some priestly representation in a religious setup. The implication is that these institutions: the educational, religious, and family are interlinked in the life experiences of rural students. That is why the student takes it as a matter of fact that I would identify with and understand the religious analogies. But that I would also understand the traditional rhetoric of building a homestead. Her education is not just for personal gain, she has children whom she must support and a homestead she must build. Dr Ntombela, her lecturer, therefore, must partner with her in all these endeavours. Education from a rural worldview, therefore, does not only consist of interactions in a lecturer hall – the lecturers and those entrusted with students enter a community where their contribution goes beyond an intellectual one. Perhaps, if the university had woken up to that reality, there would not have been a need for this student to spend up to 14 years for the first degree, or four times battling the same module to the extent of resorting to purchasing the marks.

Therefore, the whole transaction could be reduced into a plea for a pass. As mentioned above, Pillay and Ngcobo (2010) found fear of failure as one of the most common stressors among students in a rural university. Therefore, the student has taken all her energies to explain what failure would mean and the changes that would be brought by passing this course. Whilst it might seem like an automatic act of recording say 30, 35 or 40; for many students these are not just statistical figures but represent all the difference in their livelihood. Mbembe

(2016) is on point when he decries the reduction of an educational goal from that of the pursuit of knowledge to the pursuit of credits. The appeal for a 50 from this student indicates clearly that the figure far supersedes the knowledge gained. There is surely a better way of working with scores whilst at the same time acknowledging the centrality of knowledge. Ideally, knowledge should far outweigh the score to an extent that it could be represented without a grade.

Universities must also take into account the linguistic realities of rural students. Whilst universities in the metropolis, especially in South, are dominated by English and Afrikaans - traditional languages of privilege – rural students strive in their indigenous languages and there is no reason for not developing their languages into languages of intellectual pursuit. Even the French academics petitioned for scholarly publications to be in their native language because they argued that it is not possible to have a dialogue with your superior without using your own language (Phillipson, 2009). The choice that the student made to use an African language in such an important matter in her life is a testimony. But as argued earlier, the sluggishness in overhauling the language policy that promotes African languages as intellectual languages is a result of the metaphorisation of decolonisation. Akpome (2017) for instance, would call for the abandonment of the pursuit of mother tongue instruction on the ground that it would not only be herculean but has already suffered philosophical despair. He is right in his conclusions and defence of the exclusive English language medium of instruction because he stands as the beneficiary and by default the defender of his privilege – decolonisation in this instant would be brutal and unmerciful to such a privilege, but so was colonisation. It is these kinds of arguments that usurped the students' noble call for decolonisation and continue to dislocate rural students.

References

Akpome, A. 2017. How not to decolonise: old debates, new ideas. *Teaching English Today*, 7(2). [Online]. Available: https://bit.ly/2UzTDqs

Andreotti, V., Stein, S., Ahenakew, C. & Hunt, D. 2015. Mapping Interpretations of Decolonisation in the Context of Higher Education. *Decolonisation: Indigeneity, Education & Sociology*, 4(1):21-40.

Benjamin, R., Van Iran, T. & Benjamin, M.E. 1983. Alienation Among Vietnamese Students in the United States. *Free Inquiry in Creative Sociology*, 11(1):32-34.

Byun, S., Irvin, M.J. & Meece, J.L. 2012a. Predictors of Bachelor's Degree Completion Among Rural Students at four-year institutions. *Review of Higher Education*, 35(3):1-16. https://doi.org/10.1353/rhe.2012.0023

Byun, S., Meece, J.L. & Irvin, M.J. 2012b. Rural-Non-Rural Disparities in Postsecondary Educational Attainment Revisited. *American Educational Research Journal*, 49(3):1-26. https://doi.org/10.3102/0002831211416344

Danaf, M., Abou-Zeid, M. & Kaysi, I. 2014. Modelling Travel Choices of Students at a Private, Urban University: Insights and Policy Implications. *Case Studies on Transport Policy*, 2(2014):142-152. https://doi.org/10.1016/j.cstp.2014.08.006

Derrida, J. 2000. *Of Hospitality*. R. Bowlby (trans.). Stanford: Stanford University Press.

Fanon, F. 1963. *The Wretched of the Earth*. New York: Grove Press

Feris, L. & Moitui, C. 2011. Towards Harmony Between African Traditional Religion and Environmental Law. In: T.W. Bennett (ed.), *Traditional African Religions in South African Law*. Cape Town: UCT Press.

Hussain, R., Guppy, M., Robertson, S. & Temple, E. 2013. Physical and Mental Health Perspectives of First Year Undergraduate Rural University Students. *BMC Public Health*, 13(848):1-11. https://doi.org/10.1186/1471-2458-13-848

Klomegah, R.Y. 2006. Social Factors to Alienation Experienced by International Students in the United States. *College Student Journal*, 40(2):303.

Le Grange, L. 2016. Decolonising the University Curriculum. *South African Journal of Higher Education*, 30(2):1-12. https://doi.org/10.20853/30-2-709

Limanond, T., Butsingkorn, T. & Chermkhunthod, C. 2011. Travel Behaviour of University Students who Live on Campus: A Case Study of a Rural University in Asia. *Transport Policy*, 18(2011):163-171. https://doi.org/10.1016/j.tranpol.2010.07.006

Malebana, J. 2014. Entrepreneurial Intentions of South African Rural University Students: A Test of the Theory of Planned Behaviour. *Journal of Economic and Behavioural Studies*, 6(2):130-143. https://doi.org/10.22610/jebs.v6i2.476

Mamdani, M. 2016. Between the Public Intellectual and the Scholar: Decolonisation and Some Post-Independence Initiatives in African Higher Education. *Inter-Asia Cultural Studies*, 17(1):68-83. https://doi.org/10.1080/14649373.2016.1140260

Mbembe, A.J. 2015. *Decolonising Knowledge and the Question of the Archive*. [Online]. Available: https://bit.ly/2XWc2zS

Mbembe, A.J. 2016. Decolonising the university: New directions. *Arts and Humanities in Higher Education*, 15(1):29-45. https://doi.org/10.1177/1474022215618513

Mutwa, V.C. 2003. *Zulu Shaman: Dreams, Prophecies and Mysteries*. Merrimac: Destiny Books.

Nakata, N.M., Nakata, V., Keech, S. & Bolt, R. 2012. Decolonial Goals and Pedagogies for Indigenous Studies. *Decolonisation: Indigeneity, Education & Society*, 1(1):120-140.

Ntombela, B.X.S. 2017. The Double-Edged Sword: African Languages under Siege. In: V. Msila (ed.), *Decolonising knowledge for Africa's Renewal*. Randburg: Knowledge Resources. pp. 161-179.

Patton-Lopez, M.M., Lopez-Carallos, D.F., Cancel-Tirado, D.I. & Vazquez, L. 2014. Prevalence and Correlates of Food Insecurity Among Students Attending a Midsize Rural University in Oregon. *Journal of Nutrition Education and Behaviour*, 46(3):209-314. https://doi.org/10.1016/j.jneb.2013.10.007

Pillay, A.L. & Ngcobo, H.S.B. 2010. Sources of Stress and Support Among Rural-Based First-year University Students: An Exploratory Study. *South African Journal of Psychology*, 40(3):234-240. https://doi.org/10.1177/008124631004000302

Phillipson, R. 2009. *Linguistic Imperialism Continued*. New York: Routledge.

Prinsloo, E.H. 2016. The role of the humanities in decolonising the academy. *Arts & Humanities in Higher Education*, 15(1):164-168. https://doi.org/10.1177/1474022215613608

Shoho, A.R. 1996. *The Alienation of Rural Middle School Students: Implications for Gang Membership*. Paper Presented at the Annual Meeting of the American Educational Research Association, New York, 8-12 April 1996.

Tuck, E. & Yang, K.W. 2012. Decolonisation is not a Metaphor. *Decolonisation: Indigeneity, Education & Society*, 1(1):21-40.

ANNEX 1

ENQ: N. Mkhwenyana (pseudonym)
Contact: 079.......
Date: 17/11/2016

Dr B. Ntombela

Baba Ntombela ngiyakubingelela egameni lenkosi Amen. Ukhuluma nontwana omfundisayo – kodwa kodwa umntwana osekhulile umama Mkhwenyana, Mahlobo ngifikile ngolwesibili nangolwesithathu angakuthola, ngizozilahla ngehlulekile ngezwa ngomsombuluko uma ngizibalela ngifika ku 30 kodwa name anginasiqiniseko ukuthi ngizimakela ngakho, ngiyacela kulonyaka bengiyenza okwesine, 2015 ngayenza first semester and second yasala ngashayeka naku especial exam akwalunga.

Isponsor ebenginaso nakulonyaka ngasithola ngomusa ka Jehova, baba ngiyazithoba. Ngiyacela uma ngingenzanga kahle ngicela ungiphe 50 mayedlulile, ngumiswe yiyo yodwa. Nakulonyaka ngaphuthelwa itoha ebese ngilitholile ngibizwa ngoMach ngenxa yayo – ngiyazicelela Ntombela ngimdala sengizoze ngibe yihlaya nangasemakhaya, Degree yami yonke isino 65 module kusele lena, bengizele lokho, baba ngiziphethe ngiyazondla ngiphiwe nazihlobo izingane zisebenza amatoha angatheni aphelayo, kumanje omncane liphelile elakhe omdala kade ethola ethekwini ngenyanga edlule nacho akutheni udriver amatekisi bathembele kimi makulunga, baba ngishikekile, njengabafundi abathi kuJesu sishikile ubusuku bonke, kodwa, ngibona ngiphelelwa, amathemba empilo, encono, ngiyacela baba, ngiwumama oyedwa owalahlwa wumkhwenyana 1996 kade ngigana ngo 1993, ngiyaxolisa ukukwazisa izinkinga zami, wukuthi nazo zinginikeza incindezi, ngafunda ke, Sengimdala, ngabuyela esikoleni ngo 1997 ngayoqala Std 6 to STD 10 ngo 2001 – ngafika ongoye ngo 2000 – ngalimala ngo 2005 kunesiteleka, ngabuya ngo 2014 ngazoqoqa imilenze yami yonke nale Philosophy eyinkinga. Ngimisiwe eTohweni ebesengiphila ngalo bengifundisa Grade R Gobihlahla Primary and Mashoba ngo 2013 kwathiwa uhulumeni ufuna abaneziqu eziphelele, bengibuyele, ukuzoqedela nakulonyaka bebengifuna esikoleni ebengikuso, bekungefani kulowo R4000-00 bengikwazi ukuphila manje ngiyabona ikusasa lami liyafiphala uma lemodule engimise kanje ingalungi. Neminyaka isihambile 1968-11-24

Ngiyazithoba ngiyacela BABA Ntombela uma usumaka ngabona, ngehlulekele, ephepheni kodwa nje umusa wakho unkulunkulu akuthinte ngiyobuya ngizobonga Ngibhale nakabi sekushoniwe ekhaya ngiyahamba kusasa. Sifihla ngesonto, Kushone ucc wami ubese sbhedlela Eshowe. Umqondo wami waphazamiseka, ngiyacela, ngiyanxa ungiphe nje 50 angisafuni re-exam – eyango January yangichitha Ngiyakuthembisa ake uvuse leliyakaya engilikhale ngingedwa nampa ofakazi abangakuthsela ngempilo yam. Malume wami uMr Ntenga 072-------, umzala kama, wami, uzokutshela ukuthi ngiphila ngaphansi kwasiphi isipho, nangu omunye MRS Philisiwe Mpaka 082------- Sengiyabesaba, usizo lwabo, uma ngiya ekhaya yibo, uma ngibuya esikoleni yibo – umkhulu usempeshile akasasebenzi kodwa, masiswele okudliwayo, ngiphiwa kwakhe ngoba, ungumakhelwane walapho ngashadela, khona Ngiyabonga ukungizwela, ungisendele Mahlobo, mangithola itoho ngiyobuya ngizobonga, ngiyathembisa phakathi kwami nawe nonkulunkulu uyobe eyiso kimi uma ngehlulekile ukubonga

Ngiyabonga: Student 2002---- N. Mkhwenyana

ENQ: N. Mkhwenyana (pseudonym)

Contact: 079.......

Date: 17/11/2016

Dr B. Ntombela

Baba Ntombela ngiyakubingelela egameni lenkosi Amen. Ukhuluma nontwana omfundisayo – kodwa kodwa umntwana osekhulile umama Mkhwenyana, Mahlobo ngifikile ngolwesibili nangolwesithathu angakuthola, ngizozilahla ngehlulekile ngezwa ngomsombuluko uma ngizibalela ngifika ku 30 kodwa name anginasiqiniseko ukuthi ngizimakela ngakho, ngiyacela kulonyaka bengiyenza okwesine, 2015 ngayenza first semester and second yasala ngashayeka naku especial exam akwalunga.

Isponsor ebenginaso nakulonyaka ngasithola ngomusa ka Jehova, baba ngiyazithoba. Ngiyacela uma ngingenzanga kahle ngicela ungiphe 50 mayedlulile, ngumiswe yiyo yodwa. Nakulonyaka ngaphuthelwa itoha ebese ngilitholile ngibizwa ngoMach ngenxa yayo – ngiyazicelela Ntombela ngimdala sengizoze ngibe yihlaya nangasemakhaya, Degree yami yonke isino 65 module kusele lena, bengizele lokho, baba ngiziphethe ngiyazondla ngiphiwe nazihlobo izingane zisebenza amatoha angatheni aphelayo, kumanje omncane liphelile elakhe omdala kade ethola ethekwini ngenyanga edlule nacho akutheni udriver amatekisi bathembele kimi makulunga, baba ngishikekile, njengabafundi abathi kuJesu sishikile ubusuku bonke, kodwa, ngibona ngiphelelwa, amathemba empilo, encono, ngiyacela baba, ngiwumama oyedwa owalahlwa wumkhwenyana 1996 kade ngigana ngo 1993, ngiyaxolisa ukukwazisa izinkinga zami, wukuthi nazo zinginikeza incindezi, ngafunda ke, Sengimdala, ngabuyela esikoleni ngo 1997 ngayoqala Std 6 to STD 10 ngo 2001 – ngafika ongoye ngo 2000 – ngalimala ngo 2005 kunesiteleka, ngabuya ngo 2014 ngazoqoqa imilenze yami yonke nale Philosophy eyinkinga. Ngimisiwe eTohweni ebesengiphila ngalo bengifundisa Grade R Gobihlahla Primary and Mashoba ngo 2013 kwathiwa uhulumeni ufuna abaneziqu eziphelele, bengibuyele, ukuzoqedela nakulonyaka bebengifuna esikoleni ebengikuso, bekungefani kulowo R4000-00 bengikwazi ukuphila manje ngiyabona ikusasa lami liyafiphala uma lemodule engimise kanje ingalungi. Neminyaka isihambile 1968-11-24

Ngiyazithoba ngiyacela BABA Ntombela uma usumaka ngabona, ngehlulekele, ephepheni kodwa nje umusa wakho unkulunkulu akuthinte ngiyobuya ngizobonga Ngibhale nakabi sekushoniwe ekhaya ngiyahamba kusasa. Sifihla ngesonto, Kushone ucc wami ubese sbhedlela Eshowe. Umqondo wami waphazamiseka, ngiyacela, ngiyanxa ungiphe nje 50 angisafuni re-exam – eyango January yangichitha Ngiyakuthembisa ake uvuse leliyakaya engilikhale ngingedwa nampa ofakazi abangakuthsela ngempilo yam. Malume wami uMr Ntenga 072-------, umzala kama, wami, uzokutshela ukuthi ngiphila ngaphansi kwasiphi isipho, nangu omunye MRS Philisiwe Mpaka 082------- Sengiyabesaba, usizo lwabo, uma ngiya ekhaya yibo, uma ngibuya esikoleni yibo – umkhulu usempeshile akasasebenzi kodwa, masiswele okudliwayo, ngiphiwa kwakhe ngoba, ungumakhelwane walapho ngashadela, khona Ngiyabonga ukungizwela, ungisendele Mahlobo, mangithola itoho ngiyobuya ngizobonga, ngiyathembisa phakathi kwami nawe nonkulunkulu uyobe eyiso kimi uma ngehlulekile ukubonga

Ngiyabonga: Student 2002---- N. Mkhwenyana

Chapter Six

Humanising and Decolonising Adult Basic Education and Training (ABET) in South Africa

Luvuyo L Lalendle
Vuyisile Msila
Sizakele Matlabe

Genesis: Blacks and Adult Education

In chapter 1, Msila explores decolonisation in basic education. He invites the reader to investigate how the basic education sector can be indigenised and diversified to meet the needs of the learners' communities. Similarly, this chapter examines the decolonisation of adult education. Adult education is distinct from basic education, and among the differences is that it draws its learners from the adult population. Nordhaug (1986) cites Lindeman who maintains that anyone defining the concept, *adult education*, should combine the age element and/or a life cycle factor. The age determines whom an adult is and can be looked at the compulsory school age. The life cycle refers to the position where the person is in their life. Nafukho, Amutabi and Otunga (2005) point out that adult education is defined by how adulthood and maturity define its limits.

Additionally, Baatjes and Baatjes (2008) opine that adult education refers to education that is vocational and technical. Some think that adult education means literacy or Adult Basic Education and Training (ABET); some regard Adult Education and Training (AET) as synonymous to ABET (Skills-Universe, 2010; Triple E Training, 2013). However, literacy and ABET are part of adult education, but adult education is more than these. It includes peace education, cooperatives, livelihoods, environmental education, health programmes, popular education, and vocational education as well as various other forms (Baatjes & Baatjes, 2008).

Adult education includes both formal learning, non-formal learning and informal learning. In this chapter, as we define adult education, we adopt the UNESCO definition as cited by Myers, Conte and Rubenson (2014:4):

> The term 'adult education' denotes the entire body of organised educational processes, whatever the content, level and method, whether formal or otherwise, whether they prolong or replace initial education in schools, colleges and universities as well as in apprenticeship, whereby persons regarded as adult by the society to which they belong develop their abilities, enrich their knowledge, improve their technical or professional qualifications or turn them in a new direction and bring about changes in their attitudes or behaviour in the two fold perspective of full personal development and participation in balanced and independent social, economic and cultural development; adult education, however, must not be considered as an entity in itself, it is a sub-division, and an integral part of, a global scheme for lifelong education and learning.

Aitchison (2013) is more forthright albeit his narrow definition as to what qualifies as adult education; he defines adult education as "education provision for people aged 15 and over who are not engaged in formal schooling or higher education and who have an education level of less than grade 9". His definition excludes continuing education after Grade 9.

Burke (2005) states that aspects such as history, politics, economics and geography have influenced adult education in developing countries. The history of education in South Africa demonstrates that adult education has had more learners from black communities than any other over the decades. In one study, Aitchison (2012) illustrates a minimal number of whites who were illiterate in South Africa. Several chapters in this book refer to the need for a humanising and critical pedagogy that liberates and empowers. Furthermore, contributors in this volume have thrown a gauntlet of how, as we decolonise education, do we ensure that some aspects of Western education coexist with indigenous knowledges. Arguably, it remains a truism that those who have embraced Western knowledges only, whether consciously or unconsciously, marginalised indigenous knowledges are disempowered. When an adult has internalised certain cultures, it might be to the detriment of his well-being. Bad education can make one docile and not challenge the circumstances which education might misinform as acceptable. South Africa continues to need an adult education system that would enable adults to challenge the status quo. Sadly, as Biko (1987) puts it, the black man (sic) develops a two-faced attitude to accommodate the challenges in his society. Biko relates a story of how he observed a black adult whose co-worker was a white man who was constantly verbally abusing him. The white man insulted the black colleague and Biko later asked the white man why he was so hostile towards his black colleague. The white man claimed that the black man was a loafer who only understood the language of insults, and as he said this, the black man smiled. The black man retorted by stating that he was used to the white man's insults. It was clear that the black man was resigned and had accepted the conditions as unchangeable. Biko (1987:102-103) contends:

> Then I was sick. I thought for a moment I do not understand black society. After some two hours I came back to this guy, I said to him do you really mean it? The man changed, he became very bitter, he was telling me how he wants to leave any moment, but what can he do? He does not have any skills … if he does not work, he has got to take it.

Several aspects related to education are highlighted by this example. It is natural to the black man here for the white man to insult him because he is dependent upon the white man. Biko knows the black man is bitter every day but he cannot display "any form of what is called cheek to his boss". This is what Biko refers to as two-folded attitude of the black man to his existence in South Africa. Apartheid education was to prepare the black people for subservience (Biko, 1987; Kallaway, 1988; Msila, 2007). Black Consciousness (BC) seeks to correct the false images of black people in terms of their education. In a section below, we will see how Paulo Freire (1972) and his colleagues in Brazil tried to eradicate education that leads to docility by employing the concept of conscientisation. Like Paulo Freire's pedagogy, the BC philosophy sought to see education as liberating, freeing the black oppressed learner from the creations of colonialism where the black person is perpetually inferior.

This chapter explicates the role of education and what it means to decolonise adult education especially in a society like South Africa where apartheid and colonialism distorted the content of what should be learnt for decades. It focuses on how the Adult Basic Education and Training (ABET) ought to address some formal education myths that have become reality for the oppressed over the years. What is referred to as ABET today emanates from the original 'night schools' which were reserved for adult learners after work. Many adults who wanted to attain matriculation qualification (Grade 12 today) attended these night schools. The chapter is organised as follows:

o   The Night School Movement
o   Critical Pedagogy, Self-Reflection and Adult Education
o   ABET and the Current Education Policies
o   How do we Decolonise ABET
o   Decolonising through Critical Literacy
o   Conclusion

The Night School Movement

Edward Roux (1972) opines that the struggle of the black oppressed for freedom in South Africa was synonymous the struggle for education and epistemic freedom. Ndlovu-Gatsheni (2018) writes about how colonialism brought with it culturecides, historicides, and linguicides and that the search for epistemic freedom is the crux of decolonisation and epistemic freedom. Ndlovu-Gatsheni (2018) also points out how colonialism changed the first African institutions such as the university, thus making them more colonised.

When the adult education movement became popular in the 1940s, it sought to address illiteracy, among others. The Adult Committee Report in 1946 pointed out that 80% of the Africans were illiterate. The radical National Union of South African Students (NUSAS) was instrumental in developing the Night School Movement in the 1940s. However, although the night schools became strong in the 1940s the very first night schools in South Africa can be traced back to 1925. Roux (1964:346) states:

> One of the most notable achievements of the radical student movement in South Africa has been its contribution to the African night school movement. The history of these night schools begins in 1925, when the Johannesburg communist founded their first night school in a Ferreirastown slum. They taught by candlelight, without blackboards or desks. The pupils sat on benches and struggled with complicated political doctrine at the same time they learnt their letters.

Such night schools from the 1940s developed in various cities of the Union of South Africa, (known today as the Republic of South Africa). Teachers were not always qualified, and it was frequently difficult to have all learners present because others would be on night shift at work. Homework was usually impossible as workers were always tired from their shifts. The curriculum was English, Arithmetic and General Knowledge. However, as early as 1929, in Durban and Pietermaritzburg, night schools taught reading in isiZulu as well as elementary Arithmetic. As the apartheid policies intensified, government closed many adult education centres. When the Nationalist Party came to power it took control of black education and blocked all efforts at oppositional adult education (Prinsloo, 1995).

Roux (1972) points out that, although the 1955 Congress of the People's Freedom Charter called for the end to illiteracy, the National Party government that came into power in 1948 undermined adult education work and refused to subsidise night schools. The Communist Party and other liberation movements were later outlawed. Years later though, the night schools were revived in various cities in

South Africa. One of the authors of this chapter taught in several night schools in the Eastern Cape where the day curriculum was simply rehashed and taught as is to adult learners at night. The downside was that many teachers were not prepared to teach adult learners and were simply utilising the pedagogy utilised in day schools rather than the more preferred andragogy for adult learners. In fact, until recently, adult illiteracy did not interest many as the apartheid state ran poorly resourced night schools.

When 1994 came, many people thought the original model of the night schools would be improved. However, Aitchison (2013) claims that the dismal failure by government to support adult education surfaced. Aitchison also avers that there was failure by government to attain "adult education renaissance". Rule (2006) also highlights the neglect regarding the constitutional right of adults to basic education. Rule (2006:120) points out that ABET draws on the language of democracy, redress, and human rights, and that the official purpose of ABET is to:

- **Restructure and transform** programmes and centres to respond better to the human resources, economic, and development needs of the Republic.
- **Advance** strategic priorities determined by national policy directives at all levels of governance and management within the Adult Basic Education and Training sector.
- **Respond** to the needs of the Republic and the labour market and of the communities served by the centres.
- **Complement** the skills development strategy in cooperation with the Department of Labour.

Despite the above though, Rule (2006) argues that ABET has been a disservice to the poor, many of whom desperately need education empowerment.

Critical Pedagogy, Self-Reflection and Adult Learning

In addition to the above, Degener (2002) claims that there is a need for adult programmes to be designed around the backgrounds and interests of students. In addition, Degener avers that critical adult education programmes also demonstrate to students how they can use skills gained to transform their lives and the society. Progressive adult education programmes should not promote passivity and docility among learners. Degener (2002) cites Macedo who points out that non-critical programmes are criticised for ignoring the political, social, and economic factors that have schemed to marginalise people. One of adult education's main aims though should be to intensely change the learners' lives. Adult education that does not empower learners to improve their lives is futile; usually traditional education programmes, especially those under apartheid were meant to brainwash learners (Kallaway, 1988). Numerous adult learners in South Africa may be prevented from accessing education due to poverty. Degener (2002:27-28) posits:

> Too many people are prevented from reaching their full potential because they do not have access to the adequate nutrition, housing, healthcare and education that so many of us take for granted. Learning to read and write will not change this imbalance. Adult literacy programmes that make an effort to reflect a critical pedagogy try to help students understand what forces have contributed to their positions in society and to see how literacy can help them influence those forces and transform their lives.

Any transformative adult learners' programme should have teachers who are prepared to learn to unlearn old practices. Many educators in South Africa were trained as teachers in programmes that elevated the dominant culture and marginalised the indigenous African cultures. Hanson et al. (2018) spell out the definition of progressive adult education as an interdisciplinary field that often includes social justice, hence it prompts a decolonising and indigenising approach. Hanson et al. also perceive relevant adult education as a system whose programmes include indigenous epistemology and includes a culturally responsive pedagogy. These writers have also realised that there can be no decolonisation without the individuals involved having undergone the process of self-critical reflection. Hanson et al. (2018:100) argue:

> Critical reflection is understood as the process of questioning assumptions and power relations, which catalyses a change of perspective. This personal transformation brings forth emancipatory development practices that nurture social transformation. Furthermore, this process precedes indigenisation.

Literature on adult education highlights the importance of self-determination, self-regulation, and self-reflection for successful learning of adults (Kellenberg, Schmidt & Werner, 2017). Self-reflection is critical in transforming one's circumstances. When an adult learner realises the need for change and self-discovery, they will be able to understand decolonisation's transformative qualities. For self-critical reflection to happen in adult education, Freire underscores dialogic teaching, which refers to the active engagement by both teachers and learners. Darder (2017) declares that Freire opposed the limits of Western pedagogical tradition that dismembers knowledge and also supported the banking approach to education. Darder points out that Freire understood banking approach as tied to the intellectual history of the West where the mind and the body are adversaries in the process of intellectual transformation. "This tradition of disembodiment shapes anti-dialogical classroom practices and expectations that students compartmentalise themselves, without contending with the manner in which this approach to learning reproduces asymmetrical relations of power that oppress organic constructions of knowledge" (Darder, 2017:84). In decolonial classrooms, students should be able to reflect on issues of the dynamism of learning as they express their identity. Education should not lead to alienation. Freire opposed this alienating form of education as he emphasised the need for a humanising pedagogy where enquiry is problematised and dialogic teaching existed (Roche, 2016).

Problem prosing education was not only a notion, which is in conflict with the banking concept but also one which for Freire, offered hope for alleviating the situation for the oppressed of all social, cultural and racial backgrounds. Paulo Freire summed up the difference between banking education and problem-posing education: "banking education treats students as objects of assistance; problem-posing education makes them critical thinkers" (1970:71). Other educational thinkers, particularly humanists, social constructivists and those with radical or similar alternative viewpoints, shared such sentiments.

For Freire, reflection was informed by conscientisation and enabled learners for praxis; because he found an affinity between reflection and action. Furthermore, Freire found that action without reflection was merely action for action's sake (Redmond, 2016). Freire pointed out that there could be no education without reflection. Critical reflection ensures that the learner would be able to enhance own reality. Additionally, critical reflection in adult education liberates the adult learner to realise the importance of the diversity of knowledge. The adult learner should be exposed to education that demonstrates that it is not Western education only that matters in education. In fact, critical reflection in decolonisation means understanding the hierarchisation and racialisation of knowledge. In the cities or townships in South Africa, a black person might refer affectionately to another black person in Nguni as *umlungu wam* (literally meaning my white person) thus regarding the other person a provider, a master or a *baas* (boss). The equivalent in Sotho languages is *lekgowa laka*. Many adult workers grew up during apartheid times believed that the white people are superior because they have power and they provide. Even when some black people marvel at great inventions such as the television, microwave or a wonderful car, they would laud this by stating, *umlungu mdala* (the white man is dexterous). These are social constructs, and Hayes (2016) declares that the social constructs that recount people's identities impact the ways in which they perceive the world.

During similar phases of Paulo Freire's investigations in Brazil, he learned how the adult workers had internalised the superiority of the white person and they understood the superiority as a consequence of nature; that they could do nothing about the status quo. In extending the examples above, two black people may greet one another by saying to each other, *mlungu wam* (literally, my white person) thus showing respect and admiration for the other. Again, here one sees the reverence of whiteness. Without really thinking about it, even the ones who are supposed to understand the folly of the natural disposition of whiteness will use this. Freire's investigation was mainly among illiterate Brazilians, but in South Africa, even formally educated Africans fall into the trap of some of these social constructs. Numerous people may regard such as trivial everyday niceties which are harmless. Yet what one can find hidden behind these phrases, are colonial and internalised beliefs.

Maitra and Guo (2019) refer to such beliefs as Occidentalism, which is discourse about the superiority of the West and its knowledge. Maitra and Guo also point out that the Occidentalist discourse has been pivotal in dumbing down the 'other' since the first encounters between Europe and Africa as colonial power spread in Africa. The North-South global divide has been entrenched by the taking over of the Western knowledge and the domination of whiteness. Maitra and Guo (2019) raise the argument that practices of lifelong learning are associated in the perpetuation of some colonial worldviews by depicting certain groups as deficient.

Effective lifelong adult learning will purge the inferiority experienced by black workers, however subtle it can be. Progressive and decolonised adult education would oppose the hegemony of Western knowledge. The ABET centres cannot and should not pretend to offer education that is value free when colonial knowledge maintains the status quo. As decolonial education challenges the domination of Western knowledge, it should uphold the various forms of knowledge. […]"intercultural and postcolonial approaches have for many years now argued for the diversification of knowledge production and for the recognition of plural systems of knowledge" (Maitra & Guo, 2019:13). These authors also point out that there should be much emphasis to decolonise the minds of lifelong learners, practitioners, and policymakers in order to challenge the passivity, colonisation and marginalisation of learners in both classrooms and workplaces. Lifelong learning ought to accommodate cognitive justice that asserts the diversity of knowledges and the equality of knowers (Maitra & Guo, 2019).

In decolonial classrooms, the critical nature of the Anticolonial Education theory – a tool that is necessary for decolonising the classroom setting is necessary. Freire (1970) utilises this theory as he highlights the destructive nature of the oppressor.

Adult learners though, should believe in their power to change the dominating nature of the oppressor. The Anticolonial Education Theory emanates from Freire's concept of learning in order to liberate the future of the oppressed (Hayes, 2016). Hayes (2016) adds that Anticolonial Education Theory underscores that the voices of the marginalised groups are necessary to enhancing an inclusive educational environment, which has become a space of solidarity. Anticolonial Education Theory also emphasises the need for indigenous people to oppose Eurocentric knowledge that disparages and belittles other epistemologies. The indigenous people's cultures and histories are frequently obscured by 'white narratives' that 'other' the experiences of the indigenous. Furthermore, Hayes (2016) opines that the white supremacist culture seeks to marginalise the indigenous cultures. "The last and most essential element of the Anticolonial Education frames the 'undoing' or unravelling of Eurocentric social influences using it for a process of unlearning in order to transform" (Hayes, 2016:18). The adult learners should be able to see education as that which can address poverty, gender violence, patriarchy, racism, landlessness, and joblessness. Effective decolonised adult education will be based on sound principles such as these. Docile adults who do not see alternatives to whiteness and Eurocentric approaches will never be able to build a rigorous economy as well as education sustainability.

ABET and Current Education Policies

In order to attain transformation and equitable society, the South African government policy supports the idea of an empowering adult education. ABET is a concept whose ideals are to support lifelong learning and development and was conceptualised as a stream that would be available to adult learners who want to complete their basic education. ABET also provides the learners with learning tools and skills that would yield to recognised qualifications. Throughout the country, there are service providers, training companies and colleges that are ABET providers. The Skills Portal (2016) declares that there are 3.3 million illiterate adults in South Africa. ABET offers flexibility that suits specific needs of certain individuals, providing access to recognised certificates. There are however, many who question the relevance of ABET to workplace efficiency. Many believe that ABRT may be training that drills learners in routine jobs with no attention to knowledge and values (Skills Portal, 2016). ABET has four levels that are equivalent to Grades R-9. The South African Qualifications Authority (SAQA) has registered the following learning areas for level 4 or National Qualifications Framework (NQF) level 1 (Grade 12 equivalent):

- Language, Literacy and Communication – 20 credits
- Mathematical Literacy – 16 credits
- Arts and Culture – 16 credits
- Economic and Management Science – 16 credits
- Human and Social Science – 16 credits
- Life Orientation – 16 credits
- Natural Science – 16 credits
- Technology – 16 credits
- Mathematical Science -13 credits
- Additional Language – 16 credits

In addition to the above, adult learners can choose to take courses in Travel and Tourism, Agriculture, Early Childhood Development and Ancillary Health Care.

Some researchers have questioned the relevance of ABET after its initial inception (Ndlovu, 1999). Furthermore, Ndlovu conducted a study among women of the Mkhuhlu area in Mpumalanga Province and discovered that ABET was not providing relevant skills needed to develop the women participants. The women stated that ABET did not enable them to improve their quality of life. In Ndlovu's study (1999), it was found that the ABET programmes did not include effective skills training to improve the lives of learners on social, economic, and educational levels. Aitchison (2013) writes about the capacity that lacked to those who were supposed to lead adult education. He points out that the national Department of Education was unable to tackle the nationalising of education provision, resources, and teacher deployment. As a result of these challenges, ABET learners were in desperate situation where schoolteachers and higher education demanded continuation of the "lifestyle to which they had become accustomed". In Tawiah and Ngmenkpieo (2018), the researchers found that rural women who had undergone ABET training lagged behind in knowledge and skills for livelihood. The rural women were left disempowered due to the lack of relevant skills for employment or to be self-employed in the programme (Tawiah & Ngmenkpieo, 2018).

Decolonising ABET

As seen above, the original adult centres (night schools) were more focused on literacy and political education as various political activists ran them. During the apartheid times, the night schools became part of the system of segregated education offering education that is watered down. Yet when we ask today how to decolonise what is called Adult Basic Education and Training (ABET), we need to ensure that adult education addresses past imbalances as it empowers the learners. Furthermore, today decolonised adult education would also try to address the gap between the haves and the have-nots through technology use. A decolonised adult education refers to a system that treats adult learners with respect while infusing indigenous values and languages that were marginalised by apartheid and colonialism. Padayachee, Matimolane and Ganas (2018) write of a need for epistemologically diverse curricula that among others, may lead to education for sustainable development. Padayachee et al. (2018) also posit that there is strong need for a balance to be struck between theory and contextually relevant knowledge in curricula if decolonisation is to be achieved. Effective adult and basic education will lead to societal transformation. When empowered, many adults do influence the direction society adopts, and communities embrace.

The theory embedded in adult education should aspire towards liberatory education and social justice, both values that have been discussed in several chapters in this book. Additionally, because learning embraces Western knowledge and indigenous knowledge, it should address diversity as it promotes critical pedagogy. Adult learners should use the curriculum to survive in their daily lives within work environment, communities and society in general. In fact, ABET was established to support lifelong learning and knowledge required for economic and political participation and transformation applicable to a range of contexts (Skills Portal, 2016). In an age of decolonisation, these objectives are critical. Clover, Sanford, Bell and Johnson (2016) affirm about the need for critical and radical traditions of adult education. Feminist adult education, anti-racist education, decolonising methodologies, transformative, and radical learning are some of the critical themes in adult education today. Decolonised curriculum addresses apartheid and colonial vestiges.

The re-education of various adult learner's teachers is important for an education system that would truly decolonise. The social sciences are good examples for decolonising the curriculum. Through history and culture, adult learners can learn to regain their identity and self-dignity. Learning history in decolonised classrooms means reshaping knowledge. Smith (2016:30) points out why we need the shift towards decolonisation in education as she explicates the link between decolonisation and transformation:

> Decolonisation is linked to social transformation because it calls for the 'de-linking' or reshaping of societal spheres away from colonial/modern systems to allow all knowledges and systems to be given equal voice. Thereby, changing society. However, transformation stems from the need to alter past

injustices whereas decolonisation aims to dismantle them. Consequently, decolonisation is a process that can lead to societal transformation.

To redress the social sciences, adult learners would need to understand the muted voices of the oppressed as they learn to retell their own stories. Education for redress cannot be delivered for its own sake but should be seen as an instrument of social redress. The study of social sciences can address several issues including human rights, racial bigotry, and cultural domination.

Several authors have highlighted the nearness between curriculum decolonisation process and sustainable development (Padayachee et al., 2018). Furthermore, Padayachee et al. (2018) claim that curriculum decolonisation and education for sustainable development are critical for institutional and societal reform. Therefore, these are linked between curriculum transformation and sustainable development. This link has been perceived crucial in in preparing graduates for the future. In an aptly titled paper, *Decolonising Sustainable Development*, Razak (2017) writes about how Education for Sustainable Development (ESD) "blends with indigenous knowledge and wisdom with the existing 'modern' knowledge in articulating 'newer' ideas that have been cast aside by the excesses of colonisation" (Razak, 2017). Razak also points out that decolonised ESD is pivotal for a sustainable future. Adult education programmes in South Africa would be incomplete without sustainable development, for education geared towards future generations should be among the practical goals of a decolonised adult education. Adult education currently, unlike that under apartheid should play an intense transformative role.

Tikly (2019) declares that education policy should be re-oriented and harnessed to processes of economic, cultural, and political transformation. If adult education does this, learners would be able to embrace social and environmental justice. Furthermore, Tikly (2019) asserts that the vision of education for sustainable development hold an ambitious Pan-African vision of transformative change. Therefore, sustainable development is able to oppose the consequences of the colonial encounter. All learners especially the poor with no social capital, require sustainable development for it is through skills that they will be able to play part in their economy. The relevant adult learning sites should reflect the following elements as illustrated in Figure 6.1:

Learning Site

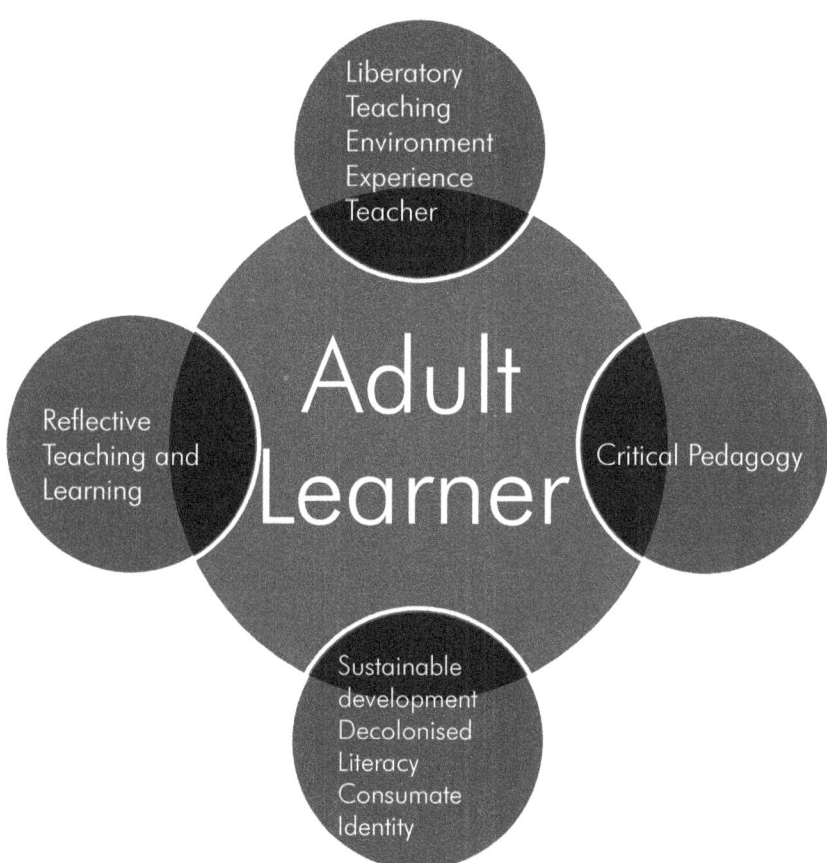

Figure 6.1   Adult Learner and Decolonisation Factors (Lalendle, Msila & Matlabe, 2020)

The figure above displays some of the elements adult learner need to decolonise education. Decolonial education should reflect the envisaged environment and the reality of the oppressed indigenous people. Numerous aspects should inform a decolonisation adult education class.

Among the values that need to be emphasised in decolonised, liberatory teaching is the will to oppose patriarchy, racism, and social injustice. Formal and informal content is needed in adult education to uplift feminist values in education. Social justice education should critically examine social relations. Schniedewind (1987) maintains that learning site interaction should always reflect feminist principles to

enhance student learning. Webb, Allen and Walker (2002) highlight six principles of feminist pedagogy, which can be useful in adult education learning sites:
1. Reformation of the teacher-learner relationship – learners need to share power.
2. Empowerment – education needs to be a practice of freedom.
3. Community building – in learning sites, learners should build community where all are equal.
4. Voice privileging – different voices should emerge in classrooms.
5. Respect for the diversity of personal experience – emphasis on personal experience and validation. This personal experience leads to respect and empathy.
6. Challenging the traditional pedagogical notions – ideas should be contested and challenged. Teachers should be prepared to relearn as they challenge the origins of knowledge.

Webb, Allen and Walker (2002) also point out that the theory of feminist pedagogy opposes the current emphasis on efficiency and objectivity that perpetuates masculine domination in rationality by bringing forth alternative views based on feminist principles. In decolonial learning sites, learners should have this experience of feminist pedagogy. The learners ought to share power and be able to challenge the notions of a patriarchal society in the learning sites. It is important for them to appreciate their active roles in learning and teaching as they contest the stereotypical portrayal presented by patriarchy. Learners should use learning sites to confront principles of a sexist society as they transform their lives. Schniedewind (1987) points out that the greatest threat to feminism at university is "the ease with which we can allow the curriculum to reflect thought without action" (Schniedewind, 1987:178). Adult education should be a source of inspiration for all communities; learners who would like to make a change in their society. Adult education centres should not mimic the miseducation that happens in learning sites that glorify banking approaches reflected by rote learning. When education does not oppose social ills, it is unlikely to challenge the status quo.

Shor (1987) contends that a curriculum that generates critical thought and leads to interactive learning should be lauded;. "The challenge to every liberal arts course is how much participation does it mobilise, how does it relate its body-of-knowledge to other disciplines, to the communities and literacies of the students, and to larger conditions of society" (Shor, 1987:21).

Arguably, language is one of the most important factors in education. In a time when the decolonisation debates have been widespread, the decolonisation of languages has also become critical. In a society where English and Afrikaans are still dominant, the adult learner might be curious to know when other indigenous languages will feature in the learning and teaching process. Language is critical to consciousness and awareness of one's society. The use of a language other than the learners' own can intensify the process of alienation. Freire's pedagogy emphasises the connection between critical use of language and a consciousness of oneself in social relations (Finlay & Faith, 1987). It is crucial for adult learners to use their indigenous languages; otherwise, if they are only forced to use English there might be less interaction in classrooms. Biko (1987:107-108) refers to this as the process of inward looking by students:

> We have a society here in South Africa, which recognises in the main two languages, English and Afrikaans as official languages. These are languages that you have to use at school, at university I mean, or in pursuit of any discipline when you are studying as a black man. Unfortunately, the books you read are in English, English is a second language to you; you have probably been taught in a vernacular [...] As a result you never quite catch everything that is in a book; you certainly understand the paragraph [...] This makes you less articulate as a black man generally, and this makes you more inward-looking; you feel things rather than say them, and this applies to Afrikaans as well---much more to English than to Afrikaans; Afrikaans is essentially a language that has developed here, and I think in many instances in its idiom, it relates much better to African languages; but English is completely foreign, and therefore people find it difficult to move beyond a certain point in their comprehension of the language.

The language shapes the dialogue and critical pedagogy in learning sites. Finlay and Faith (1987) point out that language use shapes the way people see their culture. Language also helps in transforming habitual thought into critical consciousness. Language is power and learners will feel powerlessness when learning sites marginalise their indigenous languages. Multilingual sites will empower learners who will be able to access education in their own languages. No progressive learning site will want to experience the 'culture of silence'. The exclusive use of English should not lead to illiteracy and passivity. Indigenous languages that learners speak should be part of teaching and learning. The use of indigenous languages as medium can and should challenge the dominant culture. Finlay and Faith (1987:82) claim:

> [...] our students fear and distrust the culture that runs the schools, a culture that they perceive as subordinating individual activity to the needs of a consumer economy. Since our students are not children, however, their education is complicated by their awareness that they have become accomplices in maintaining this culture and its values.

When adult learners use their indigenous languages such as isiXhosa, Xitsonga and isiNdebele in decolonial learning sites, they are able to bring their cultures and epistemologies as well. Language is the basis of literacy and constitutes the learners' reality. Freire believes that the goal of a literacy programme is to help learners to be critically conscious of their connection between their lives and the larger society and to empower them to change their environment (Fiore & Elsasser, 1987).

Decolonisation through Critical Literacy

If adult learners are able to attain social justice and freedom from the dominant culture, they should have the literacy skills that would equip them. From the very first night schools discussed above, the idea to bring forth learning to read was a political act. The activists who championed night schools sought to create adult learners who would share power. Brown (1987) proclaims that a non-literate person may have power within a non-literate subculture but within the dominant culture, a non-reader is marginal. "Learning to read gives access to information, protection against fraud, and participation as a citizen. Miller (nd) also points out that education is a political act because literacy builds an engaged, informal and participatory citizenry." Through literacy, people are able to access democracy and social justice. Literacy makes a huge difference to the learners, their families and their communities. Adults who are literate are able to be vocal in society and may play and active role in progressive groups as they access their right to voice their opinions.

All educators should understand their job as a political act. Brown (1987) writes about how Paulo Freire developed materials that made it possible for adult learners to learn to read in 30-40 hours. Freire achieved this after he understood the political dimensions of reading. Freire also discovered that nonliterates, through reading, became aware that they could change their lives although at first they thought that their lives were due to God's will (Brown, 1987). When the nonliterates became literate, they could distinguish between nature and culture and got to understand that there was a distinction because they were the makers of culture. They realised that they could change their circumstances. Literacy made the adult learners realise the importance of conscientisation because they could analyse reality and transform their lives. For Paulo Freire, education is either liberating or domesticating and if literacy is not domesticating, it must then be part of conscientisation (Brown, 1987).

The struggle for literacy in South Africa has been equivalent to the struggle for freedom. Carroll (2018) states that there is an improvement in literacy rates among adults in South Africa. In 2017, adult literacy rate was 87%. This increased from 76,2% in 1980 (Knoema, n.d.). This includes numeracy, which is the ability to make basic arithmetic calculations.

As we agree about the need to decolonise adult education, some experts such as Aitchison (2012) point out that South Africa has failed to achieve the "golden future of literacy and adult basic education". Aitchison laments that fact that the right to adult basic education is not yet real as long as it is not quickly achievable or enforceable. Yet, the history of Black Consciousness has shown how Biko and his peers used Freire's concept to build successful community programmes in the Eastern Cape Province where black people became self-reliant. Recent studies however demonstrate that there is still much room for improvement for South Africa's literacy. In 2016, a study by the Central Connecticut University showed that South Africa is ranked as one of the illiterate countries in the world (BusinessTECH, 2016). The study examined the literate behaviour rather than the country's ability to read. The five categories on which the study was based on were libraries, newspapers, education inputs and outputs, and computer availability. South Africa was ranked 56th overall among 61 countries (BusinessTECH, 2016).

Conclusion

Like other forms of education in South Africa, Adult Education was negatively influenced for decades by the legacies of apartheid and colonisation. Yet, today Adult Education can be a conduit of addressing several social ills including patriarchy, illiteracy, racism and sexism. Furthermore, progressive adult education can help entrench the culture of lifelong learning that would yield empowered and liberated citizenry. In this chapter, we concentrated more on the decolonisation of ABET and demonstrated why decolonisation is so critical today. Western knowledges or Eurocentric philosophies have dominated in South Africa for years, and arguably, some may contend that today those legacies are stalling meaningful changes in not only adult education but also all forms of education including basic education and higher education. When students started the #FeesMustFall campaign in 2015, it was an attempt to speed the transformation process by also calling for a decolonised system. Many African countries continue to struggle as they seek lasting solutions to decolonise education. Lifelong learning is critical in that it focuses mainly on workers who want to improve qualifications for better living. Yet, decolonisation needs new intellectuals who will understand diversity and ways to use indigenous knowledges as some form of an antidote to the internalised Western knowledges. Decolonised lifelong learning should be able to address the social ills brought by Eurocentrism. Adult learners must through critical pedagogy be able to decolonise the ideological underpinnings of colonial domination especially racialised privileging of whiteness (Maitra & Guo, 2016).

The need to decolonise all forms of education in Africa has never been as urgent as various African states seek to topple the exclusive recognition of Western knowledges which disempower the historically oppressed. All adult learners should be exposed to decolonised education that magnifies their purpose in life to improve their communities and enhance their self-identities. Decolonisation needs to seep through all institutions in the society. It is now apt to close the chapter by citing Maitra and Guo (2019:16) who posit:

> By decolonisation, we are not calling for an uncritical acceptance of knowledge systems. Rather, the emphasis should be on being open-minded enough to acknowledge the value of lifelong learning systems based on 'objectively ascertained merits […] We believe lifelong learning practices need to embrace cognitive justice that asserts the diversity of knowledges and equality of knowers.

References

Aitchison, J. 2012. Where are We Now with Literacy in South Africa? *KC Journal*, 31.

Aitchison, J.J.W. 2013. *A Review of Adult Basic Education and Training in South Africa*. [Online]. Available: https://bit.ly/2UAhVAk

Baatjes, B. & Baatjes, I. 2008. *The Right to Adult Community Education*. Centre for Education Rights and Transformation. Auckland Park: University of Johannesburg.

Biko, S. 1987. *I Write What I Like*. Oxford: Heinemann.

Burke, M.C. 2005. *Post-Colonialism: Informing Adult Education Research in Developing Countries*. Adult Education Research Conference. [Online]. Available: https://bit.ly/3dVtmKR

BusinessTECH. 2016. *South Africans among the most illiterate in the world*. [Online]. Available: https://bit.ly/2UzWdNa

Brown, C. 1987. Appendix: Literacy in 30 Hours: Paulo Freire's Process in Northeast Brazil. In: I. Shor (ed.), *Freire for the Classroom: A Sourcebook for Liberatory Teaching*. Portsmouth: Heinemann.

Carroll, J. 2018. Literacy and Skills are the Power for Good. *Mail and Guardian*.

Clover, D.E., Sanford, K., Bell, L. & Johnson, K. 2016. Introduction. In: D.E. Clover, K. Sanford, L. Bell & K. Johnson (eds.), *Adult Education, Museums and Art Galleries: Animating Social, Cultural and Institutional Change*. Rotterdam: Sense Publishers. https://doi.org/10.1007/978-94-6300-687-3

Darder, A. 2017. *Reinventing Paulo Freire: A Pedagogy of Love*. New York: Routledge. https://doi.org/10.4324/9781315560779

Degener, S.C. 2002. *Making Sense of Critical Pedagogy in Adult Literacy Education*. Volume 2. [Online]. Available: http://www.ncsall.net/?id=562

Finlay, L.S. & Faith, V. 1987. Illiteracy and Alienation in American Colleges: Is Paul Freire's Pedagogy Relevant? In: I. Shor (ed.), *Freire for the Classroom: A Sourcebook for Liberatory Teaching*. Portsmouth: Heinemann.

Fiore, K. & Elsasser, V. 1987. Strangers No More: A Liberatory Literacy Curriculum. In: I. Shor (ed.), *Freire for the Classroom: A Sourcebook for Liberatory Teaching*. Portsmouth: Heinemann.

Freire, P. 1970. *Pedagogy of the Oppressed*. New York: Continuum.

reire, P. 1970. The Adult Literacy Process as Cultural Action for Freedom. *Harvard Educational Review*, 40 (2): 205-225. https://doi.org/10.17763/haer.40.2.q7n227021n148p26

Freire, P. 2019. Oppression, Freedom and Critical Approaches to Education. In: K. Aubrey & A. Riley (eds.), *Understanding and Using Educational Theories*. Los Angeles: SAGE.

Hayes, C.C. 2016. How to Decolonise a Classroom. Unpublished Masters Dissertation. Vermont: SIT Graduate Institute.

Kallaway, P. 1988. *From Bantu Education to Peoples Education*. Cape Town: UCT.

Kellenberg, F., Schmidt, J. & Werner, C. 2017. The Adult Learners: Self-determined, Self-regulated, and Reflective. *Signum Temporis*, 9(1):23-29. https://doi.org/10.1515/sigtem-2017-0001

Knoema. n.d. *Adult (15+) Literacy Rate*. [Online]. Available: https://bit.ly/2UCq07X

Maitra, S. & Guo, S. 2019. Theorising Decolonisation in the Context of Lifelong and Transnational Migration: Anti-colonial and Anti-racist Perceptions. *International Journal of Lifelong Education*, 38(1):5-19. https://doi.org/10.1080/02601370.2018.1561533

Miller, D. n.d. *Education is a Political Act*. [Online]. Available: https://bit.ly/2YsMoS3

Msila, V. 2007. From Apartheid Education to the Revised National Curriculum Statement: Pedagogy for Identity Formation and Nation Building in South Africa. *Nordic Journal of African Studies*, 16(2):146-160.

Myers, K., Conte, N. & Rubenson, K. 2014. *Adult Learning Typology: Adult Learning and Returns to Training Project*. Ottawa: Social Research and Demonstration Corporation.

Nafukho, F., Amutabi, M. & Otunga, R. 2005. *Foundations of Adult Education in Africa*. New York: UNESCO.

Ndlovu, B.G. 1999. The Role of ABET Programmes in the Development of Rural Black Women in the Mkhuhlu Area. Unpublished Masters Dissertation. Auckland Park: Rand Afrikaans University.

Ndlovu-Gatsheni, S.J. 2018. *Epistemic Freedom in Africa: Deprovincialization and Decolonization*. London: Taylor and Francis. https://doi.org/10.4324/9780429492204

Nordhaug, O. 1986. The Concept of Adult Education. *Scandinavian Journal of Educational Research*, 30(4):153-165. https://doi.org/10.1080/0031383860300401

Padayachee, K., Matimolane, M. & Ganas, R. 2018. Addressing Curriculum Decolonisation and Education for Sustainable Development Through Epistemically Diverse Curricula. *South African Journal of Higher Education*, 32(6):288-304. https://doi.org/10.20853/32-6-2986

Prinsloo, M. 1995. Provision, Acquisition and Culture: Literacy Research in South Africa. *International Journal of Educational Development*, 15(4):449-460. https://doi.org/10.1016/0738-0593(95)00022-U

Razak, D.A. 2017. Decolonising Sustainable Development. *Global RCE Network – Education for Sustainable Development*. [Online]. Available: https://bit.ly/37n06tX

Redmond, B. 2006. *Reflection in Action: Developing Reflective Practice in Health and Social Services*. Aldershot: Ashgate.

Roche, M. 2016. What is Action Research? In: B. Sullivan, M. Glenn, M. Roche & C. McDonagh (eds.), *Introduction to Critical Reflection and Action for Teacher Researchers*. London: Routledge.

Roux, E. 1964. *Time Longer Than Rope: A History of the Black Man's Struggle for Freedom in South Africa*. Madison: University of Wisconsin Press.

Rule, P. 2006. The Time is Burning: The right of Adults to Basic Education in South Africa. *Journal of Education*, 39:113-135.

Schniedewind, N. 1987. Feminist Values: Gudelines for Teaching Methodology in Women's Studies. In: I. Shor (ed.), *Freire for the Classroom: A Sourcebook for Liberatory Teaching*. Portsmouth: Heinemann.

Shor, I. 1987. Educating the Educators: A Freirean Approach to the Crisis in Teacher Education. In: I. Shor (ed.), *Freire for the Classroom: A Sourcebook for Liberatory Teaching*. Portsmouth: Heinemann.

Skills-Universe. 2010. *Understanding Adult Education and Training (ABET and/or AET)*. [Online]. Available: https://bit.ly/3dYeew5

Skills Portal. 2016. *What is Adult Basic Education and Training (ABET)*. [Online]. Available: https://bit.ly/30z6CMD

Smith, C.J. 2016. Decolonising the South African Art Curriculum. Unpublished masters Dissertation. Johannesburg: Wits University.

Tawiah, S. & Ngmenkpieo, F. 2018. Adult Basic Education and Training in South Africa: The Perspectives of Rural Women in Khotso. *Mediterranean Journal of Social Sciences*, 9(1):57-64. https://doi.org/10.2478/mjss-2018-0005

Tikly, L. 2019. Education for Sustainable Development in Africa: A Critique of Regional Agendas. *Asia Pacific Education Review*, 20(2):223-237. https://doi.org/10.1007/s12564-019-09600-5

Triple E Training. 2013. *ABET/AET Basic Education and Training for Adults*. [Online]. Available: https://bit.ly/30CiQ79

Wallerstein, N. 1987. Problem-Posing Education: Freire's method for Transformation. In: I. Shor (ed.), *Freire for the Classroom: A Sourcebook for Liberatory Teaching*. Portsmouth: Heinemann.

Webb, L.M., Allen, M.W. & Walker, K.L. 2002. Feminist Pedagogy: Identifying Basic Principles. *Academic Exchange*, Spring:67-72.

Chapter Seven

Fostering Collective Teacher Efficacy Through Values-Based and *Ubuntu*-Inspired Leadership: Implications for Decolonisation

Terefe F. Bulti

Getting back to African Values: Solidifying Organisations

Conscientious leaders today are constantly asking themselves as to what values and which kind of leadership they need to follow as they head their organisations. This volume has examined various ways in which teacher education can decolonise institutions, programmes, and people. These are all themes that are necessary to be addressed in Africa as we embolden the dream of an African Renaissance. Leadership institutes should also be open about decolonising leadership models that would embrace innovative leadership practices. Without effective leadership, institutions would not be able to have people who will spread the tenets of decolonisation. Many African leaders have begun to dig deep into African values and ethics as they build institutions.

With the advent of decolonisation and African Renaissance, leaders are more open to experiment with various models, including African leadership models. There are a few of these values, which are universal, and these include the values around servant leadership and ethical leadership to a certain extent. Intentional leaders will seek relevant values that would contradict poor leadership that debilitates many dysfunctional organisations. We have arrived at an age when nothing should preclude leaders in bringing the historically marginalised African values to enhance the organisation. Boon (2001) writes about the need to create an interactive leadership system, which begins with values. He distinguishes principles from values for principles are regarded as fundamental truths that do not change with time. Boon (2001) argues that there are two ways to create values; the one is democratic whilst on the other involves autocratical decisions. Boon (2001:35) writes:

> Many management teams create values and then thrust them on the organisation. I heard this comment from a senior leader of a well-known international corporation: "We [the management] listed the values and then went to each factory and office, and spent a lot of time explaining them to each group. Nothing really changed though and, quite frankly, other than the team building senior management experienced during the time in the bush, when we listed the values, I think it was a bit of a wasted effort."

Boon (2001:85) goes on to explain that one group cannot create values but need to emanate from the people's belief system. "To be accepted by a community, values have to be created and shared by that community". Viljoen (2015) underscores the need for inclusivity in organisations. Inclusivity releases energy in an institution and this is likely to enhance performance and productivity. All leaders' behaviour is critical for effective leaders can use values that, when cascaded down the ranks of an organisation, can help curb ills such as corruption in organisation (Hendrikz & Engelbrecht, 2019). Numerous values could be used to build ethical organisations. Several writers have drawn African-inspired models that are driven by African values. One of these African values highlighted in literature is *Ubuntu/Huhnu/Umunthu*, which refers to humaneness – reflected in the maxim "I am because you are". *Ubuntu* is a unique African value which shares certain characteristics with servant leadership. This old African philosophy is based on ethical leadership and values of dependability, solidarity, and commitment. Hendrikz and Engelbrecht (2019) point out that, "*Ubuntu* could transform the way in which leadership development takes place. As a basic tenet of African philosophy and ethics, *Ubuntu* suggests that basic life goals should be to realise excellence".

Broodryk (2006) lists a number of values that make up *Ubuntu*, and among these is humanness. He then discusses various components of humanness and these include human rights, tolerance, understanding, peace, and humanity. All these are vital to living whether it is in the home or workplace. Msila (2015) points out that *Ubuntu*-inspired workplace thrives on teamwork, solidarity, interconnectedness, loyalty, openness, and honesty. Organisations and communities with these characteristics will thrive hold together by the belief system in *Ubuntu*. *Ubuntu* models can be amenable to Collective Teacher Efficacy discussed in this chapter.

This chapter examines the role Values-Based Leadership (VBL) in influencing Collective Teacher Efficacy (CTE) in education institutions. What is clear in this chapter is the ideal of decolonisation; to show that African leadership models can co-exist with Western models. The chapter emphasises what other chapters have referred to and that is the need for the use of collective ecologies of knowledge instead of marginalising some knowledges. The preface of this book briefly raises the argument of the need to decentre the West as we include all knowledges, including those historically marginalised.

Teaching is one of the core missions that every education institution strives to accomplish. To this effect, the role of teachers, particularly in the conventional mode of delivery, is not substitutable. Teachers do have a primary and direct role in influencing students' learning. If any other variable must be mentioned as attributing to the success of students, leadership should come next. This implies leadership does have an influence over students' learning by influencing teaching or the teachers' role. Nevertheless, there no single route to bring such an influence; hence different leadership efforts are made in this regard. However, the influence that gears towards building the confidence of the teachers and attempts to cultivating the belief and efficacy of the teacher work group must be considered as bottom lines to such leadership efforts. Obviously, not all leadership styles and behaviours do have equal impact in terms of fostering this desired efficacy and hence VBL is proposed here as having a significant role in fostering CTE.

Values-Based Leadership (VBL)

When we talk about values, we cannot miss the fact that some values are universal and Africa shares these with many other countries. Crossan, Gandz and Seijts (2018) differentiate between values and virtues. These authors define values as those beliefs that people embrace and these are also vital to them; for they influence behaviour. Virtues are close to values but are defined as behavioural habits – actions that are displayed consistently over time (Crossan et al., 2018). Leaders who focus on long-term performance display ten virtues and these are humility, integrity, collaboration, justice, courage, temperance, accountability, humanity, transcendence, and judgement (Crossan et al., 2018). Values are those moral beliefs and attitudes held by an individual person or a collective to which people appealed for the ultimate rationales that guide behaviour or action (Busher, 2006). These values are relatively stable beliefs that certain modes of behaviour or end-states are desirable (Grojean, Resick, Dickson & Smith,

2004; Buchko, 2006). Such values are the essence of leadership in educational institutions (Frank, 2005; Greenfield, 2005; Haydon, 2007; Gold, 2010) because the values that people emphasise may influence the actions they engage in (Grojean et al., 2004). It implies that VBL is about leading through those moral beliefs, behaviours to influence actions and decisions. Broadly, however, VBL can be conceptualised in terms of the following aspects: leader-follower relationships; a path that connects moral orientation and principles to stewardship decisions and actions; and a leadership that involves a set of distinguishable behaviours.

As evident above, several writers from Africa have written about values in organisations, showing how Africans upheld and strengthened their societies through values of the society (Mbigi, 1997; Mbigi & Maree, 1995; Broodryk, 2006; Msila, 2015). Broodryk (2006) perceives *Ubuntu* philosophy as crucial in Africa and maintains that the values enshrined in *Ubuntu* are pivotal life-coping skills from Africa. Furthermore, Broodryk (2006) like Mbigi (1997) contends that *Ubuntu* management philosophy that contains the necessary leadership values is imperative for improved staff performance. Humanness, caring, sharing, respect, and compassion are values that he highlights in the book.

Similarly, in his book, *Ubuntu: Shaping the Current Workplace with (African) Wisdom*, Msila (2015) writes about the values underscored in Mbigi (1997); Prinsloo (1998); Broodryk (2006); Mbigi (1995) and Msila (2008). Many of these values as highlighted above are universal and are various ways shared by the world. Nussbaum (2003) argues that African values such as *Ubuntu* are solid and can teach the world consciousness much if only the West did not misunderstand or ignore Africa for a number of reasons. Therefore, the knowledge or the epistemic freedom that seeks to underscore these African values will bring them to the centre sharing with the West under the ecologies of knowledge. Discussing servant leadership, Msila (2008) reflects how the qualities of this concept are also present in African models, including *Ubuntu*.

Msila (2008) opines that the value of dependability in *Ubuntu* manifest itself as the virtue of servant leadership which is shown by caring leaders around the world. Management practices in our world have always been dominated by Western philosophies although we now know of the need to also incorporate traditional African wisdom. It is a fact that we cannot discard Western strategies of management because these can be enhanced by African styles of leadership and values. Reuel Khoza of the Nedbank Group in South Africa was quoted as saying we should not place too much confidence in traditional wisdom (Mgayi, 2013).

There seems to be consensus that values of diverse and dynamic organisations should be extrapolated from Western approaches as well as traditional Africa, thus combining the best of both worlds can build the organisation. Organisations are in a state of flux and it will always help to glean from a variety of approaches to build institutions and organisations. Combining Western and traditional African models means the appeasement of individual goals and community ideals on the other. Leadership based on a combination of values will be beneficial to the 21st century organisation in Africa; organisations that strive for inclusivity, social justice, cognitive justice, and high performance. Van Coller-Peter states that it is mostly second generation of third generation of management coaches who realise the richness of diversity brings to the workplace (Mgayi, 2013). For example, what Mbigi and Maree (1995) is complementary to what other Western experts are saying. Mbigi and Maree argue that for organisations to thrive they must be based on values that would build teamwork and solidarity. The leader is very central in this regard. Mbigi (1997) claims that five key values are essential for VBL and these are:

1. **Survival** – ability to live despite challenges.
2. **Solidarity spirit** – difficult goals can be overcome through collectiveness.
3. **Compassion** – understanding and empathising with others.
4. **Respect** – respecting others is also key to building organisations. In affective teams, people know, "I exist because of others – I live through others".
5. **Dignity** – when people see that they are respected they grow dignity within. Through dignity, they will show commitment and a sense of responsibility.

VBL will be propelled by these values. These values will lead to solidarity, dependability, humanity, leadership that is based on social justice principles (Msila, 2015).

VBL is one of the contemporary leadership theories meant to contribute to institutional success, particularly in terms of establishing a desired relationship among the working staff, as well as between leaders and followers. According to Rhode (2006:5) in the past few decades the rise, fall, and resurrection of many leadership theories have been revealed. Currently, however, VBL theories have received increased attention (Copeland, 2014). To this effect, Segon and Booth (2013) assert that for higher education institutions to foster right actions, they are required to adopt the philosophy of VBL and ensure its institutionalisation. The specific benefits of VBL to organisational operations include enhancing trust on leaders (Adei, 2010; Viinamäki, 2011) fostering accountability (Viinamäki, 2011; 2012); and establishing a basis upon which stakeholders can collaborate (Mills & Spencer, 2005).

Collective Teacher Efficacy (CTE): What's Value-Based Leadership (VBL) got to do with it?

CTE can be defined as the confidence that teachers develop in a group about their ability to organise and implement tasks pertaining to improvement of students' learning experiences (Leithwood, Patten & Jantzi, 2010; Angelle, Nixon, Norton & Niles, 2011). Goddard, Hoy and Woolfolk Hoy (2000) also define CTE as the perceptions of the teachers about their collective capability that their efforts can result in improvement in students' achievement. It is also referred to as "a specific form of self-efficacy in which the target of the beliefs is the organisation to which the individual belongs" (Ross & Gray, 2006:801). It is the beliefs that typically reflect individual teachers' perceptions of group-level attributes at organisational level (Ross & Gray, 2006). These authors argue that CTE is a specific form of self-efficacy in which the beliefs gear towards the organisation to which the teacher belongs. The general implication is that CTE mainly deals with teachers' mental state (perceptions, beliefs, and attitude) and gears towards the group, to the collective or to the entire organisation. Accordingly, it involves a view that 'together we can make a significant improvement to students' learning experience.

Scholars suggest some defining features about CTE, i.e. the teacher work groups having a strong CTE are identified with some characteristics. These may include: the acceptance of challenging goals (Goddard et al., 2000); strong organisational efforts, and greater motivation to persist for a better performance (Goddard et al., 2000; Angelle et al., 2011); collective responsibility/collegial accountability (Angelle et al., 2011); and strong teachers' commitment to institutions (Brinson & Steiner, 2007). In line with investigations pertaining to CTE, findings consistently show that in an institution where CTE is strong, there is a better learning (Cybulski, Hoy & Sweetland, 2005; Adams & Forsyth, 2006; Ross & Gray, 2006). Moreover, Leithwood et al. (2010:676) assert that Collective Teacher Efficacy:

> [...] creates high expectation for students' learning and encourage teachers to set challenging benchmarks for themselves [...] High-CTE are more likely to engage in student-centred learning [...] High CTE is associated with teachers adapting a humanistic approach to student management, testing new instructional methods to meet the learning needs of their students, and providing extra help to students who have difficulty.

These findings all affirm that CTE has a crucial role to play in promoting better learning experiences for students. Being cognisant of the potential outcome of this sort of efficacy, Brinson and Steiner (2007) also contend that educational leaders currently have shown keen interest in building such an efficacy. However, most of the investigations in this regard have been focusing on elementary and high schools. The need to extend this knowledge to the level of higher education has been addressed by some researchers. For instance, in their attempt to endorse the need to foster CTE at a university level, Fives and Looney (2009:82) postulate: "In a time when more and more students are coming to the university and concerns such as grade inflation[...] and academic dishonesty are becoming more salient, it seems pertinent that we begin to look at the motivations and beliefs of the professionals who guide the learning process."

Furthermore, Chakravarthi, Haleagrahara and Judson (2010) also conducted a study in the context of higher education and found out that a lecturer's efficacy is one of the few lecturer characteristics consistently related to student achievement. It has been noted here that effective teaching and those who have confidence in their ability to teach persist longer in their teaching efforts, provide greater academic focus in the classroom, give different types of feedback, and ultimately improve student performance can influence lecturers who believe that student learning. Shambaugh (2008:135) also notes: "Collective Teacher Efficacy seems to have the most robust impact on student achievement, school climate, faculty morale, and the organisation's ability to manage stress." In general, CTE refers to individual teachers' belief about the collective capability of the teacher work group to bring the desired change in students' learning. The building of confidence (efficacy) is a process that involves many inter-related efforts and thus it is worthwhile to identify and start with the bottom line. To instil confidence in teachers, a leader may click on the mind and heart of the teachers. Since CTE is a group property that must be seen in terms of group level attributes, it is imperative to raise group norms and professional values as a relevant subject of discussion here.

Accordingly, there have been many research undertakings about which leadership models are linked to and would foster CTE. For instance, it has been found that there is a positive and significant linkage between CTE and transformational leadership (Demir, 2008); between CTE and teacher leadership (Angelle et al., 2011); and between CTE and instructional leadership (Fancera, 2009; Vari, 2011). However, the effect sizes of these leadership models were found to be different. The fact that different leadership models could have different effect sizes implies the need to explore the roles of other contemporary leadership models in this regard. In line with this, Copeland (2014:106) maintains that VBL has a high potential in overcoming the limitations associated with charismatic and seemingly transformational leadership that lack moral, authentic, and ethical dimensions. It means that, if properly institutionalised, VBL would result in positive outcomes.

Leader-follower Relationship based on Ideological Values

VBL is defined as "a relationship between a leader and followers that is based on shared strongly internalised ideological values adopted by the leader and strong followers' identification with those values" (Daft, 2008:439). This implies that it is the ideological values that bind the leaders and the followers together. It is also implied herein that vision is the end value/the-ultimate rationale that guides the behaviours of leaders and the followers. To this effect, the instrumental means to realise the vision is also stated by the author. With this respect, three issues are addressed as a basic requirement. The first one is the exceptionally strong identification of followers with the collective vision espoused by the leader and the collective.

The second requirement is internalised commitment of followers to the vision of the leader and to the collective (followers' willingness to make substantial self-sacrifices to serve beyond the call of duty). The implication here is the commitment of the follower is the key instrumental value to realising the vision, which is the end value. The third requirement is arousal of follower motives that are relevant to the accomplishment of goals. This means that after the vision is shared and owned, and after the followers internalised their commitments, the leaders is also required to arouse the interest of the working staff and increase their confidence. Consequently, VBL can be conceptualised as a leader-followers relationship whereby a leader formulates a vision and values to which the followers identified with, are committed to, and motivated by.

VBL refers to the moral foundation underlying stewardship decisions and actions of leaders (Ahn, Ettner & Loupin, 2012). It is also called the leadership path wherein the fundamental moral orientation of self-fullness leads to complete stewardship decisions and actions (McCuddy, 2008). It centres, among others, on the philosophical reality (moral orientation) adopted by the leader (Fairholm & Fairholm, 2009). This moral orientation can be of three types (McCuddy, 2008): selfishness, selflessness, and self-fullness. These qualities, especially selflessness, is underscored in African models of management (Mbigi & Maree, 1997; Msila, 2015).

Nevertheless, whether a leader espouses selflessness or self-fullness, it is assumed that the leader adopts VBL as long as stewardship is reflected in the leader's decisions and actions. In self-fullness, the leader pursues reasonable self-interest to ensure the sustainability of the business and pursues reasonable concern for the staff's current affairs (McCuddy, 2008). However, in selflessness, the leader forgoes his personal interests in the interest of the staff and of the company (Taylor, 2010). The point here in general is stewardship is inculcated in the leader's moral orientation and serves as the driving force when the leader takes action/makes a decision. Hence, VBL can be conceptualised as a leadership philosophy whereby a leader forgoes a certain level of selflessness and takes decisions in the sense of stewardship.

A Set of Distinguishable Behaviours

As noted above, VBL can be conceptualised in terms of the leader-follower relationship and in terms of the leader's moral orientation or philosophy. To this end, it is also possible to view VBL as a leadership model that has its own unique sets of behaviour by which the leader is characterised. According to Taylor (2010:6):

> Organisations live and die by their leadership ultimately; it is the leader's effectiveness in creating vision for a preferred future and establishing an appropriate values-driven culture that determines organisational results. Leaders and their organisations can best execute their mission and achieve superior results by first addressing the foundation of behaviour and performance-personal and shared values. Values determine behaviour and behaviour determines performance.

Taylor's assertion implies that VBL leaders do have their own unique sets of behaviour that can be sensed and learnt from their personal and shared values. This means that there is some behaviour by which the values-based leaders are identified or characterised. To this end, Daft (2010:395) articulates the specific characteristics or behaviours of values-based leaders as:

> They treat others with care, are helpful and supportive of others, and put efforts into maintaining positive interpersonal relationships. They treat everyone fairly and with respect. They accept others' mistakes and failures and are never condescending. They hold themselves to high ethical standards; continuously strive to be honest, humble, and trustworthy and to be consistently ethical in both their public and private lives […] they also clearly articulate and communicate an uncompromising vision for high ethical standards in the organisation, and they institutionalise the vision by holding themselves and others accountable and by putting ethics above short-term personal or company interests. They continuously strengthen ethical values through every day behaviours, rituals, ceremonies, and symbols, as well as through organisational systems and policies.

From the descriptions given by Daft in the above, it is possible to identify the following phrases as linked to the behaviours of values-based leaders: respect and fair treatment; accepting others' mistakes and being humble; encouraging and supporting others; and being honest, trustworthy, and commitment to higher ethical standards. Ahn et al. (2012) also affirm that VBL can be characterised by such behaviours as: integrity; good judgment; leadership by example; decision-making; trust; justice/fairness; humility; and sense of humour. Similarly, the following are also identified as values that are characterising VBL: integrity, compassion, humility, courage, and respect (Sarros & Cooper, 2006; Segon & Booth, 2013). This implies that a leader utilising values requires a level of commitment to institutionalise such values.

Finally, Taylor (2007) also stipulates seven characteristics of values-based leaders. The first is that they set an uncompromising example through demonstrating integrity. Secondly, they serve the organisation and its constituents in a selfless fashion and raise-up others (followers) in genuine humility. Thirdly, they show compassion by caring for others and developing their potential. Fourthly, they are purpose-driven, aligning with corporate mission, vision, and values. Fifthly, they demonstrate courage and persevere to do the right thing. Sixthly, they are self-disciplined, holding themselves and others accountable. Lastly, they show gratitude and appreciation, acknowledging the contributions of others. As a result, VBL can be conceptualised as a leadership model that is characterised by the aforementioned leadership behaviours.

From the above noted assertions, it can be inferred that there are some values and behaviours that are assumed to form VBL and would result in positive organisational outcome. That is, some values are found to have critical importance in every organisational operation. In line with this, Fairholm and Fairholm (2009) assert that there is growing consensus over the values of VBL. Several scholars have identified many values that have been highlighted over the years and these include; integrity, compassion and sense of gratitude, accountability and self-discipline, humility/selflessness and humbleness, and envisioning. Validation of these values is based on their frequent citation in reputable journals and books. To this end, at least six references are made about the relative importance of each of these values.

Integrity

Northouse (2013:25) defines integrity as "the quality of honesty and trustworthiness and notes that leaders with integrity inspire confidence in others because they can be trusted to do what they are going to do." Integrity means adhering to moral principles and acting based on those beliefs (Daft, 2008), or consistently adhering to strict moral or ethical standards (Sarros & Cooper, 2006; Ahn et al., 2012). This is directly related to role modelling/setting uncompromised examples (Haydon, 2007; Taylor, 2007; Taylor, 2010; Ahn et al., 2012; Segon & Booth, 2013). For example, one of the desirable behaviours or instrumental values that a leader wants his/her followers to espouse may be job commitment. However, a leader cannot win such a commitment from followers through a mere desire or by using word of mouth. As Albion (2006) advocates, the leader's commitment can determine the followers' level of commitment. Moreover, it is asserted that the best leaders are distinguished by relentless effort, steadfastness, competence, and by paying attention to detail (Kouzes & Posner, 2008). In support of this, Taylor (2007) also contends that integrity is the most widely endorsed values of VBL.

According to Kouzes and Posner (2008), to demonstrate integrity or to model behaviours in a credible way requires two things; primarily a leader is required to espouse integrity as his/her leadership value, and secondly he/she is expected to set a complementary example to ensure that words and deeds are aligned. In their attempt to emphasise this concept, Kouzes and Posner (2012:17) note "leaders' deeds are far more important than their words when constituents want to determine how serious leaders really are about what they say. Words and deeds must be consistent." In an education setting, integrity is indicated by "the shared belief that a good balance is struck at a given school among external demands, professional values, and student needs" (Mintrop, 2012:702).

In relation to the significance of integrity for employees' morale and confidence, Taylor (2007:43) notes that when the leader behaves with integrity, he/she earns trust. As integrity and trust become the norm, two things happen relative to organisational performance. The first one is, employees throughout the organisation practice ethical behaviour and seek to do what is right – not what is expedient or convenient for short-term gains. The second is employees will experience new and heightened levels of emotion. "Employees learn about values from watching leaders in action. The more the leader 'walks the talk', by translating internalised values into action, the higher level of trust and respect he generates from followers." (Mihelič, Lipičnik & Tekavčič, 2010:33). Therefore, from the discussions made thus far, it is possible to infer that a leadership in which integrity is reflected has a strong potential to foster CTE.

Compassion and Sense of Gratitude

Sarros and Cooper (2006) view compassion as "concern for the suffering or welfare of others and to provide aid or show mercy for others". These authors also point out that the real reflection of compassion is stewardship, which is a unique character of a leader. Similarly, Albion (2006) contends that a key part of being a values-based leader is stewardship and providing a community where every individual counts, and the boundaries of that community include all the company's internal stakeholders. Furthermore, Fairholm and Fairholm (2009:86-87) affirm: "Values leaders come to see the organisation, its people, and resources in stewardship terms. As stewards, leaders take responsibility to care for and develop the people they work with and the team they represent. They are creating an environment conducive towards improvement of team work." In connection to this, it is advocated as a principle that "the leader's role is stakeholder development/empowerment."

In a similar fashion, Daft (2010:395) also contends that values-based leaders "treat others with care, are helpful and supportive of others, and put efforts into maintaining positive interpersonal relationships. They also treat everyone fairly and with respect." A compassionate values-based leader acts in the best interest of all members of the organisation who could be impacted by the decisions made at a given organisation (Albion, 2006). Accordingly, Taylor (2007; 2010) endorses this value as one of the most important elements of VBL. The author also endorses a sense of gratitude as one essential value of VBL noting that values-based leaders show gratitude and appreciation, acknowledging the contributions of others.

Humility/selflessness

Another frequently referred to value in relation to VBL is humility and/or selflessness. This value is addressed as a key to the implementation of VBL, without which this implementation looks ingenuine in the eyes of the followers. For instance, Taylor (2010:23) contends, "values-based leaders selflessly serve and raise-up others in genuine humility." Furthermore, Kouzes and Posner (2012:341) describe the essence of this value as:

> You can avoid excessive pride only when you recognise that you are human and need the help of others. Exemplary leaders know that 'you cannot do it alone,' and they act accordingly. They lack the pride and presence displayed by many leaders who succeed in the short term but leave behind a weak organisation that fails to remain viable after their departure. Instead, with self-effacing humour, deep listening to those around them, and generous and sincere credit to others, humble leaders realise higher and higher levels of performance.

From the description given by Kouzes and Posner, it can be implied that humility and selflessness are about having a modest sense of one's significance and recognising the significance of others genuinely. They are about serving others by forgoing personal interests. In this case, selflessness and humility are presented as inseparable words and are jointly applied in practice. However, Sarros and Cooper (2006:8) conceptualise selflessness as "being genuinely concerned about the welfare of others and willingness to sacrifice one's personal interest for others and their organisation" and humility as "the quality of being humble or a modest sense of one's own significance." Although it is possible to describe them differently, both humility and selflessness are the desirable behaviour of a value-based leader. In relation to the significance of humility/selflessness, Taylor (2010) contends that humility is the indispensable value of VBL and serves as the basis for any other values. He also contends that humility is the one indispensable trait of values-based leaders because leaders who demonstrate true humility are best able to motivate followers to high levels of execution and performance (Taylor, 2007).

The polar extreme of selflessness and humility is selfishness. It is about pursuing one's personal desires at the expense of others. According to McCuddy, (2008:12) selfishness exists in a variety of degrees. Its worst extreme is "about the unbridled pursuit of greed and the uncaring exploitation of others". A relatively less extreme form of selfishness is about "making decisions and taking actions that provide a person with satisfaction … in the conduct of one's life". The author notes that selfishness can be socially acceptable when it involves decisions and actions that are intended to ensure one's physical survival. This implies that a modest sense of selfishness can also be reflected in VBL, as long as it is done reasonably and is socially acceptable. When a modest sense of selfishness is reflected in leadership jointly with a reasonable concern for others, McCuddy calls it 'self-fullness', which he asserts as the most rational approach to result in a VBL with a better outcome.

Accountability and Self-discipline

Accountability and self-discipline are two seemingly different but inseparable words. In connection to this, Taylor (2010) notes that self-disciplined leaders dare to hold themselves and others accountable for their action. This implies that self-discipline can be manifested in terms of the leader's readiness to take personal responsibilities and to delegate responsibilities to others. Taking an initiative and moral courage to lead the followers towards a desirable end is responsibility of a value-based leader. In line with this, O'Toole (2008:90) asserts that "the role, task, and responsibility of values-based leaders is to help followers realise the most important ends that they hold dear but cannot obtain by themselves." Furthermore, Daft (2010:395) notes that values-based leaders "institutionalise the vision by holding themselves and others accountable and by putting ethics above short-term personal or company interests." Therefore, self-disciplining and shouldering a responsibility to discipline the followers to collectively move to a certain end are among the key values in VBL.

Some scholars argue that there is a delicate demarcation between and among compassion, accountability, and responsibility. For instance, Albion (2006:41) asserts, "compassion is the quality of empathy that leads to a healthy respect for others and a sense of accountability. A cousin of responsibility, compassion often leads to what society calls more responsible action." Thus, for a leader to effectively shoulder accountability, he/she needs to be compassionate to others, but the fact that accountability involves an aspect of sustainability may help the leader balance the future fate of a company with the current concern of its employees. A leader is accountable to ensure that the personal and organisational values are enforced and key organisational issues are continually addressed (Taylor, 2012).

Envisioning and Moral Courage

Vision is the end value or the ultimate rationale for deriving any other values. As a concept, it refers to a mental picture of what lies at the end of a road that has never been travelled or a dream just beyond an institution's current reach (Calder, 2006). It is based on and reflects a company has stated beliefs and values, and conveys the future status of an institution and the end of the journey. Yoeli and Berkovich (2010) view such a vision as an organisation's compass that points in the direction the organisation should aim at and that reflects a desired ideal for the organisation's activity. This implies that vision is a mental affair that drives institutional stakeholders to travel to a desired end on a challenging but defined path.

A vision should be set in a way that it is powerful enough to upscale the expectations, aspirations, and performance of relevant stakeholders (Calder, 2006). This depicts that moral courage or inspiration is one important element that followers usually expect from their leaders. This is because "inspiring leaders breathe life into people's dreams and aspirations, making them much more willing to sign on for the duration" (Kouzes & Posner, 2008:3). As asserted by Calder (2006), a vision is grounded in an institution's beliefs and values. Moreover, a clearly articulated vision would inform the major stakeholders of a given institution about what an institution values (believes in).

A key element in envisioning is moral courage. Courage, according to Sarros and Cooper (2006:8), refers to "setting a direction for the long term and taking people along without being hampered by fear". Accordingly, whether it stands out as a value in its right or is considered as an aspect of envisioning, courage is a key issue in VBL (Sweeney & Fry, 2012; Segon & Booth, 2013). Similarly, Taylor (2010) asserts that values-based leaders demonstrate courage and persevere to do the right thing. Moral courage exists at the intersection of three domains: a commitment to moral principles; an awareness of the dangers involved in supporting those principles; and willingness to endure the risks (Taylor, 2007; Daft, 2008; Taylor, 2010). This means that when a moral leader takes the courage of leading the followers on a journey that has never been travelled before, he/she is not blind to the risks associated with this initiative. Rather, the leader is conscious of the risks involved and is passionately willing to show perseverance along the way.

The Path-goal Theory of Leadership in Explaining the Relationships between Values-Based Leadership (VBL) and Collective Teacher Efficacy (CTE)

The theory addresses the effects of leaders on the motivation and abilities of immediate subordinates and the effect of leaders on work unit performance (House, 1996). The stated goal of this theory is to enhance employee performance and satisfaction by giving due emphasis to their motivation (Northouse, 2013). The leader's responsibility in this case is to increase the subordinates' motivation to attain both personal and organisational goals (Daft, 2008). The defining terms here are goal, motivation, satisfaction, empowerment, ability, and performance. The underlying concept of this theory is that leaders define a path along which the subordinates are going to attain a certain goal. Hence, the role of a leader in this case is to link the performance of the members to a realistic goal through working on their motivation, satisfaction, empowerment, and abilities.

Generally, the theory has two main constructs: goal setting theory which suggests the relevance of challenging and realistic goals to motivate people; and expectancy theory which explains why people work hard to attain work goals. It has been claimed here that people work hard when they are convinced two things will happen: on the one hand, goal attainment leads to something they value and, on the other hand, the behaviours they engage in have a high chance (expectancy) of leading to the goal (Martin, 2012). In the expectancy theory, what matters is the perception of the constituents about the relevance of their current behaviours to their goal attainment and the relevance of matching the goal with their personal or shared values. This requires a leader to cultivate and clarify the behaviour that leads to an intended goal and to build confidence in the followers that this goal attainment will bridge them to their desired values.

House (1996), in the reformed path-goal theory of leadership, stipulated eight classes of leader behaviour that may help the subordinates' effort to attain a certain organisational goal. These include path-goal clarifying behaviour; achievement-oriented leader behaviour; work facilitation; supportive leader behaviour; interactive facilitation; group-oriented decision process; representation and networking; and values based leader behaviour. It means that the reformulated theory involves four additional behaviours. It can be explicated here that each of these leader behaviours is a derivative of the path-goal theory of leadership. Hence, VBL is proposed as one of the paths that connect subordinates to organisational goals. In each class of leader behaviour House tries to stipulate the specific behaviours that a leader is expected to exhibit to connect the subordinates to the commonly defined goals.

Regarding the select sets of conditions or contingency variables influencing the application of these leadership behaviours, House (1996:345) proposes that the emergence and effectiveness of VBL will be enhanced to the extent that three conditions are met. The first one is that extrinsic rewards cannot be, or are not made, contingent on individual performance. Secondly, there are few situational cues, constraints, and re-enforcers to guide behaviour and provide incentives for specific performance. Finally, the leader refrains from the use of extrinsic rewards contingent on subordinate performance. These propositions are in line with the assertion that VBL strengthens collective identification and the motivation for work unit members to contribute to collective goals (House, 1996:347). The author further argues that VBL is more likely to be relevant under conditions that do not favour transactional leadership which relies on contingent rewards as inducement for performance that goes along with cognitive dissonance theory. VBL mainly focuses on group norms through promoting the constructive collectivism perspective (Greenfield, 2005). Similarly, Fairholm and Fairholm (2009:16) suggest the following conditions:

> First, the members of the organisation must share common values. Second, leadership has to be thought of as the purview of all members of the group and not just the heads. Third, the focus of leadership must be individual development and the fulfilment of the group goals. And fourth, shared, intrinsic values must be the basis for all leader action.

According to path-goal theory of leadership, to be motivated employees must feel certain that they shall receive commensurate reward if they attain their commonly held goals, but the reward is directly attributed to values held to be significant among the subordinates in their personal and group affairs. Similarly, although the value of reward for motivation has not been overlooked in VBL, it looks like the value of extrinsic reward for motivation is negligible and is not recommendable, particularly if related to individual performance. The essence of extrinsic motivation is that staff members need some external rewards from their leaders or employers so that they are motivated and committed.

The acceptability and motivational effect of path-goal theory clarifying behaviours depends on subordinates' perception of their abilities to perform effectively and to resolve task and role ambiguity independently of their superiors (House, 1996). It means that, for the teachers to exert their efforts towards their goal attainment, they must believe that they are on the right journey that takes them to their desired educational goal and that they are able to move on the journey to get to that desired end. This belief is so important in that "individuals who feel that they will be successful on a given task are more likely to be so because they adopt challenging goals, try harder to achieve them, persist despite setbacks, and develop coping mechanisms for managing their emotional states" (Ross & Gray, 2006:801). Therefore, the path-goal theory has a direct implication for the concept of teachers' efficacy in general and to CTE in particular.

CTE is the beliefs that typically reflect individual teachers' perception of the capability of the teacher work group to bring a significant change to their students' learning experiences. Holanda Ramos, Costa Silva, Ramos Pontes, Fernandez and Furtado Nina (2014) note that the perceptions of efficacy are determined by judgment of capabilities, environmental conditions, and expected results. In fact, in relation to an investigation of teachers' perception of their abilities, the social cognitive theory has been widely used as a theoretical framework. The sources for such a perception have been widely contested by scholars. For instance, Adams and Forsyth (2006) classify factors influencing CTE broadly into two: proximate source (teaching task and teaching competence), and remote source (mastery experience, vicarious experience, social persuasion, and affective states). It has been argued here that leaders have the potential to influence all these situations.

Final Thoughts

At the beginning of this chapter, I explored the values from African leadership models including *Ubuntu*. That discussion highlighted several values endemic in African societies. Humility, respect, compassion, sharing, caring, and solidarity are among these. All these reflect the traditional life and ways of coping in Africa. These values have existed in Africa since time immemorial. Therefore, as the discussion above deliberated on Western ideas and philosophies, one could see that there are various commonalities between Global North and Global South divide. The strength of our world depends on appreciating the complementing ways in Western and African philosophies. Some experts have written at length about the differences between the two worlds; African philosophies are more inclusive whilst the West emphasises the individual. African philosophers are said to reflect inclusivity and solidarity of the group. Boon (2001:54) spells out the power of interactive leadership in Africa when he points out:

> Western management runs work groups and individuals in terms of *role* and *function*. 'Joe Ndlovu' is given a task or role. He understands exactly what his role and function is, and he is measured against this. It is an individually oriented approach to management. The African work group, however, assesses itself on moral and emotional grounds […] In this work group there needs to be a superordinate goal for the collective to aspire to.

Despite the differences though, it is evident that we can learn much in using eclectic approaches as we enrich the best of African philosophy with the best from the West in leading successful organisations. The decolonial thinking seeks to see each one borrowing from the other. The transformation of the new organisations in postcolonial Africa will be as successful as how we blend African philosophies with Western philosophies. The years of colonisation and apartheid have marginalised the indigenous ways of thinking. Therefore, as leaders shirk colonialism, they need to consciously merge indigenous knowledges. In 'Western' literature examined above, we witnessed how these values reflect the African philosophies in a number of ways. As we merge the knowledges, we can see how institutions such as education and government institutions can transform internalised institutional cultures by using cultures of inclusivity. Viljoen (2015:13) opines:

> In a culture of inclusivity, the energy in the system may be perceived as positive. Everybody is involved and shares his or her different viewpoints, non-performance is not tolerated and everyone assumes personal authority. These are high levels of support, trust and respect. Leadership may be human and vulnerable as mistakes may be shared and speedily resolved. The energy in the system is in a virtuous cycle and all the emotions mentioned in this content again reinforce the climate of inclusivity.

Education institutions, as explored in this chapter can grow with the use of the necessary values highlighted in the discussions. *Ubuntu* for example, is one philosophy that could promote working together of teams (Mbigi, 1997). Mbigi (1997) also raises an important point when he argues that *Ubuntu* is uniquely African and universal for this philosophy is implicitly expressed elsewhere in the world. The latter is what we see as we read the 'Western' literature.

This chapter exemplifies what many decolonial scholars are saying about combining Western and African approaches for decolonised, transformed and diversified environments (Heleta, 2016; Ndlovu-Gatsheni, 2018). The preface of this volume also emphasised the need to use the historically marginalised knowledges alongside the Western knowledges. This chapter demonstrates how in a time of decolonisation as we move the centre, we are able to see the value in knowledges as we utilise them in a socially just manner informed by democracy and cognitive justice. This chapter demonstrates that there is no need to marginalise African knowledges; we can build all institutions through a combination of best approaches from Africa and the best from the West. Progressive leaders will be able to glean from both worlds in building better performing institutions that are sensitive to democratic leadership using critical thinking to advance the goals of successful organisations. Leaders whose leadership development understand African values and how these can be utilised to enhance communities in the workplace will sustain CTE. On the other hand, leaders should be able to understand when to support individual efforts for growth in the workplace as well as when to expect community work and individual effort.

References

Adams, C. & Forsyth, P. 2006. Proximate Sources of Collective Teacher Efficacy. *Journal of Educational Administration*, 46(6):625-642. https://doi.org/10.1108/09578230610704828

Adei, S. 2010. *Institutionalizing Values-based Leadership in the Public Service*. A public lecture report organized by Kenya Association for Public Administration and Management presented at Kenya Institute of Administration.

Ahn, M.J., Ettner, L.W. & Loupin, A. 2012. Values vs Trait-based Approaches to Leadership: Insights from an Analysis of the Aeneid. *Leadership & Organization Development Journal*, 33(2):112-130. https://doi.org/10.1108/01437731211203447

Albion, M. 2006. *True to Yourself: Leading a Values-based Business*. The Social Venture Network Series. San Francisco: Berrett-Kohler Publishers.

Angelle, P., Nixon, T., Norton, E. & Niles, C. 2011. *Increasing Organizational Effectiveness: An Examination of Teacher Leadership, Collective Efficacy, and Trust in Schools*. Paper presented at the Annual Meeting of the University of Council for Educational Administration. Pittsburgh.

Boon, M. 2001. *The African Way: The Power of Interactive Leadership*. Cape Town: Zebra Press.

Brinson, D. & Steiner, L. 2007. *Building Collective Efficacy: How Leaders Inspire Teachers to Achieve*. The Center for Comprehensive School Reform and Improvement. October Issue Brief. Administered by Learning Point Associates in partnership with the Southwest Educational Development Laboratory (SEDL).

Broodryk, J. 2006. *Ubuntu: Life-Coping Skills from Africa*. Randburg: Knowres.

Buchko, A. 2006. The Effect of Leadership on Values-based Management. *Leadership and Organization Development Journal*, 28(1):36-50. https://doi.org/10.1108/01437730710718236

Busher, H. 2006. *Understanding Educational Leadership: People, Power, and Culture*. New York: Open University Press.

Calder, B. 2006. Educational Leadership with a Vision. *ProQuest Educational Journals*, 12(2):81-89.

Chakravarthi, S., Haleagrahara, N. & Judson, J. 2010. Enhancing the Efficacy of Lecturers in Educating Student Cohorts Consisting of Cultural Diverse Groups in a Medical University. *International Education Studies*, 3(2):161-166. https://doi.org/10.5539/ies.v3n2p161

Copeland, M.K. 2014. The Emerging Significance of Values-based Leadership: A Literature Review. *International Journal of Leadership Studies*, 8(2):105-135.

Crossan, M.M., Gandz, J. & Seijtz, G. 2018. Developing Leadership Character. In: G. Seijts & K. Macmillan (eds.), *Leadership in Practice: Theory and Cases in Leadership Character*. London: Routledge. https://doi.org/10.4324/9781315405629-4

Cybulski, T., Hoy, W. & Sweetland, S. 2005. The Role of Collective Efficacy of Teachers and Fiscal Efficiency in Student Achievement. *Journal of Educational Administration*, 43(4/5):439-461. https://doi.org/10.1108/09578230510615224

Daft, R.L. 2008. *The Leadership Experience*. Mason, OH: Thomson.

Daft, R.L. 2010. *Organisational Theory and Design*. Mason: South-western Cengage Learning Publishing.

Demir, K. 2008. Transformational Leadership and Collective Efficacy: The Moderating Roles of Collaborative Culture and Teachers' Self-efficacy. *Eurasian Journal of Educational Research*, 33:93-112.

Fairholm, M. & Fairholm, G. 2009. *Understanding Leadership Perspectives: Theoretical and Practical Applications*. New York: Springer Science and Business Media, LLC. https://doi.org/10.1007/978-0-387-84902-7

Fancera, S. 2009. Instructional Leadership Influence on Collective Efficacy and School Achievement. Unpublished Doctoral Dissertation-The State University of New Jersey. Ann Arbor: University of Michigan.

Fives, H. & Looney, L. 2009. College Instructors' Sense of Teaching and Collective Efficacy. *International Journal of Teaching and Learning in Higher Education*, 20(2):182-191.

Frank, J. 2005. Transformational Leadership and Moral Discourse in the Workplace and Civil Society. Unpublished Doctoral Dissertation, University of North Florida. Ann Arbor: University of Michigan.

Goddard, R., Hoy, W.K. & Woolfolk Hoy, A. 2000. Collective Teacher Efficacy: Its Meaning, Measure, and Impact on Student Achievement. *American Educational Research Journal*, 37(2):479-507. https://doi.org/10.3102/00028312037002479

Gold, A. 2010. Leading with Values. In: M. Coleman & D. Glover (eds.), *Educational Leadership and Management: Developing Insights and Skills*. Berkshire: Open University Press.

Greenfield, W. 2005. Leading the Teacher Work Group. In: L. Hughes (ed.), *Current issues in School Leadership*. New Jersey: Lawrence Erlbaum Associates. https://doi.org/10.4324/9781410611901-14

Grojean, M., Resick, C., Dickson, M. & Smith, B. 2004. Leaders, Values, and Organizational Climate: Examining Leadership Strategies for Establishing an Organizational Climate Regarding Ethics. *Journal of Business Ethics*, 55(3). https://doi.org/10.1007/s10551-004-1275-5

Haydon, G. 2007. *Values for Educational Leadership*. Los Angeles: Sage Publications.

Heleta, S. 2016. Decolonisation of Higher Education: Dismantling Epistemic Violence and Eurocentrism in South Africa. *Transformation in Higher Education*, 1(1):1-9. https://doi.org/10.4102/the.v1i1.9

Hendrikz, K. & Engelbrecht, A.S. 2019. The Principled Leadership Scale: An Integration of value-based Leadership. *South African Journal of Industrial Psychology*, 45(0). https://doi.org/10.4102/sajip.v45i0.1553

Holanda Ramos, M.F., Costa Silva, S.S., Ramos Pontes, F.A., Fernandez, A.O. & Furtado Nina, K.C. 2014. Collective Teacher Efficacy Beliefs: A Critical Review of the Literature Review. *International Journal of Humanities and Social Science*, 4(7):179-188.

House, R. 1996. Path-goal Theory of Leadership: Lesson, Legacy, and a Reformulated Theory. *Leadership Quarterly*, 3:323-352. https://doi.org/10.1016/S1048-9843(96)90024-7

Kantaburta, S. 2010. Vision Effects: A Critical Gap in Educational Leadership Research. *International Journal of Educational Management*, 24(5):376-390. https://doi.org/10.1108/09513541011055956

Kouzes, J. & Posner, B. 2008. The Leadership Challenge. A Summary of the Original Text. *Audio-Tech Business Book Summaries*, 17(8):1-16.

Kouzes, J. & Posner, B. 2012. *The Leadership Challenge: How to Make Extraordinary Things Happen in Organisations*. San Francisco: Jossey-Bass.

Leithwood, K., Patten, S. & Jantzi, D. 2010. Testing a Conception of How School Leadership Influences Student Learning. *Educational Administration Quarterly*, 46(5):671-706. https://doi.org/10.1177/0013161X10377347

Martin, R. 2012. Path-goal Theory of Leadership. In: J.M. Levine & M.A. Hogg (eds.), *Encyclopaedia of Group Processes and Intergroup Relations*. Thousand Oaks, CA: Sage.

Mbigi, L. 1997. *The African Dream Management*. Pretoria: Sigma.

Mbigi, L. & Maree, J. 1995. *The Spirit of African Transformation Management*. Pretoria: Sigma.

McCuddy, M. 2008. Fundamental Moral Orientations: Implications for Values-based Leadership. *Journal of VBL*, 1(1):9-19.

Metz, T. 2014. Harmonising Global Ethics in the Future: A Proposal to Add South and East to West. *Journal of Global Ethics*, 10(2):146-155. https://doi.org/10.1080/17449626.2014.931875

Mgayi, B. 2013. *Does African Wisdom Have a Place at Work?* USB Agenda from www.howwemadeitinafrica.com

Mihelič, K., Lipičnik, B. & Tekavčič, M. 2010. Ethical Leadership. *International Journal of Management & Information Systems*, 14(5):31-42. https://doi.org/10.19030/ijmis.v14i5.11

Mills, A. & Spencer, E. 2005. Values-based Decision- making: A Tool for Achieving the Goals of Health Care. *HEP Forum*, 17(1):18-32. https://doi.org/10.1007/s10730-005-4948-2

Mintrop, H. 2012. Bridging Accountability Obligations, Professional Values and (Perceived) Student Needs with Integrity. *Journal of Educational Administration*, 50(5):695-726. https://doi.org/10.1108/09578231211249871

Msila, V. 2008. *Ubuntu* and School Leadership. *Journal of Education*, 44:67-84.

Msila, V. 2015. *Ubuntu: Shaping the Current Workplace with (African) Wisdom*. Randburg: Knowres.

Ndlovu-Gatsheni, S.J. 2018. *Epistemic Freedom in Africa: Deprovincialization and Decolonization*. London: Routledge. https://doi.org/10.4324/9780429492204

Northouse, P.G. 2013. *Leadership: Theory and Practice*. Los Angeles: Sage Publications.

Nussbaum, B. 2003. *Ubuntu*: Reflections of a South African on Our Common Humanity. *Reflections*, 4(4):21-26. https://doi.org/10.1162/152417303322004175

O'Toole, J. 2008. Notes towards a definition of values-based leadership. *The Journal of Values-Based Leadership*, 1:84-92.

Prinsloo, E.D. 1998. *Ubuntu* Culture and Participatory Management. In: P.H. Coetzee & A.P.J. Roux (eds.), *The African Philosophy Reader*. London: Routledge.

Rhode, D.L. 2006. *Moral Leadership: The Theory and Practice of Power, Judgment, and Policy*. San Francisco: Jossey-Bass.

Ross, J.A. & Gray, P. 2006. School Leadership and Students Achievement: The mediating effects of teacher beliefs. *Canadian Journal of Education*, 29(3):798-822. https://doi.org/10.2307/20054196

Sarros, J.C. & Cooper, B.K. 2006. Building Character: A Leadership Essential. *Journal of Business and Psychology*, 21(1):1-22. https://doi.org/10.1007/s10869-005-9020-3

Segon, M. & Booth, C. 2013. Values-based Approach to Ethical Culture: A Case Study. *Ethics, Values and Civil Society Research in Ethical Issues in Organizations*, (9):93-118. https://doi.org/10.1108/S1529-2096(2013)0000009011

Shambaugh, R. 2008. *Teacher Self-efficacy, Collective Teacher Efficacy, Automatic Thoughts, States of Mind, and Stress in Elementary School Teachers*. PCOM Psychology Dissertation. Philadelphia, Philadelphia College of Osteopathic Medicine.

Sweeney, P.J. & Fry, L.W. 2012. Character Development through Spiritual Leadership. *Consulting Psychology Journal: Practice and Research*, 64(2):89-107. https://doi.org/10.1037/a0028966

Taylor, D. 2007. *The Imperfect Leader: A Story about Discovering the Not-so-secret Secrets of Transformational Leadership*. Bloomington: Author House.

Taylor, D. 2010. *The Power of Values-based Leadership: A Leader's Guide to Sustainable and Extraordinary Results*, Booklet. [Online]. Available: https://bit.ly/3cZ3z2S

Vari, T. 2011. Collective Efficacy and Instructional Leadership: A Cross-sectional Study of Teachers' Perceptions. Unpublished Doctoral Dissertation-Wilmington University, Ann Arbor: University of Michigan.

Viinamäki, O. 2011. Embedding Value-based Organization: An Identification of Critical Success Factors and Challenges. *The International Journal of Management Science and Information Technology*, 1(3):37-67. https://doi.org/10.5539/ijbm.v7n9p28

Viinamäki, O. 2012. Why Leaders Fail in Introducing Values-based Leadership? An Elaboration of Feasible Steps, Challenges, and Suggestions for Practitioners. *International Journal of Business and Management*, 7(9):28-39.

Viljoen, R. 2015. *Organisational Change & Development: An African Perspective*. Randburg: Knowres.

Yoeli, R. & Berkovich, I. 2010. From Personal Ethos to Organisational Vision: Narratives of Educational Leaders. *Journal of Educational Administration*, 48(4):451-467. https://doi.org/10.1108/09578231011054716

Chapter Eight

Reflections on Programming in an Afrocentric Distance Education Certificate Programme: A Case Study

Zamo Hlela

Introduction

The intention of the chapter is to critically engage with issues of curriculum or what I call programming using a Certificate Programme (CP) in distance education offered in over 10 African countries using South Africa as an example. Issues of distance education are not the intention of the chapter, but programming the vehicle through which content, the 'script' is passed on or disseminated and the implications thereof on students and local communities. Put differently, how far does the CP, through programming, contribute to the humanisation project? The chapter highlights the significant contribution of CP in the provision of the much-needed education qualification. This is done through unpacking the pulls and the pushes on programming models that inform the CP. This chapter seeks to identify the pulls and pushes to programming/curriculum design in a distance education programme that locates itself in Afrocentrism. The chapter seeks to pursue scholars, practitioners, and policy makers in education, in particular distance education, to continuously engage and deliberate about how programming in education or distance education education facilitate the humanisation project agenda.

My discussion draws its reflections from empirical data in the form of document analysis (academic papers, evaluation reports); a three-day 2015 alumni workshop; a report thereof that I conducted and wrote that 33 former students from 12 African countries (Lesotho, Kenya, Zimbabwe, Mozambique, Botswana, Malawi, Namibia, Tanzania, Uganda, Zambia, Swaziland and South Africa) participated in which included semi structure questionnaires; focus groups; and life histories. I also reflect on my own experience since being part of the project at pilot phase in 2009, and in 2019 it is at its 5th cycle of delivery.

I first present an historic case study of CP through a brief context of distance education in Africa, and an Afrocentric perspective. The discussions that follow argue that a single theoretical background only offers partial and limited perspectives; that recognition or infusion of theoretical African perspective does not mean inclusion. On the contrary, I argue that locating Afrocentrism at the centre of programming will help facilitate transformative learning that inform development cultural identity and communal agency. I close the chapter by looking at recommendations.

The Context of Programming

On the onset, I must state that, similar to Boone et al. (2002), I have taken the term 'programming' to mean curriculum, which according to Jarvis (1995), is a contested assumption. It is not the intention of this chapter to enter this debate, save to say that, for me, programming/curriculum are interchangeable concepts because they are all-inclusive terms covering a variety of activities and assumptions, reflecting different ideologies, partnerships, implementations, and evaluations in the delivery. Onyemuwa (1997) views activities in programming as directed towards a clearly articulated goal or task to be performed and, importantly, maintaining viability of the agency or institution as a social entity. Programming therefore becomes the blueprint of any educational provision whether in formal, informal or non-formal education. Programming/curriculum, however, like an iceberg has above the surface as well as below the surface activities. In the context of globalisation and neoliberalism, programming/curriculum have come to be viewed almost as universal, one size fit all, scientific (which often hid the human factor, cultural context, ideology) to name but a few.

According to Bourdieu and Passeron (1977), programming becomes a mechanism through which ideology of legitimation is attained rewards are distributed unevenly – when one works hard one benefits accordingly. Yet, for Abdi and Cleghorn (2005), programming in education becomes a mechanism for social control. In the context of globalisation or neoliberalism, programming/curriculum has played a major role in 'educating' society that education or education provision is scientific, contextless, and universal.

Looking at programming historically, it is easy to understand what this phenomenon entails. Programming, as defined or understood by Nyerere (1968:268) is:

> The educational systems in different kinds of societies in the world have been, and are, very different in organisation and content. They are different because the societies providing the education are different, and because education, whether formal or informal, has purpose. That purposes is to transmit from one generation to the next the accumulated wisdom and knowledge of society, and to prepare the young people for their future membership of the society and their active participation in its maintenance and development.

In the context of globalisation, there is a need for a middle ground. It is important to note that I have intentionally dropped the neoliberal term because, in my view, globalisation is upon us but we can still reject neoliberalism. It is this context of programming that lays firm foundation for this chapter.

The Certificate Programme (CP)

The Certificate Programme is a distance education offering in over 10 African countries. Initially called "Working with Children, Families, and Communities affected by HIV & AIDS, Conflict, Poverty, and Displacement in Africa", the "Community-Based Work with Children and Youth (CBWCY)" certificate programme is a collaborative process between key partners: the United Nations Children's Fund (UNICEF), Regional Psycho Social Initiative (REPSSI) Academic team of consultants, and later the Africa Centre for Childhood (ACC), as well as the University of KwaZulu-Natal (UKZN) academic team and teams from other counties. The stated intentions of the CP are:

1. to provide access to adults who are already doing this work and might be employed or volunteering,
2. to professionalise this area of work, and
3. to strengthen educational institutions across Africa, by indigenisation of the CP over time.

The CP is formally accredited by the University of KwaZulu-Natal as a short course pitched at level 4 (South African Qualification Authority), or equivalent to the end of high school (ISCED level 3) or entry into tertiary study (ISCED level 4) according to the International Standard Classification of Education (UNESCO, 1997). The programme is made up of six multi-disciplined developed modules based on a constructivist design.

The constructivist delivery model or Situated Supported Distance Learning (SSDL) is supported by five equally important components:
1. Learning materials developed and redeveloped by the University of KwaZulu-Natal academics.
2. At local level, students are supported by local mentors trained on the model and supported by the University of KwaZulu-Natal through mentor training and a minute per minute structured mentor guide/booklet.
3. Students at local level attend 4 organised minute per minute structured daylong contact sessions per module.
4. Each module has two continues assessments designed by the University of KwaZulu-Natal academics for facilitation of (v) applied theory and practice component. Through minute per minute structured material learning and teaching environment are participatory and experiential yet are remotely controlled from South Africa.

In terms of retention and throughput, the CP has attained much success. In Cycle 1 (2010) of the CP offering, 484 learners had successfully completed the programme, only one had failed and 68 discontinued their studies, this achieving an overall 87.5% throughput rate. In Cycle 2 (2010), 1062 learners registered and 933 (87.9%) passed and completed. In Cycle 3 (2012), 897 students commenced with their studies and 699 (78%) successfully completed. In Cycle 4 (2015), 1604 enrolled, 1137 graduated, and 604 remained active. Similarly, in Cycle 5 there are close to 1000 registered students. Therefore, in less than 10 years, 4,852 students from various African countries have had direct contact with the CP learning material, an opportunity to learn, improve quality of their lives as well as the communities they live in. The success of the CP programme is obvious in terms of throughput and retention. Importantly, the CP is growing and extending its reach. The question is, given its ability to attract and keep its learners, how much does the CP contribute to the project of humanisation?

The Context of the Distance Education (Rationale for Problematising Programming in Distance Education)

In Africa, the need to provide access, particularly higher education opportunities to those who continue to be at the margins – the previously disadvantaged and adult learners as a whole – is unquestionable. Distance education in Africa often purports that it creates real and meaningful educational opportunities for poor and marginalised (Prinsloo, 2017). Jegede (2011:1) cites Pityana who states that open distance learning widens access and increases participation in higher education in a cost effective manner. However, issues such as high dropout and student retention in Africa are a major hindrance and far more complex than those in Europe. In Africa, underdevelopment and less resources imply inaccessibility to technology that Distance education depend on, and poverty, which affects the ability to buy education are key factors (Sondlo, 2013). Furthermore, in Africa, issues of retention and dropout rates take a different slant (Letseka, 2007; Sondlo, 2013). Sondlo (2013:33) defines retention rate as "the number of students who enrol in a programme in a particular year and are actively engaged in learning and teaching without discontinuing their studies in that year and proceed to the following at the same institution". Letseka (2007), in support of Sondlo, claims that there is correlation between retention and dropout rates and students from low socio-economic backgrounds, those from less economically developed regions, and female students.

In my view, empirical studies in Distance education appear to overlook the role of how Distance education can turn into the 'sprinkler' of imported knowledge, therefore contributes to high dropout rates, as passage to Western enculturation or worse still, dehumanising project. Distance education through programming is a sprinkler of borrowed axiology, ontologies, and epistemologies. It is a clear example of how knowledge generated somewhere "is undone from its context and ideology, its 'embodiedness' and 'situatedness', and presented as neutral and universally good" (Van der Velden, 2004:74). This is a modernist approach to knowledge. The modernism movement designed knowledge to liberate humanity from ignorance and irrationality. Its principles included the power of knowledge over ignorance, the power of order over disorder, and the power of science over superstition. The implication is that the African learner must forego his/her socio-cultural context as he/she is unable to draw freely from his/her African experience (Zulu, 2006; Ngara, 2007; Oloruntoba, 2015). This is alienation of an African person and enculturation into Westernisation, or the Trojan house to Westernisation. It is dehumanisation of the African learner. The Distance education or the 'sprinkler' in this context is under the control of the provider or by proxy consequently in Gboku and Lekoko (2005) view Distance education by its very nature is top-down for the purposes of (i) minimising cost, maintaining total control (hegemony), (ii) provision of approved content (knowledge), (iii) and impositions of Western models. Clearly, Distance education programming deserve scrutiny. In the context of paper chase, it is easy to overlook other implicit functions of education in society. Education must serve society in the first place, helping people meet their daily lives. This is the function of programming.

African-centred programming places Africa at the centre. It is not infusion or hybridity. Infusion approach could signal good intentions or window dressing in programming. Jansen, (2017) whose views on the decolonisation of the curriculum are ciontentious makes a valid argument that, in South Africa, there has been curriculum change. He cites examples of projects where South Africans are interacting with the Northern counterparts as equal partners in the production of knowledge, such as Professor Mayosi at University of Cape Town (UCT) advancing the cardiovascular research; AIDS research by Karim and Karim at the University of KwaZulu-Natal, and the history of mining in SA by Phimister at University of the Free State (UFS) (Jansen, 2017). This I call a hybridity approach, that is a space where different meaning-making processes and knowledges meet and are accorded equal status (Kanu, 2011). In my view, these rare examples where the knowledge space is entered into as equal partners.

What Jansen fails to recognise is also a need for programming projects that foreground Africa as the centre of curriculum as yet another approach to the decolonisation project. This causes total shift from dominant categorisation of Eurocentric thought and engagement explicitly with Afrocentric discourse. For example, the work of Gqaleni (Gqaleni et al., 2011) in biomedical and traditional healing; Ngara (2007) Lekoko and Modise (2011), Preece, (2009), Ntseane (2011), Hlela (2017) defining learning, meaning making and knowledge; Reviere (2001), Hlela (2016) seek to locate research and research process within African perspectives. This is a move away from arguing for Afrocentrism to the imposition of Afrocentrism in knowledge systems, curriculum and every aspect of living, *we make the road by walking it.*

The chapter makes a clear distinction between infusion, hybridity, and for grounding of ideology. The next section unpacks Afrocentrism as an ideology.

Afrocentricism

Afrocentrism, Afrocentric, Africentric or African-centred are interchangeable terms because of how they relate to the stated purposes. The terms refer to the categorisation a quality of thought rooted in the African culture reflecting life experiences, history, African traditions, and African futures in the globalising word as a centre of analysis and thought (Hill, 1995; Hlela, 2017). Three key components are highlighted and relevant for programming.

Firstly, common amongst Afrocentrists is the acknowledgement and recognition of common ethos, ethics, and values as reflected in *Ubuntu*, which incorporate interconnectedness and interdependence of all things and spirituality. *Ubuntu* states that a person is a person through others or 'I am because we are' expressed as *Umuntu ngumuntu ngabantu* in isiZulu languages, *botho* in Pedi, *munthu* in

Malawi or *Harambee* in Kiswahili, *ujamaa* in Tanzania (Ntuli, 2002; Preece, 2009; Ntseane, 2011; Ngara, 2007; Asante, 1987; 1990; Pietersen, 2005; Dei, 2002; Mangaliso & Damane, 2001).

Secondly, common amongst Afrocentrists are the impacts of colonialism or neocolonialism on Africa and the African. For example, Nandy (1983:xi) states, "this colonialism colonises the minds in addition to bodies and it releases forces within colonised societies to alter their cultural priorities once and for all". Consequently, "The West is now everywhere, within the West and outside, in structures and in minds" (Eze, 1998:213). Like Nandy above Ngugi wa Thiong'o (1986:16) states that "its most important domination was mental domination of the colonised, the control, through culture, of how people perceived themselves and their relationship to the world". The consequence is dehumanisation of the African. In Fanon's view dehumanisation is when the African's identity becomes a white construction (Fanon, 1968). Similarly, Biko (2004:30) claims, "to a large extent the evil-doers have succeeded in producing at the output end of their machine a kind of black man who is a man only in form". This implies that the Afrocentrist's mission entails the humanisation of Africans in a globalising world.

The humanisation attainment project is summarised by Tolliver (2015:63) as:
> A response to the need for agency and self-determination among people of African descent; Reaffirms the positive aspects of indigenous African cultural values and ways of being, positioning us to use the best from the past; Promotes resistance against violence of hegemonic philosophies and global racist structures, ideologies, and attitudes; Purposefully supports the development of positive self-perceptions that can benefit from and be motivated by the strengths and beauty of the traditions and cultures of people of African ascent; Enables people of African ascent to become warriors, healers, and builders in their lives and in their communities.

These purposes of Afrocentrism dictate that the actualisation of the humanisation project in programming means locating programming in the *Ubuntu* principles and values. That's is recognition of collective identity; the collective nature; and the value of interdependence of all things (ontology) and the oneness of mind, body, and spirit in meaning making (Epistemology).

The Road to Hell is Paved with Good Intentions

In this section, I present a potted history of the CP since first implementation in relation to theoretical orientation. The history is divided into two, the first part on programming informed and based on constructivism and the second part on

Afrocentrism. Each part seeks to explore the extent to which each theory averted or contributed the 'sprinkle' effect in the distance education certificate programme.

The Constructivist Programming (2009-2011)

Constructivist programming means a structured design informed by certain assumptions of meaning making. Gravett defines learning from a constructivist point of view as "a process of constructing meaning, or put differently a process of knowledge construction" Gravett (2001:74). For Nagowah and Nagowah is a "theory that is actively constructed in the mind of the learners out of their experiences in the world" (Nagowah & Nagowah, 2009:280). Applefied, et al., 2001 present four assumptions that inform constructivism: (1) learners constructing their own learning; (2) the dependence of the new learning on learners' existing understanding; (3) the critical role of social interaction; and (4) the need of authentic learning tasks for meaningful learning. In short, constructivists believe that specific experiences in contexts shape individual's experiences in meaning making, learning becomes a scaffolder process.

The six modules were designed as a learning scaffold:
1. Module 1 – 'Introduction to personal development' (Psychology).
2. Module 2 – 'Introduction to Human Rights based approach' (Law).
3. Module 3 – 'Youth and development' (Social Work).
4. Module 4 – 'Care and support for children at risk' (Psychology).
5. Module 5 – 'Integrated Community development' (Community Development).
6. Module 6 – a capstone module, 'Service-learning' (Adult Education). The design is base prior knowledge (module) setting up necessary foundations for new knowledge (next module). The curriculum design finds its origins in social constructivist and experiential learning theories.

The scaffolding of each module to the next was attained through a cartoon story line called the Kibali story as well as house construction analogy. Kibali is a typical rural village. The story revolves around the Phiri family; Gogo (granny) Phiri as she struggles with her grandchildren. The story was carefully constructed to reflect the African experience through names of different characters and realities that characters face. The story develops with each module. The story deals with major issues that each module covers. The Phiri family faces the kinds of challenges typical to a rural village in Africa, such granny headed families, migrant labour, early pregnancies, addictions, and all forms of abuse. It is a story or vulnerability and poverty. The Kibali story served as a golden threat of all modules. For example, in Module 4, one character from the story starts the modules by say "Remember in Module 1 and 3 there were questions about this story that guided your thinking for the modules. In this module the questions related to Kibali are in the content of the module. Look out for them" (Module 4:7). In the final module, Module 6, a different cartoon character introduces the chapter by saying: "So, how this story ends is up to you. What service-learning project are you going to be involved in for families that are closest to you who also have problems and issues like the Phiri's." (Module 6:6). Finally, constructivism was also attained through the house construction analogy where Module 1 is understood as foundation of the house, the 4 next modules as we seen as the four walls of the house and Module 6, the roof.

The Afrocentrism Infusion (2011-)

Winds of change were very strong at the University of KwaZulu-Natal during this period. The university positioned itself at the centre of the African scholarship. This has positively impacted on all the University of KwaZulu-Natal engagements including the CP at both leadership and module coordinator level. At leadership level, it meant that African leadership took over. The implication of this was a total change in the complexion of module coordinators, which previously had been predominantly white.

At module coordinator, level common issues take a different turn and become urgent. Common issues, such as implications of the CP on learners and their communities; indigenisation of the CP in the host country a stated intention of the programme; and if the CP is that good, why not offer it in South Africa? What message does this send out there? A concept paper on an additional module with an intention to contextualise the programme in the continent was prepared and presented. The module was never realised mainly because of cost as well the fact that it was going to prolong the qualification further. Next, an internal workshop on Afrocentrism is conducted for the coordinators. This is followed by a three days' workshop on the same topic. The final product was the six modules that were infused with Afrocentrism.

At content and programme level, infusion of Afrocentrism did not affect content or the Kibali story which are both the golden thread of what is to be learnt and how. In all six modules, the introduction foregrounds Afrocentrism, here below is an example from module 6.

> You and your students are now familiar with Afrocentrism, which was introduced in Module 1 and has been repeated in every module. The concept of *Ubuntu* in Nguni languages – *botho* in Pedi, *munhtu* in Malawi, *harambee* in Kiswahili, *Ujaama* in Tanzania – states that *Umuntu ngumuntu*

> *ngabantu*; a person is a person through others or "I am because we are".
> This view demonstrates that Africans whether in the south or north, east or
> west, share a common culture. (Mentor Guide:1)

The infusions created opportunities to explore concepts such as social, cultural, and cognitive justice. The principles of what or how content is taught remained unchanged, in other words individualism, the autonomy, and rational self remain the implicit goal.

Afrocentrism infusion has good intentions, but locating Afrocentrism at the core will present a different CP. Locating the CP in Afrocentrism will require a total re-conception of what is to be considered knowledge, facilitation of learning, assumptions made about meaning making, as well as assessment regime. In my view, it is in programming is made up of different components which must be dealt with holistically, for example the Kibali story or infusion of Afrocentric text does not make the programme Afrocentric. In the next section, I present five tenets to Afrocentric programming.

Discussion: 'We Make the Road by Walking it'

Indeed, the process of locating programmes in Afrocentrism will be attained by reflecting in and on the action in our different practices. It cannot be a one size fits all. Through a CP, I have presented a case for infusion approach. The infusion approach is an indicator of good intentions which can easily remain at that and therefore become window-dressing. It is an important step nevertheless. Noteworthy, is recognising that Afrocentrism in programming does not seek to take over from Eurocentrism. Afrocentrism argues for acknowledgement of African knowledge, it is an African contribution to the globalising world. Hence, hybridity in programming becomes relevant. However, to attain true hybridity, one must be clear on the possibilities of African contribution. Below, I present salient points that pave the way to hybridity. The section presents my recommendation of what an Afrocentric programming could look like:

Firstly, an Afrocentric programme cannot take modernist view of knowledge. Modernity, as commonly understood, emerged into being in the 18th and 19th centuries, the period of the Enlightenment in Europe, and was strengthened through the development of industrial society in the 20th century. It was a philosophical and scientific worldview, which saw itself as a movement designed to liberate humanity from ignorance, and irrationality. Its principles included the power of knowledge over ignorance, the power of order over disorder, and the power of science over superstition. Included amongst its ideas was that of the individual, the autonomous and rational self, acting in a natural world that was knowable. Over time, knowledge would increase, and humanity, as well as civilisation would progress. An Afrocentric programme cannot subscribe to these principles mainly because there are key to cognitive and cultural injustice. On the contrary, Afrocentrism subscribes to the view that they are many knowledges that it may co-exist with.

Secondly, at the centre of Afrocentric programming must be relevant African axiology, epistemology, and ontology. The notion that "what is good for the group will eventually be good for the individual" – not the opposite. *Umuntu* (a human person) in Africa perspectives, according to Ramose (2004), is the maker of knowledge and truth. In other words, the notion that "what is good for the individual will be eventually be good for the group" is human made and therefore can be changed. *Ubuntu* is the creator of *Ubuntu* values; I am because you are (interconnectedness) and interdependence of all things living, dead and yet to be born, become truth. Consequently, knowledge, truth and reality are value-laden, referred to as axiology (Chilisa & Preece, 2005; Hlela, 2016). In the African context knowledge, reality and truth is holistic (ontology) that is the interconnectedness and interdependence and spirituality (Ngara, 2007; Preece, 2009; Ntseane, 2011; Lekoko & Modise, 2011). In short, ontology is informed by context, environment, culture, and spirituality. Acknowledgement of this ontology dictates an equal valuing of the body, mind, and spirituality as sources and sites of meaning making, a recognition of diunital logic or diunitism – the union of opposites. This is a tall order for programming in the context of neo liberalism, informed by individualistic conceptions of learners and learning, shaped by industrial and post-industrial political economy, liberal democratic politics and consumerist culture. However, we derive solace from Biko (1978:51):

> We believe that in the long run the special, contribution to the world by Africa will be in this field of human relationship. The great powers of the world may have done wonders in giving the world an industrial and military look, but the great gift still has to come from Africa – giving the world a more human face.

Thirdly, in Afrocentric programming, the history of Africa becomes important – precolonial, as well as postcolonial history. In programming the colonial period becomes more relevant mainly because of the immense impact that period had and continue to have on Africa. The starting point is recognition and acknowledgment that African existed before colonialism and therefore had knowledge. Second is acknowledgement of the impacts of colonialism on the continent and its people (Nandy, 1983; Ngugi wa Thiong'o, 1986; Eze, 1998). Mignolo (2009) argues that colonialisation cohere with geo-politics of knowledge particularly the domination of Eurocentric and the inability to confront the injustices of that history. Afrocentrism positions history as critical springboard for the development of critical consciousness, and humanisation project. It confronts issues of social, cognitive, and cultural injustices by foregrounding these in programming.

In my own work theorising about Afrocentric programming, I also emphasise three concepts: collective history, mutual dialogue, and collective enquiries (Hlela, 2017). The three are cyclical and interactive guide with no clear start or end. Collective history is a critical in programming. In practice, it is a structured process of recreating history from the local people's point of view. It is a means of developing critical consciousness towards humanisation of the African person historically, in the present, and into the future, which Fanon (1968) describes as 'self-consciousness' or 'liberatory praxis', and Ngugi wa Thiong'o, (1986) as 'decolonising the mind', or what I refer to as critical memory. It's not about romanticising the past and/or apportioning blame, but critical ownership of the past and recreation of the imagined future.

Fourthly, current and dominant programming models for an African learner, knowledge is foreign – there is no connection between what is assumed knowledge and the socio-cultural context of the learner. Too often, the learner is assumed a blank slate. Asante (1990) reminds us that centricity as a concept locates students/learners within their cultural context and references, enabling students to relate socially and psychologically to other cultural perspectives. Centricity is recognition of the other as human in a particular place and time, and that constitutes the socio-cultural context. It accepts the view that learners learn best when they draw from their own repertoire of local cultural expressions and traditions. Acknowledgement that each place has its own knowledge systems implies acknowledgement of different ontologies such as iintuition as significant in meaning making (Mazama, 2003); diunitism (Ngara, 2007; Karanja, 2010), that is 'both ... and' rather than 'either ... or' and all-inclusive, it is "something apart and united at the same time" (Karanja, 2008:13). Alternatively, extra-cognitive phenomena (Shavinina & Seeratan, 2004). Extra-cognitive refers to "a particular cognitive mode of human thinking that appears in advance of any logical, conscious account of any individual's intelligence" (Shavinina & Seeratan, 2004:93). Conversely, in the African context, centricity in curriculum or programming assumes that we are all share the colonialists socio-cultural background so are the meaning making processes.

Fifthly, is hybridity defined as 'a third space' where different meaning-making processes and knowledges meet and are accorded equal status (Kanu, 2009). Hybridity must demonstrate the following characteristicts as summarised succinctly by Burbules (2000:2):

> a way of reconciling differences; a means of promoting empathy and understanding for others; a mode of collaborative inquiry; a method of critically comparing and testing alternative hypotheses; a form of constructivist teaching and learning; a forum for deliberation and negotiation about public policy differences; a therapeutic engagement of self- and other-exploration; and a basis for shaping uncoerced social and political consensus.

This third space is a space that ought to be explored and utilised for advancing cultural and cognitive justice and advancing African values in learning. These include collectivism rather than individualism (Lekoko & Modise, 2011), sacred rather than secular (Chile & Simpson, 2004), interconnectedness rather than disconnectedness (Ntseane, 2007) and Afrocentric rather than Eurocentric. The paradoxes or tensions between Western centrism and Afrocentrism are acknowledged.

Conclusion

In this chapter, I present the success of a distance education programme offered in over 10 African countries. Furthermore, I present a well thought out distance learning model of distance education; a model that facilitates participatory learning at a village context. Moreover, I present a Certificate Programme that is informed by constructivist theory of learning, meaning that foreign ontology and epistemology continue to be spread and maintained by Africans. Therefore, even though curriculum issues in the Certificate Programme are seemingly in the hands of Africans, fundamental changes are hard to come by. Cosmetic changes remain at the infusion level. A critical area the chapter did not cover is the examination of the role of funders or funding in education provision such as Certificate Programme. This was not the focus of the chapter, however, without looking at this critical aspect it is easy to 'bark up the wrong tree'. This does not exonerate African lethargic response to programming or curriculum issues. In the context of globalisation and Africa, seeking to make its own contribution in the area of education, knowledge, and learning, the chapter presents five salient points to the road to hybridity in programming and this, is a call to action!

References

Abdi, A.A. & Cleghorn, A. 2005. *Issues in African Education: Social Perspectives*. New York: Palgrave Macmillan. https://doi.org/10.1057/9781403977199

Agada, A. 2013. Is African Philosophy Progressing? *Journal of African Philosophy, Culture and Religions*, 1(2):239-274.

Anyidoho, N.A. 2010. Communities of Practice': Prospects for Theory and Action in Participatory Development. *Development in Practice*, 20(3):318-328. https://doi.org/10.1080/09614521003710005

Applefield, J.M., Huber. M. & Moallem, M. 2001. Contsructivism in Theory and Practice: Toward a Better Understanding. *The High School Journal*, 84(2): 35-53.

Asante, M.K. 1987. *The Afrocentric Idea*. Philadelphia: Temple University Press.

Asante, M.K. 1990. *Kemet, Afrocentric and Knowledge*. Trenton, NJ: Africa World Press. https://doi.org/10.1215/10439455-4.2.47

Burbules, N.C. 2000. The Limits of Dialogue as a Critical Pedagogy. In: P.R. Trifonas (ed.), *Revolutionary Pedagogies*. New York & London: Routledge.

Biko, S.B. 2004. *I write what I like*. Johannesburg: Picador Africa.

Boone, E.J., Safrit, R.D., & Jones, J. 2002. *Developing Programs in Adult Education: A Conceptual Programming Model*.

Bourdieu, P. & Passeron, J.C. 1977. *Reproduction in Education: Society and Culture*. California: Sage.

Chile, L.M. & Simpson, G. 2004. Spirituality and Community Development: Exploring the link between the Individual and the Collective. *Community Development Journal*, 39(4):318-331. https://doi.org/10.1093/cdj/bsh029

Chilisa, B. & Preece, J. 2005. *Research Methods for Adult Educators in Africa*. Cape Town: Pearson.

Dei, G.J.S. 2002. Spiritual Knowing and Transformative Learning. The Research Network for New Approaches to Lifelong Learning, NALL Working Paper #59. *The research network for New Approaches to Lifelong Learning*. [Online]. Available: https://bit.ly/2YqRoH3

Eze, E.C. 1998. Modern Western Philosophy and African Colonialism. In: E.C. Eze (ed.), *African Philosophy: An Anthology*. Massachusetts: Blackwell Publishers.

Fanon, F. 1968. *The Wretched of the Earth*. C. Farrington (trans.). New York: Grove Press.

Foucault, 1991. Governmentality. In: G. Burchell, C. Gordon & P. Miller (eds.), *The Foucault Effect: Studies in Governmentality*. Hemel Hempstead: Harvester Wheatsheaf.

Freire, P. 1975. *Pedagogy of the Oppressed*. Harmondsworth, UK: Penguin.

Gboku, M.L.S. & Lekoko, R.N. 2007. *Developing Programmes for Adult Learners in Africa*. Hamburg: UNESCO Institute for Lifelong Learning.

Gqaleni, N., Hlongwane., Khondo, C., Mbatha, M., Mhlongo, S., Ngcobo, N., Mkhize, V.T., Mtshali, N., Pakade, R. & Street, R.A. 2011. Biomedical and Traditional Healing Collaboration on HIV and AIDS in KwaZulu-Natal, South Africa. *Universitas Forum*, 2(2): 1-9.

Gravett, S. 2001. *Designing and Implementing Learning Events: A Dialogic Approach*. Pretoria: Van Schaik.

Hill, P. 1995. African Centred Paradigm. *The Drum*, 2(1):4.

Hlela, Z. 2016. Learning through the Action of Research: Reflections on an Afrocentric Research Design. *Community Development Journal*, 50(2):196-212. https://doi.org/10.1093/cdj/bsw033

Hlela, Z. 2017. Participatory Community Learning for Community Empowerment: A Case Study in Maputaland. Unpublished Doctoral Thesis. Edgewood: University of KwaZulu Natal.

Jansen, J. 2017. Introduction – Part II Decolonising the University Curriculum given a Dysfunctional Schooling System. *Journal of Education*, 68:3-14.

Jarvis, P. 1995. *Understanding Adult and Continuing Education : Theory and Practice*. London: Kogan Page.

Jegede, O. 2011. When the Unthinkable Happens. Editorial, *Open Praxis*, October 2011:1-4.

Kanu, Y. 2011. *Integrating Aboriginal Perspectives into the School Curriculum: Purposes, Possibilities and Challenges*. Toronto: University of Toronto Press.

Kaphagawani, D.N. 2000. What is African Philosophy? In: P.H. Coetzee & A.P.J. Roax (eds.), *Philosophy for Africa*. Cape Town: Oxford University Press.

Karanja, K. 2010. A Genealogical Analysis of the Worldview Framework in African-centered. Psychology. *The Journal of Pan African Studies*, 3(8):109-129.

Legum, C. 1990. *Africa since Independence*. Indiana: Indiana University Press.

Lekoko, R. & Modise, O. 2011. An insight into an African Perspective on Lifelong Learning: Towards Promoting Functional Compensatory Programmes. *International Journal of Lifelong Education*, 30(1):23-35. https://doi.org/10.1080/02601370.2011.538176

Letseka, M. 2007. Why Students Leave: The Problem of High University Drop-Out Rates. *HSRC Review*, 5(3):8-9.

Mangaliso, M.P. & Damane, M.B. 2001. Building Competitive Advantage from *Ubuntu*: Management Lessons from South Africa. *Academy of Management Perspectives*, 15(3):23-34. https://doi.org/10.5465/ame.2001.5229453

Mazama, A. 1998. The Eurocentric Discourse in Writing: An Exercise in Self-glorification. *Journal of Black Studies*, 19(1):3-16. https://doi.org/10.1177/002193479802900101

Nagowah, L & Nagowah, S. 2009. A Reflection on the Dominant Learning Theories: Behaviourism, Cognitivism and Contsructivism. *International Journal of Learning*, 16(2):279-285. https://doi.org/10.18848/1447-9494/CGP/v16i02/46136

Nandy, A. 1983. *The Intimate Enemy: loss and Recovery of Self Under Colonialism*. Delhi: Oxford University Press.

Ngara, C. 2007. African Ways of Knowing and Pedagogy Revisited. *Journal of Contemporary Issues in Education*, 2:7-20. https://doi.org/10.20355/C5301M

Ntseane, P.G. 2011. Culturally Sensitive Transformational Learning: Incorporating the Africentric Paradigm and African Feminism. *Adult Education Quarterly*, 61(4):307-323. https://doi.org/10.1177/0741713610389781

Ntuli, P. 2002. Indigenous Knowledge Systems and the African Renaissance. In: C.A. Odora-Hoppers (ed.), *Indigenous Knowledge and Intergration of Knowledge Systems: Toward a Philosophy of Articulation*. Claremont: New African Books.

Nyerere, J. 1968. *Freedom and Socialism*. New York: Oxford University Press.

Ozomon, H. & Craver, S. 1998. *Philosophical Foundations of Education*. Englewood Cliffs: Prentice-Hall.

Odora Hoppers, C.A. 2009. *Engaging Critically with Tradition, Culture, and Patriarchy through Lifelong Learning: What Would Julius Nyerere say?* Paper presented in 6th Julius Nyerere Annual Lecture on Lifelong Learning. University of the Western Cape, 3 September.

Oloruntoba, S. 2015. Pan-Africanism, Knowledge Production and the Third Liberation of Africa. International Journal of African Renaissance Studies-multi-, inter-and transdisciplinarity, 10(1):7-24. https://doi.org/10.1080/18186874.2015.1050212

Onyemuwa, S.G. 1997. Appropriate Adult Education Programme Planning and Implementation Framework for Nigeria in the 21th Century. In: A. Ayodele & I. Biao (eds.), *Policy Issues in Adult and Community Education*. Maidururi, Nigeria: Mainasara Publishing.

Pietersen, H.J. 2005. Western Humanism, African Humanism and Work Organisations. *South African Journal of Industrial Psychology*, 31(3):54-61. https://doi.org/10.4102/sajip.v31i3.209

Preece, J. 2009. *Lifelong Learning and Development A Southern Perspective*. London & New York: Continuum International Publishing Group.

Prinsloo, P. 2017. Online Distance Education in South Africa: Past Practices and Prognosis. In: O. Zawacki-Richter & A. Qayyum (eds.), *National Systems in an Era of Global Online Distance Education*. Alberta: Athabasca University Press.

Ramose, M.B. 2004. In Search of an African Philosophy of Education: Perspectives on Higher Education. *South African Journal of Higher Education*, 18(3):138-160. https://doi.org/10.4314/sajhe.v18i3.25487

Reviere, R. 2001. Toward an Afrocentric Research Methodology. *Journal of Black Studies*, 31(6):709-728. https://doi.org/10.1177/002193470103100601

Shavinina, L.V. & Seeratan, K. 2004. Extracognitive Phenomena in the Intellectual Functioning of Creative and Talented Individuals. In: L.V. Shavinina & M. Ferrari (eds.), *Beyond Knowledge, Extracognitive Aspects of Developing High Ability*. Mahwah: Erlbaum Publishers. https://doi.org/10.4324/9781410610041

Sondlo, M. 2013. A Comparative Study of Student Retention and Throughput in Postgraduate Distance Education Programme. Unpublished Master's Thesis. Pretoria: University of Pretoria.

Tolliver, D. 2015. Afrocentrism - Standing on its Own Cultural Ground. *New Directions for Adult and Continuing Education*, 1015(147):59-69. https://doi.org/10.1002/ace.20142

UNESCO. 1997. *International Standard Classification of Education (ISCED) 1997*. New York: The Author.

WaThiongo, N. 1986. *Decolonising the Mind: The Politics of Language in African Literature*. London: James Currey.

Zulu, I. M. 2006. Critical Indigenous African Education and Knowledge. *The Journal of Pan African Studies*, 1(3):32-48.

Chapter Nine

Heutagogy, Decolonisation and Rethinking Knowledge: Voices of University Teachers

Luvuyo L Lalendle
Vuyisile Msila

Introduction

One of the factors that higher education institutions need to change if their mission is to be achieved, is effective teaching. In many African states, the calls to transform the university through decolonisation will not be realised without the conscious efforts to transform teaching and learning. For the new world of the fourth industrial revolution, countries would need graduates who are empowered with knowledge and skills to be able to create a better future. Bidabadi, Nasrisfahan, Rouhollahi and Khalili (2016:171) point out that the university's imperative is to be a space where creative minds meet and "established notions of truth are challenged in the pursuit of knowledge. To be able to do all this, getting help from experienced teachers can be very useful and effective".

Today's higher education institutions seek to improve not only the quality of graduates but also the entire university curriculum, as well as scholarship and teaching. Bidabadi et al. (2016) also add that good teaching methods help the students to question their preconceptions and motivates them to learn. Serdyukov (2017) concurs with the above stating that education should serve the needs of the society and must evolve to meet the challenges of the fast-changing world. Serdyukov contends that there is a constant need for innovations in education and that education today has to be ready always for educational innovations. This, however, calls for the involvement of all stakeholders for meaningful innovations need a multidimensional approach to revitalise the educational system so that it leads to students' autonomy (Serdyukov, 2017).

Current education demands educators who will be conduits of decolonising education by using their consciousness to promote progressive classrooms that reflect the necessary epistemic freedom. Consciousness is critical in this regard for a conscientised teacher would be able to lead transformed classrooms that promote critical thinking and new identity formation. Stokes (1997) contends that progressive teachers with vision would be able to enable their learners to be critical and active in reshaping their own education. Progressive teachers are those who are sensitised around issues of gender, race, history, language, teaching methodologies and class. Not only will these teachers understand the past struggles to liberate education, but they would also understand the new struggles for a decolonised future of education. Shor (1987:14), writing about Freirean approaches in the classroom states, "[…] one way to touch the real potential of teaching is to see that education can either confirm or challenge socialisation into equality". bell hooks (1994:10) opines, "To emphasize that the pleasure of teaching is an art of resistance countering the overwhelming boredom, and apathy that often characterise the way professors and students feel about teaching and learning, about teaching and learning, about the classroom experience". bell hooks (1994) points out that the classroom should be exciting and never boring, and that the classroom is the most radical space of possibility in the academy.

Fry, Ketteridge and Marshall (2009) raise a salient argument when they argue that it is unfortunate that, in higher education institutions, some academics teach students without any expertise on how students learn. In a country like South Africa for example, massification has ensured that diverse students learn in different ways as many aspects, such as socio-economic status, social capital, and several others have an impact on learning. Knowles (1995) has argued in his andragogical approach that adults tend to be self-directed and autonomous. The teacher should always know how her teaching helps students to learn and this can only happen if they understand the effectiveness of certain learning styles that would suit the students. Hoskins and Newstead (2009) postulate that the strategies used in teaching and learning can make students lack motivation: "There is also evidence that what we do to students at university can lead to their becoming motivated." (Hoskins & Newstead, 2009:33). Stefani (2009) points out that the culture and the ethos of the higher education institution will influence the curriculum and the way it is delivered. Furthermore, Stefani (2009:40) argues:

> […] our knowledge and understanding of student learning gleaned from the research literature indicates that the attention given to curriculum design and development, the planning experiences and assessment of student learning all have a significant impact on students' approaches to learning.

This study looks at the propinquity between decolonisation of higher education institutions and heutagogy. In search for democratic liberatory teaching and learning models, heutagogy appears to have some qualities of a strategy that prevents alienation of the student, thus leading to epistemic freedom. The questions posed by the study is, which factors of heutagogy are interrelated to decolonisation of higher education institutions in Africa?

The secondary question was: Can heutagogy be utilised to fit in the process of decolonisation of knowledge?

Brief Literature Review

Two concepts that are critical in this study are *heutagogy* and *decolonisation*. The latter has been used frequently in the debates for a transformed education in South Africa. In fact, most South African students have stated it categorically that they want more than transformation of education; they want a total overhaul of education and this can be achieved through decolonisation. Joseph (2018) argues that it appears as if transformation has failed and should be replaced by decoloniality. Among the demands of the #RhodesMustFall and #FeesMustFall movements (mainly in 2015 and 2016) were the calls for free education, destruction of colonial effigies, as well as a decolonised university in all its forms including teaching, curriculum, and the materials used for learning and teaching.

Heutagogy is a teaching and learning strategy that comes after pedagogy and andragogy, and it wants the student to be a self-determined learners. Heutagogy is different from andragogy, which seeks students to be self-directed in their learning. As decolonisation appears to be taking centre stage for future African higher education institutions, so is heutagogy. Blaschke (2012) sees heutagogy as of special interest to distance education as she points out that it possesses key characteristics linking it to distance education institutions; learner autonomy and self-directedness are among these. The educators have a mammoth task in developing students for the future. Again, Blaschke (2012:57) succinctly captures this:

> Educators today are tasked with developing lifelong learners who can survive and thrive in a global knowledge economy – learners who have the capability to effectively and creatively apply skills and competencies to new situations in an ever-changing, complex world (The World Bank, 2003; Kuit & Fell, 2010). Pedagogical, even andragogical, educational methods are no longer fully sufficient in preparing learners for thriving in the workplace, and a more self-directed and self-determined approach is

> needed, one in which the learner reflects upon what is learned and how it is learned and in which educators teach learners how to teach themselves (Peters, 2001; 2004; Kamenetz, 2010).

Among others, heutagogy seeks to bring relevant education to the student, one in which s/he can be empowered as they study the present and are able to project into the future. These are critical for the rapidly changing society in which the students live. Mann, Ker, Eden-Mann and O'Brien (2017) point out that heutagogy is an approach based on a learner-determined approach which recognises a transformation of learning processes beyond a teacher-centric focus on content. Capability and capacity to learn and mature into autonomy are some of the factors that are critical in heutagogy.

Decolonisation, like heutagogy, seeks to redress several aspects of teaching and learning in university learning sites. Ndlovu-Gatsheni (2018) points out that epistemological decolonisation can be fully realised when it is coupled with decolonial pedagogy. Decolonial pedagogy is associated with re-humanisation in teaching and learning. In the short discussion above, we have seen how heutagogy seeks to break alienation as it brings students to work with teachers in formulating the curriculum. Decolonial pedagogy speaks to inclusion and understanding, to relevance, and quality. We also see the infusion of decolonisation as an area of study that calls for *Decolonial Heutagogy*; this means a heutagogical approach that will help anchor decolonisation for distance learning students in particular. Decolonial heutagogy require the need for re-education of teachers as well as the move to change consciousness. Ndlovu-Gatsheni (2018) addresses the problem of consciousness of university teachers: "There is a lot that is wrong with the academics produced by Western-style universities. The key problem is their mentalities and consciousness cascading from what carter G. Woodson (1933) termed miseducation" (Ndlovu-Gatsheni, 2018:84). Ndlovu-Gatsheni adds that this miseducation experienced by African academics in particular is that it promotes arrogance, which may be inimical to decolonial heutagogy. This arrogance creates toxic environments where the teacher still thinks they are the 'alpha and omega' of knowledge. In decolonial heutagogy, the student should be encouraged to lead in the process of formulating knowledge that confronts Western hegemonies. They should formulate curricula and work a programme that is relevant to their communities in the process unmasking the positive aspects of decolonisation thus demonstrating how the world can be changed through understanding what African knowledges can bring as people try to dismantle Eurocentrism and epistemic violence in society. It should also be in this process that students should see how to use eclectic approaches from Africa and the West to solve certain challenges in society. Decolonisation is not about disregarding Western knowledges, but it seeks to bring all marginalised knowledges in an ecology of knowledges where all knowledges will compete on an equal level. Students should be given this opportunity, and this is the true meaning of education.

Others such as Heleta (2016) have posed questions of whether our teachers at university are ready to teach at decolonised institutions of higher learning. Heleta poses a question of whether those who do not care about the indigent in society educate students to become virtuous, ethical, change agents and vital citizens. Heleta (2016:3) posits:

> Decolonisation of higher education is "about justice that addresses the epistemic violence of colonial knowledge and colonial thought" (Pillay 2015). South Africa needs a higher education system to develop graduates and intellectuals who can address the epistemic violence of the past and present and who will go on to rewrite the "histories and humanity [of both South Africa and Africa] so cruelly seized and denied by Europe" (Zeleza, 2009:116) throughout centuries. However, where to find leaders, administrators and academics capable of addressing deep-rooted epistemic violence? Where to find academics who possess knowledge and passion about the African continent?

Therefore, decolonised curriculum is a meaningful transformation of education. Sayed, Motala and Hoffman (2017:60) define the concept by citing #FeesMustFall and #RhodesMustFall Movements and explicates decolonisation as "treating African discourses as the point of departure – through addressing not only content, but languages and methodologies of education and learning – and only examining western traditions in so far as they are relevant to our own experience". The calls for a decolonised university is a call to include all students not only the elites in institutions that are opposing epistemic violence. The student in higher education institution should consciously move to change the ills of colonisation. Mudimbe (1994) argues that the society cannot speak of decolonisation when there is no understanding of the psychology of colonisation. Like heutagogy, decolonisation has become as urgent as Africa seeks to deal with the complexities of a changing society that experts such as Barnett (2015) talked about.

Methods

This qualitative case study used purposive sampling which is a form of non-probability sampling. This is used by researchers whilst aware that it does not represent the entire population and simply represents itself. Purposive sampling is also less complicated and is less expensive although it does have some disadvantages. These disadvantages include the fact that it is deliberately selective and biased (Cohen, Manion & Morrison, 2004). We selected the participants by handpicking those we judged by their typicality. We focused on a number of lectures who had used heutagogical approaches and were teaching in post-graduate distance programmes whose duration was from six months to a year. Purposive sampling is also critical where data gathering is meant to contribute to a better understanding of a theoretical framework (Etikan, Musa & Aikassim, 2016). As part of qualitative studies, purposive sampling is meant to achieve depth of understanding of the phenomena under study.

Purposive sampling was conducted in three universities where the teachers (lecturers) used heutagogic principles in teaching three different postgraduate modules; Business Management and Entrepreneurship, School Management, and Leadership and African Philosophy. Two of the modules are one-year modules (School Management and Leadership, as well as African Philosophy) and the other a six months module. This was a qualitative study, hence only six teachers/lecturers and 12 learners were interviewed; two teachers from each university as well as four learners from each university.

In each of the universities, the teachers were interviewed individually first and then in two focus groups. Data analysis was done through constant comparative analysis. "This strategy involves taking one piece of data (one interview, one statement, one theme) and comparing it with all others that may be similar or different in order to develop conceptualisations of the possible relations between various pieces of data" (Thorne, 2000:3). A researcher may compare the accounts of two participants who had identical experiences and then pose analytic questions, e.g. *why is this the same with that one?*

After the analysis, we were able to interpret the data and identify patterns to enhance verifiable conclusions. After the organisation of the data, we coded the data to compress it in understandable concepts. We used pattern coding as we found patterns in the data and used these as the basis of the coding.

Findings

There were several aspects that reflected elements of a transformative education in all three universities represented by the sample: the African Philosophy class, School Management and Leadership class, and the Business Management and

Entrepreneurship class. What was striking in the findings was to learn that both the teachers and their students shared similar experiences about the heutagogical approaches in their learning groups.

Whilst all the learners were aware of the demands of heutagogy because a number of them were the best, heutagogy might not have worked in their undergraduate classrooms because they were used to teacher-centred approaches, as well as study guides that prescribed what needed to be learnt. Five learners though pointed out that learning by rote, which was supported by study guides, made it easy for them to prepare for exams. They were saying that they sometimes found the exam-driven approaches working for students whose schooling careers all about rote was learning. These five pointed out that they were still in the process of appreciating heutagogical principles and two of the five stated that heutagogy "enhanced their creativity and ability to think broadly about the subject matter". The teachers also underscored the fact that heutagogy transformed the way they perceived and practiced teaching. They also talked of the way they looked at curriculum, for now they found curriculum that does not change the student's life, is futile. The six teachers who emphasised the need for teachers to accept innovative ways of teaching also highlighted the maturity that students talked about. All found heutagogy unsettling at first because, as two of them stated, "It appeared as if teachers did not have much to do and students were rendering the teachers' work redundant". Yet all the teachers concurred of the need for teachers to relook at teaching with new eyes to discover new challenges.

Therefore, both the teachers and the learners saw the richness in teaching and learning. The teachers mentioned several aspects when they talked about teaching and learning. These included, changing scholarship, conducting relevant research on teaching and learning, and changing the ingrained cultures of what teaching and learning means. One teacher pointed out:

> When you use heutagogical principles, you realise how much we need to focus on novel ways. You see many of us still struggle to move away from the past practices. We want to do things the way we used to, with the guides, usually dated guides and wrong activities even in these guides.

Another from a different institution said something similar stating:

> It becomes difficult when colleagues are asked to change the way they set questions class activities or exam questions. It is rote learning; list, name and so on. Many a times they do not change not because they are not aware of the need to change but they are struggling to teach and assess differently. Yes, there are those who still believe in old ways and who do not want to change.

Several student participants concurred with the teachers on the potential of heutagogical approaches. One student participant seemed to summarise what others believed:

> The heutagogical models are very useful in making all those involved in education to be thinkers, to be part of the creation knowledge as they learn. This empowers for the student is not a mere receiver of knowledge on whom the teachers impart knowledge. In fact, this is the crux of heutagogy, making all of us to be worthy creators of our curriculum.

In addition, all the participants contended that heutagogy is a useful method that ensures that the students and the teachers are not alienated by the content of the modules they studied. They also opined that the heutagogical approach ensured that there was no domination of anyone in the learning encounter for the teacher and the students were almost peers in the creation of knowledge. Participants repeated this in different ways. One teacher participant claimed:

> This (heutagogy) is really empowering and there is nothing so pleasant as when as a teacher you see your student developing, this is even so in heutagogy because I found my students as consultants, as peers as experts who enabled me to frequently rethink about my module. This has hanged my teaching philosophy and my approach.

Most critically, another facilitator spoke of the way heutagogy has changed his ways of thinking about teaching. He also added that one needs to be ready for this kind of teaching and learning approach. She said:

> Two things happened in many of us using this heutagogy, we changed our consciousness to be receptable to heutagogy or it changed our consciousness. It was such a great experience trying things anew and heutagogy will be one of the critical elements in decolonisation approaches as we transform the curriculum inn (South) Africa. It makes all involved think about ways of improving the curriculum. Even teachers become lifelong learners.

The idea of consciousness was very critical in all modules because teachers used novel ways of teaching which included all groups work among learning communities. Students formed learning communities with group leaders who were coordinators. In their communities, the students were responsible in setting questions for assessment. The groups were also responsible for leading discussions on certain topics with minimal but critical teacher guidance. The students were also responsible in applying the knowledge gained in a module to their communities. This was close to experiencing epistemic freedom where the students found learning boundless. Both the teachers and the students found it fulfilling for them to be able to develop knowledge that is relevant to their environment. This was critical in selecting various kinds of knowledge as they explored both Western and Indigenous Knowledge Systems. It was also clear though among other students, that it would take quite some time to be assertive to try to argue for knowledge different from what they were used to in traditional classrooms. Of the 12 students, four stated that they did not always feel free to use examples from communities because that is not what they are used to in their textbooks and most of them are from Europe.

They all found heutagogical principles espousing the ideals of lifelong learning where the students were to take learning outside the learning groups to workplace and the communities.

Finally, the idea of collaboration was inevitable in heutagogy and the participants praised the ways in which this method supports the views of diverse students. Some opined that it was collaboration that enhances the value of heutagogy because it enables the students to work together "as they unbundle the learning materials debating amongst themselves". Collaboration enabled them to express themselves freely as they identified themes that are relevant to their lives thus making them ready for the life outside the modules and higher education institution.

All participants concurred that heutagogy enabled them to face alienation that characterises institutions of learning. The students also expressed that "getting a degree or a qualification in a distance education institution is usually a lonely road that alienates". Student participants also proclaimed that the teachers who use 'power-over' students frequently filled this road with domination. The idea of community brought by the methodology of heutagogy is able to overcome the experiences of teacher-centred classes because teachers become part of these communities. The participants also found this method very amenable to a transforming higher education institution that was trapped in 'traditional' teacher-centred approaches.

Yet, although all the participants saw the positive role that heutagogy can play in their studies some had reservations. Six students stated that they still believed that the teacher-centred approaches should balance the peer-led discussions. They also stated that sometimes students could "move at a tangent and miss the objectives of the modules". One teacher also pointed out that to some extent heutagogy can make teachers helpless and impotent when students lead. Furthermore, this participant stated that heutagogy would best suit the new teachers who may change easily but those who had been teaching for more than a decade, they might struggle changing their practice. Despite these reservations though, the participants found much value in the novel ways used in heutagogy.

Another aspect that the participants found illuminating was the flexibility of heutagogy. Almost all were pointing out how they came from education culture that is rigid and prescriptive.

Themes were teased from the study's findings and the researcher used categories to highlight several themes found in the study. Out of this categorisation, the themes below emerged:

- Heutagogy as Liberatory Teaching
- Heutagogy: enabling epistemic freedom
- Heutagogy leading to rethinking of teaching and learning

Heutagogy as Liberatory Teaching

The heutagogical approaches are relevant to distance education programmes. It is also a relevant approach for liberatory teachers. Some of the qualities of liberatory teachers include teachers who promote democracy, cognitive justice, social justice, and classes that challenge the status quo. All these are elements that the teachers in particular talked about. These are also the elements that were highlighted although some participants reiterated the need for professional maturity as well which they described as being able to guide learning utilising various novel strategies. By its own nature, heutagogy appears 'synonymous' with liberatory teaching. Liberatory teachers seek to see the dialogic activities for learning to occur. The use of resources such as social media, learner-centred activities, and the emphasis on learner capacity shows how open learning is and how teachers make their learners the core of learning activities. These enable learners to prepare themselves well for workplace realities and complexities.

Heutagogy is perceived as a methodology that has revolutionised teaching and learning. Snowden and Halsall (2016:4) cite research that discovered that "the heutagogical approach enables the student to control their learning, reflect, and expand professional development. The key to success of the heutagogical approach relies on reflective practice because it helps the student to control their learning …". Heutagogy changes the culture of teaching and learning – this is relevant to what colonisation seeks to do and this is to disrupt how things are done, the routine of Western epistemologies. Liberatory teaching enables the students and the teacher to adopt the right consciousness because as Freire says they would have been conscientised.

Heutagogy prepares students for the workplace in a fashion where they learn about various ecologies of knowledge as they enhance the planetary system. What is critical for heutagogical approach is the non-linear teaching and learning found in traditional approaches. Decolonisation is opposed to teacher-centric approaches. McPherson (2016) posits that in a heutagogical approach, the learners set their own path. Heutagogy changes traditional teaching, as we know it where the teacher has all the knowledge and the learners nothing. In fact, traditional pedagogy under apartheid was unjust and one-dimensional – regarding the learner as a tabula rasa or a blank slate. Freire et al. (1997:xv) write about ways in which traditional pedagogy denies the active involvement of the learner who receives learning:

> [...] in a manner that denies the validity of the ontological and epistemological productions of the learner and the learner's community. This is an authoritarian, manipulative, 'banking' pedagogy, which negates the possibility of democracy and distorts the lived experiences of the learners who are silenced and denied the opportunity to be authors of their own histories.

Heutagogy addresses the past inactivity of the learner who is now expected to work with the teachers as cocreators of knowledge. This method addresses social injustices and the silence that leads to miseducation as well as manipulation in the classroom. It is vital for the learner to be able to bring her lived experiences to the classroom. Progressive educators using pedagogy constantly promote dialogue, which is in contrast to the banking approaches. Frere et al. (1997) explain that progressive classrooms should neither display authoritarianism nor permissiveness, for the latter can develop when the extreme of no authority exists. Decolonisation needs these elements; addressing epistemicides, culturecides and linguicides requires empowered learners who will appreciate the co-responsibilities with the teacher and other learners. Learners and teachers who both see the purpose of democratic education in classrooms will appreciate the rehumanising goals of education based on social justice and the promotion of dialogic learning. The essence of heutagogy has all elements that seek to free the learners who is a trusted role-player in the education process. Heutagogy emphasises the idea of knowledge as shared experience by the role-players. This is also the idea of liberatory teaching where knowledge is understood to be "socially constructed in the negotiation of experience with other knowers" (Freire, Fraser, Macedo, McKinnon & Stokes, 1997:xvi). What needs to develop in this negotiation process is a critical pedagogy devoid of methodological inflexibility. Macedo (1997) explicates the need to use anti-method pedagogy to improve classroom practice – this opposes domesticating education that seeks to retain the status quo. Heutagogy employs anti-pedagogy, which seeks to rehumanise and is amenable to decolonisation, which seeks to reclaim history and knowledge.

Heutagogy: Enabling Epistemic Freedom

Liberatory teaching discussed above requires the idea of epistemic freedom where knowledge has been decolonised. Decolonisation pursues the decentring of Eurocentrism and Western knowledges whilst opening up for indigenous knowledges that have been marginalised. It is critical for decolonial theory to bring the North and South knowledges on an equal pedestal. Over the decades of colonisation, the West has been the sole point of reference we used to view the world. The classrooms today need broad learners who will open up to new knowledges. Liberatory teaching starts here, with epistemic freedom. Ndlovu-Gatsheni (2018:3) points out, "Thus epistemic freedom speaks to cognitive justice. Epistemic freedom is fundamentally about the right to think, theorise, interpret the world, develop own methodologies and write from where one is located and unencumbered by Eurocentrism". Heutagogy by its nature is about this cognitive justice as learners are free to express themselves as cocreators of knowledge with their teachers. It revolutionises the classroom as learners learn to think freely as they generate theory.

Heutagogy shows the necessary epistemic freedom as learners can create knowledge towards self-directed learning. Epistemic freedom will also 'level the playing field' for learners to be able to embrace heutagogcal principles. Epistemic freedom is a starting point for heutagogy as it is for decolonised system of education. A number of aspects can shock learners who are to engage in a transformed system encompassing heutagogy and/decolonised system. Many learners and their teachers are likely to have been used to Western knowledges in classrooms that are teacher-centred, devoid of social justice, cognitive justice, and democracy. Epistemic freedom should empower learners so that they could see and appropriate their role in creating knowledge. Stoszkowski and McCarthy (2018) learners may like the autonomy and self-determined learning although they may lack the desired attributes such as knowledge, skills, and attitude they need. In fact, Joshi (2018) contends that, by using heutagogy pedagogical approach, we can prepare our learners to survive in the global economy and enable them to apply the skills learnt. Furthermore, Joshi (2018) states that the heutagogical approach focuses on learning the content to learning to learn. In the process, it develops life skills through active learning.

Epistemic freedom raises critical consciousness as well as Freire's conscientisation about the world. Murrell (1997) links critical consciousness to Africanist critical pedagogy. Citing Freire, Murrell writes that critical pedagogy should promote the value of self-generativity as well as self-agency. Learners should understand that they are the creators of culture and that their work can be creative. Critical pedagogy also needs to promote humanisation "so that dehumanisation can be exposed whenever it occurs, and learners can see connections and actually decide whether or not they want to be complicit in a dehumanising social and political system without seeking to change it" (Murrell, 1997:54).

Heutagogy Leading to Rethinking of Teaching and Learning

It was clear in the study how the participants saw the vital role of education as lifelong learning and a noble idea linked to decolonisation's search for relevance as well as the application of knowledge. Heutagogical approaches expect learners to apply skills learnt creatively. The use of new technologies also brings forth the idea of rethinking about teaching and learning heutagogy has ensured that adult education's rethinking is taken seriously as people shifted from andragogy. In fact, Blaschke (2012) cites Wheeler when she avers that andragogy has been outmoded in light of the rapid development in teaching. The rethinking of teaching of teaching and learning has been enhanced by new learning resources and digital media. Rethinking of education also means that there is a shift from self-directed learning (andragogy) to self-determined learning (heutagogy).

The above subsections demonstrate that heutagogy is about thinking and rethinking of the curriculum as well as the university at large. Some speak of the curriculum that is dehumanising and alienating in our institutions of higher learning. This makes the university irrelevant as it also marginalises some other knowledges. Ndlovu-Gatsheni (2018) speaks of the need to bring to the fore knowledges that have been marginalised in an "ecology of knowledges basket". Heutagogy seeks to address the anomalies that have always been there in education around the world. In Africa, the way colonisation has shaped education will always get a special attention, as conscientious practitioners would want to free education from various ills. Barnett (2015) writes about the world's *supercomplexity* and the curriculum and how education needs to prepare the student for this supercomplexity. Barnett contends that, for over a century, academics have been the ones who shape the curricula in their fields of study. Barnett (2015:180) argues:

> The challenges of understanding the changing patterns of the curriculum in higher education are, however, even more severe. Higher education is faced not just with preparing students for a complex world but is faced with preparing them for a supercomplex world. It is a world where nothing can be taken for granted, where no frame of understanding or of action can be entertained with any security. It is a world in which we are conceptually challenged, and continually so.

As curriculum patterns are changing, there needs to be change, a rethinking of teaching and learning to also confront the supercomplexity. Sayed et al. (2017) write about the need for teacher educators to understand what their underlying curriculum decisions "and the broader institutional and policy dynamics that impact on efforts to rethink curricula". Heutagogy would include the relooking and reshaping the intellectuals who work with students in distance education programmes. A meaningful, decolonised curriculum will be entrenched in some relevant philosophy or practice. Sayed et al. (2017) cite Mafeje who pointed out that "we must be rooted in something" and that something is the decolonised African conditions. In this study, the students used their ideas to experiment with epistemic freedom as they took lead in the teaching and learning encounter. Many teachers were somehow 'relieved' to find that their students are taking the lead showing signs of decolonising the curriculum. Yet findings paths towards decolonisation and epistemic freedom is complex and supercomplex to cite Barnett above. Sayed et al. (2017:84) claim:

> Lecturers characterised the process of decolonising the curriculum as a form of struggle with the self, one, which involves coming to terms with the brokenness of our knowledge, and requires us to cultivate the virtues of epistemic tentativeness, humility and courage. However, while lecturers engage in this personal struggle, they must also grapple with an institutional context of dwindling resources and increasing workloads.

Heleta (2016) states that South Africa needs a higher education system to develop graduates who can address epistemic violence of the present and the past. Heutagogy has this responsibility in African institutions. It should free the students and their teachers to struggle for relevant liberatory curriculum undergirded by epistemic freedom.

McPherson (2016) contends that collaboration is a powerful tool in heutagogy because students learn much from one another as they do from the facilitator. Heutagogy also uses connection with others utilising many tools in distance education; twitter, Facebook, LinkedIn, and WhatsApp are some examples. It is opposed to colonial and Western hegemonies in education that seek to promote the individual over the collective.

Finally, what is clear in the model of heutagogy above is that it is more focused on learning than teaching, something that teachers in the study understood. Therefore, one would agree with the participants who talked about the need to develop their teachers and be professionally matured. Yaduvanshi and Singh (2017) state that teacher education ought to develop competent future teachers and teacher educators. These writers point out that competent future teachers should create healthy living environments. "As prospective teachers are adult learners and are nation builders of the twenty first century, therefore heutagogical approaches are appropriate for developing professional competencies among them" (Yaduvanshi & Singh, 2017:3690). Yaduvanshi and Singh also mention the approach of double-loop theory that is based upon 'theory of action' focused on solving complex and ill-structured problems. These authors also highlight four basic steps that are crucial in the process of action theory:

o   detection of support and theory-in-use;
o   creation of new meanings;
o   construction of new actions; and
o   simplification of outcomes.

Yaduvanshi & Singh, 2017

The four steps above are encompassed by Double-loop learning. Learning becomes an active process in which the individuals seek education or gain feedback and do assessment as they move through life experiences (Yaduvanshi & Singh, 2017). The use of double-loop learning ensures that teachers are able to create competent and capable learners. Teachers can and should play a role in developing double loop learning, for it requires that learners be both psychologically and behaviourally engaged (Blaschke & Hase, 2012).

Conclusion

Decolonisation is not heutagogy and vice versa. However, as seen in the debates about the heutagogical approaches reflect many decolonisation practices hence heutagogy can be useful in the decolonisation of knowledge and scholarship. The approaches used in heutagogy are amenable to epistemic freedom, which respects the position of the learner. The objectives of heutagogy include learners being involved in negotiating what and how they learn. This collaboration between the teacher and the learner implies social justice, democracy, relevance thus addressing anomalies in teaching and learning of the past. Decolonisation embraces democratic practices that seek not only to utilise various knowledges but also to involve learners in addressing epistemicides and culturecides that have excluded the majority of learners from being responsible in the creation of knowledge.

Decolonial classrooms need collaborative learning, communities, and social justice in learning sites. As evident in this study, all these are critical aspects of heutagogy. Furthermore, it is vital for a learner to be responsible or matured in heutagogy to be able to break the rigid, structured curriculum. In heutagogy, learners must unlearn individualism and rote learning. Furthermore, in heutagogy, empowering education promotes critical thinking, flexible democratic learning as well as relevant application of knowledge. All these are imperative especially when one examines ways in which decolonisation seeks to decentre Western knowledges as they are positioned among other knowledges. In this way, education will be humanising – recognising all those who are part of the teaching-learning process. Education that has only recognised Western knowledges has dehumanised the indigenous people. The latter included historicides, culturecides, and linguicides. To be a free, decolonial education learners can be co-creators of anti-colonial and anti-racist education. Heutagogy could play a central role in decolonising lifelong learning approaches and decolonisation can make use of heutagogy in espousing its principles.

References

Barnett, R. 2015. *Thinking and rethinking the University: The selected Works of Ronald Barnett*. London: Routledge. https://doi.org/10.4324/9781315768045

Bidabadi, N.S., Nasrisfahan, A., Rouhollahi, A. & Khalili, R. 2016. Effective Teaching Methods in Higher Education: Requirements and Barriers. *Journal of Advances in Medical Education & Professionalism*, 4(4):170-178.

Blaschke, L. 2012. Heutagogy and Lifelong Learning: A Review of Heiutagogical Practice and Self-determined Learning. *International Review of Research in Open and Distance Learning*, 13(1):56-71. https://doi.org/10.19173/irrodl.v13i1.1076

Cohen, L., Manion, L. & Morrison, K. 2004. *Research Methods in Education*. London: Routledge Falmer.

Etikan, I., Musa, S.A. & Aikassim, R.S. 2016. Comparison of Convenient Sampling and Purposive Sampling. *American Journal of Theoretical and Applied Statistics*, 5(1):1-4. https://doi.org/10.11648/j.ajtas.20160501.11

Fry, H., Ketteridge, S. & Marshall, S. 2009. Understanding Student Learning. In: H. Fry, S. Ketteridge & S. Marshall (eds.), *A Handbook for Teaching and Learning in Higher Education: Enhancing Academic practice*. New York: Routledge. https://doi.org/10.4324/9780203891414

Heleta, S. 2016. Decolonisation of Higher Education: Dismantling Epistemic Violence and Eurocentrism in South Africa. *Transformation in Higher Education*, 1(1):1-8. https://doi.org/10.4102/the.v1i1.9

hooks, b. 1994. *Teaching to Digress: Education as The Practice of Freedom*. New York: Routledge.

Hoskins, S.L. & Newstead, S.E. 2009. Encouraging Student Motivation. In: H. Fry, S. Ketteridge & S. Marshall (eds.), *A Handbook for Teaching and Learning in Higher Education: Enhancing Academic Practice*. New York: Routledge, pp. 27-39.

Joseph, T.R. 2018. *Decolonising the Curriculum: Transforming the University: A Discursive Perspective*.

Joshi, R. 2018. Cybergogy to Heutagogy: For Engaged Learning. *The Himalayan*.

Kallaway, P. 1988. From *Bantu Education to People's Education*. Cape Town: UCT.

Knowles, M.S. 1995. *Designs for Adult Learning*. Alexandria: Amer Society for Training.

Mann, S., Ker, G., Eden-Mann, P. & O'Brien, R. 2017. Designing for Heutagogy: An Independent Learning Pathway Approach. *Capable-Scope (Flexible Learning)*, 2:59-70.

Mudimbe, V.Y. 1994. *The Idea of Africa*. Indiana: Indiana University Press.

Murrell, P.C. 1997. Digging Again The family Wells. In: P. Freire, J.W. Fraser, D. Macedo, T. McKinnon & W.T. Stokes (eds.), *Mentoring the Mentor: A Critical Dialogue with Paulo Freire*. New York: Peter Lang.

Ndlovu-Gatsheni, S.J. 2018. *Epistemic Freedom in Africa: Deprovincialisation and Decolonisation*. London: Routledge. https://doi.org/10.4324/9780429492204

Sayed, Y., Motala, S. & Hoffman, N. 2017. Decolonising initial teacher education in South Africa Universities: More than an event. *Journal of Education*, 68:59-91.

Serdyukov, P. 2017. Innovation in Education: What Works, What doesn't, and What to do About it? *Journal of Research in Innovative Teaching & Learning*, 10(1):4-33. https://doi.org/10.1108/JRIT-10-2016-0007

Shor, I. 1987. Educating the Educators: A Freirean Approach to the Crisis in Teacher Education. In: I. Shor (ed.), *Freire for The Classroom: A Sourcebook for Liberatory Teaching*. Portsmouth: Heinemann.

Snowden, M. & Halsall, J.P. 2016. Self-determined Approach to Learning: A Social Science Perspective. *Cogent Education*, 3(1). https://doi.org/10.1080/2331186X.2016.1247608

Stefani, L. 2009. Planning Teaching and Learning. In: H. Fry, S. Ketteridge & S. Marshall (eds.), *A Handbook for Teaching and Learning in Higher Education: Enhancing Academic Practice*. New York: Routledge.

Stokes, W.T. 1997. Progressive Teacher Education: Consciousness, Identity, and Knowledge. In: P. Freire, J.W. Fraser, D. Macedo, T. McKinnon and W.T. Stokes (eds.), *Mentoring the Mentor: A Critical Dialogue with Paulo Freire*. New York: Peter Lang.

Stoszkowski, J. & McCarthy, L. 2018. Who Wouldn't Want to take Charge of Their Learning? Student Views on Learner Autonomy, Self- Determination and Motivation. *Journal of Perspectives in Applied Academic Practice*, 6(2):104-107. https://doi.org/10.14297/jpaap.v6i2.330

Tabata, I.B. 1979. *Education for Barbarism: Bantu (apartheid) Education in South Africa*. Pennsylvania: Unity Movement of South Africa.

Thorne, S. 2000. Data Analysis in Qualitative Research. *Evidence Based Nursing*, 2000(3):68-70. https://doi.org/10.1136/ebn.3.3.68

Torres, C.A. 2014. *First Freire: Early Writings in Social Justice Education*. New York: Teachers College Press.

Yaduvanshi, S. & Singh, S. 2017. Developing Professional Competencies Among Prospective Teachers Through Heutagogical Practices. *International Journal of Information Research and Review*, 4(2):3690-3694.

New Epistemologies
and Society

Chapter Ten

Decolonising Epistemologies: The Paradoxes of a Self-Colonised State

Philip M. Ramadikela
Vuyisile Msila
Teshome Abera

Introduction and Background

In his book, *Epistemic Freedom in Africa*, Ndlovu-Gatsheni (2018) writes about how Ethiopia colonised itself as he advances arguments raised by Woldeyes (2017) in his work, Native *Colonialism: Education and the Economy of Violence Against Tradition in Ethiopia*. Ethiopia is always lauded as one African country that was never colonised by European powers like other African states. The Italian occupation from 1936-1941 was short-lived. Earlier in the 1880s, Italy tried to colonise Ethiopia, but the Italians failed to conquer Abyssinia (as it was called then). The resistance posed by the Emperor Menelek II was enough to ward off the enemy, as his army was ready and able to defeat the Italians at the Battle of Adwa. Therefore, there was never any physical colonisation although epistemic freedom was to be stolen by self-colonisation.

Terefe (2017) explains how growing up in Ethiopia meant that, at school, she had to learn the English language although, from Grade 1 to Grade 6, she was taught in Amharic. However, in the upper grades, English was a mark of success and as a class monitor, she remembers being asked by the teacher to write the names of those who conversed in Amharic instead of English. "Our teacher would enforce a 5-cent penalty for every Amharic word that slipped through our lips during lessons" (Terefe, 2017). Furthermore, the school taught them Western history and literature; their education promoted the mimicry of Western life. Terefe points out that the many aspects of her Ethiopian culture were neglected by the school system.

This chapter looks at how and why Ethiopia needs decolonisation or, as our title suggests, to demarginalise the marginalised Indigenous Knowledge Systems. When one looks at the country, because it was never colonised, it was supposed to be among the most successful countries having never experienced epistemic violence like other African states that were under severe colonial administrations. How did such a country end up with colonialism is the question? Ndlovu-Gatsheni (2018) cites Woldeyes (2017) to argue how Ethiopia ended up in the unenviable position of other African states that were former colonies under European powers. Ndlovu-Gatsheni (2018:164-165) contends:

> Ethiopia could not successfully escape the impact of the Western Metaphysical empire. Consequently, Ethiopia is one of those countries that deliberately colonised itself with foreign Western institutions and Eurocentric ideas (see Woldeyes, 2017). This amounts to a paradoxical situation in the African struggles for decolonisation and deprovincialization, worthy detailed exploration before one turns to reflect on the rise of the modern Westernised education in Africa.

Woldeyes (2017) perceives Ethiopians complicit in the colonisation of their country because they voluntarily rebelled against the indigenous epistemologies and marginalised them in preference of Western knowledges. As a result, traditional philosophies, indigenous languages, and indigenous knowledge inspired education were all marginalised. Ethiopia has a deep history that goes back to the story of the Bible. The original indigenous Ethiopian education comprised of ancient Hebrew, Aramaic, Greek, Syriac, Muslim, and various other knowledges (Woldeyes in Ndlovu-Gatsheni, 2018).

The chapter examines a few themes and brief accounts; the original Ethiopian education, the marginalisation of indigenous knowledges, the West vs Africa, the language dilemma and finally, there are recommendations on what Ethiopia can do to decolonise education and resist the self-inflicted epistemic violence.

Self-colonisation and Denigration

Kiossev (1998) defines the concept self-colonising as referring to cultures that give in to Eurocentrism and West without having been invaded and turned into colonies. Furthermore, Kiossev refers to this as 'hegemony without domination'; the countries that self-colonise find themselves having to Europeanise themselves as they assimilate foreign cultures. The paradox in this picture is the invitation of the ills of colonisation including epistemic violence; Ethiopia was like a body that mutilated itself. Nayyar (2016) states that the colonised people feel grateful to their generous rulers as they carry modernisation. All the ills are likely to bring the social and cognitive injustice. Kiossev (1998) points out that, for the self-colonised state, all the ills are self-inflicted; no military occupation, no political dominance, no administrative rule, and economic exploitation – social imagination had a crucial role to play in self-colonisation. Kiossev (1998) explains social imagination as that which implies:

> [...] a background intuitive knowledge, a body of stereotypes shared by a community [...] Supported and reproduced by everyone, such community shared notions encourage individuals in imagining participants in communities and processes beyond the limited horizon of their immediate experience whereas primary groups are stimulated to perceive themselves as being part of a larger and sometimes unfathomable societies – nations, races, classes, historic periods, and even "humankind acting upon 'the world stage' and producing 'world history'".

The modern age has taught societies that which is colonial forms a collective imagination. Its main objective is to explain and defend European expansionism from the 16th until the 20th century, which is why these perceptions "ranked peoples and geographic spaces as 'superior' and inferior', delineated them not only geographically but in terms of value into 'Western', 'Eastern' and 'Southern', defined them as 'big' and 'small, historic and non-historic'" (Kiossev, 1998).

Nayyar (2016) states that the perception of Europe/West/White is rarely based on reality – the imagined modern West is always larger than the actual West. The self-colonising states seek the idea of a gigantic West with a lot of opportunities. Nayyar (2016) contends that the self-colonised have a grim view of their political past as being despotic for example. They detest their cultural past because it has always been not modern and also immoral. Furthermore, Nayyar (2016) postulates that the self-colonisers vouch that their languages were not developed enough for the global world; the languages cannot communicate science "and their emancipation solely depends on following the path of the West and Europe adopted during her renaissance". Furthemore, the paradox of self-colonised states is clear as self-colonising nations imported everything from the West, and this included elements that derided their own beings. "The borrowings from the European cultures made them to be culturally dependent upon the West" (Kiossev, 1998).

Spicer (2015) writes about the evils of colonialism in Liberia where black people colonised other black people, a different kind of self-colonisation. Spicer dispels the myth of Liberia as the oldest independent black republic in Africa. She adds that Liberia was entangled in colonial history. As the 'coloured' settlers established themselves in Liberia, they started imitating the habits of their colonisers and oppressors in America. When 185 000 blacks were shipped to Liberia, they started to experiment with black colonisation upon the indigenous people, such as the Groba. In fact, the black colonisers or Americo-Liberians were mixed race and lighter skinned than the indigenous Liberians and used this fair skin as a characteristic that demonstrated their superiority over the darker skinned indigenous people. Spicer (2015:37) argues, "Despite being idealised as the land of the free, the black settlers introduced to Liberia an experience of colonialism which mirrored conventional features of European colonisation".

The Americo-Liberian (the black settlers) who were as black as the indigenous people were, but this did not deter them from being the black colonisers who exhibited various characteristics of European colonisation. Furthermore, Spicer (2015) contends that the Americo-Liberian colonisers did not cherish the objectives and meaning of liberty; they only treasured their own liberty from America, hence their freedom was a paradox. In colonising the indigenous blacks, they were colonising themselves. Spicer highlights the way the Americo-Liberians continued to idolise America and referred to indigenous blacks as barbarians; they became a curse to the indigenous people who they frequently attacked. It is clear that this self-colonisation led to self-hate of all indigenous blacks and their cultures in Liberia. The Americo-Liberians were so brutal to the native Kru and Grebo that they excluded them birth right citizenship until 1904 when America revised the rights of Native Americans (Snapp, 2019).

The attitude of the Americo-Liberians might not have shocked some because many blacks from America at the time worshipped America and felt that they belonged to America not Africa. Several prominent blacks in America identified with America, so much so that they appeared to despise Africa. Their allegiance was more to America. The illustrious American black abolitionist, Frederick Douglass, was opposed to black Americans going back to Africa unlike people such as W.E.B. DuBois, Wilmot Blyden, and Marcus Garvey. Douglass dispelled the arguments that the black American had any connection with African people and maintained that they were Americans. Kilbride (2014) contends that Douglass rejected this connection to Africa because he believed that this distracted black Americans from the resistance against slavery in America. He also believed that the Anglo-American civilisation provided more opportunities for black Americans and a better life which Africa could never provide. Martin Luther King Jr speaks eloquently about the ambivalence of the black American; something that impact on her/his identity; Luther Jr (1995) points out:

> The Negro's greatest dilemma is that is that in order to be healthy he must accept his ambivalence. The Negro is the child of two cultures – Africa and America. The problem is that in search for wholeness all too many Negroes seek to embrace only one side of their natures. Some seeking to reject their heritage, are ashamed of their colour, ashamed of black art and music, and determine what is beautiful and good by the standards of white society.

In Liberia, the Americo-Liberians chose one culture – one that was against the indigenous Liberians. In doing so, they were to be black settlers who colonised other black people. In a true Fanonian sense, these blacks hated themselves. In oppressing other blacks in Liberia, they were in fact oppressing themselves, colonising themselves. The Americo-Liberians instilled new cultures and new dominant epistemologies in Liberia.

Indigenous Ethiopian Education

The traditional Ethiopian education was steeped into wisdom and the church was responsible for formal education. The Ethiopian Orthodox Church was leading, and schools under churches prepared children for religious positions in society. Education started through the learning of the alphabet. The second stage comprised the rote learning of the first chapter of the Epistle of John whose main themes are love and a relationship with God. It also teaches about the evil world and the children of God who are righteous and free from the world's tribulations. Writing was also introduced at this stage. The third stage was about the Acts of the Apostles and prayers were learnt as well as arithmetic. The fourth stage began with the study of the Psalms of David and this was the crux of the learners' education. Those who reached this level of education would be able to write and could be letter writers or would be able to study Praise to God and the Virgin Mary, the Song of Solomon and the Songs of Prophets (Pankhurst, 1968). Ethiopia is the only African country that has practiced Christianity for more than a millennium.

Since the fourth century, Christianity played a huge role in traditional education. The Aksumite Kingdom introduced Christianity and later introduced monasteries and churches, which became pivotal in planning Ethiopian education. In addition to the discussion above about school curricula, Dagne (1970) states that the church system after the 17th century had the following divisions:

1. Nebab Bet (Reading School);
2. Qedasse Bet (Liturgy school); and

3. higher schools, namely
    (i) Zema Bet (Music school);
    (ii) Quene Bet (Poetry school); and
    (iii) Metsehaf Bet which again have different sub-divisions. (Literature school).

It is interesting to note that, in Ethiopia, the church was the main guardian of traditional culture and for centuries, all schools were under churches as pointed out above. Again, Ndlovu-Gatsheni (2018:165) summarises some aspects of Ethiopian education when he posits:

> At the centre of Ethiopian indigenous knowledge is the importance of wisdom. To the Ethiopians knowledge is wisdom not power. Therefore, they consistently and systematically sought wisdom wherever it existed. *Kebre Nagast* is one of the most revered indigenous Ethiopian books, which contains all the tenets of Ethiopian philosophy and life including that nation's myth of foundation as a chosen place by God. It occupied the same status that Plato's Republic enjoyed in Western tradition of political thought (Woldeyes, 2017:23).
>
> The *Kebra Nagast* (Glory of Kings) was written from 1314 to 1322 and relates to the birth of Menelik, the son of King Solomon and the Queen of Sheba, Makuda. This book became vital as the source of literature and culture of Ethiopia. It is also in the Kebra Nagast that the discussion of how the Ethiopians changed from worshiping the Sun, Moon and Stars to the God of Israel (Ullendorff, 1968).

Woldeyes (2017) explains that the total years of study under the indigenous education system in Ethiopia spanned over 30 years. Woldeyes (2017) concurs with Dagne (1970) above although his explication of the curriculum is more elaborate, and it includes timelines as well. Additionally, Woldeyes (2017:59) illuminates the Ethiopian indigenous schooling system originating from the *Kebra Nagast* as follows:

Table 10.1 The Kebra Nagast (Woldeyes, 2017:59)

Form of Schooling	Duration of Study
Nibab Bet (Reading School)	2 years
Zema Bet (Music School)	4 years
Kidassie (Holy Mass)	6 months
Zema Bet *zimare and mewasit zema*	1 year
Zema Bet akwakwam	3 years
Quene Bet (Poetry school)	5 years
Liqawunit (Interpretation of scholarly books)	3 years

Merha Ewur (Computation)	6 months
Yetarik Tinat (Study of history)	1 year
Yategibare'ed Timhirt (Art and handcraft)	4 years
Masmesker (Certification)	2 years
Total Years of Study	**30 years**

All this demonstrated rigorous scholarship from indigenous knowledges. This indigenous knowledge was soon to be destroyed by the ruling elite who sought to mimic the West hence they abandoned even Ethiopia's indigenous languages in preference of English in schools. This chapter examines the struggle to decolonise Ethiopia's education as some critics argue for the decentring of Western education.

Marginalisation of Indigenous Knowledge Systems in Ethiopia

The Organisation for Social Science Research in Eastern and Southern Africa (OSSREA) (2002) states that there is no question about Ethiopia having had an indigenous philosophy. The report points out, "If in one African country, Ethiopia, there are written historical documents where the words 'philosophy' and 'philosopher' appear many times why question the existence of philosophy and philosophers in the continent?"

Many have considered Ethiopia as a country that symbolises black people's freedom and is an example of how the nation warded off European colonisation. However, the Ethiopian education system does not reflect the country's authentic history and civilisation. The country had, over decades, adopted Western practices and infused these into the traditional education thus dominating indigenous epistemologies. The latter led to the mental colonisation that created Africans who believe in the supremacy of Western-oriented education.

Ferede and Haile (2015) concur as they argue that Ethiopia imported Western education that marginalised its traditional education system. There was a failure to combine the traditional education system with the missionaries' Western education. As a result, Ethiopia's traditional education system was "de-Ethiopianised or de-Africanised and that triggers many social evils as it has been witnessed since the 1960s" (Ferede & Haile, 2015:39). These authors also point out that the 'modern' curriculum alienated Ethiopian elite from their original system of education. "Thus, such educational system was calculated means that served for the colonisation of non-colonised state and citizens" (Ferede & Haile, 2015:39). The Western-oriented education system left the Ethiopian learners with no knowledge of their history an aspect Walter Rodney (1973) and Molefi Asante (1995) express so eloquently as they write about the effects of Western education on African learners. Ethiopia modernised its traditional system of education; the traditional system of education was dismissed abruptly as the new colonial education was embraced. "The path traversed by Ethiopia was not to modernise the traditional system rather it was to erase past practices so as to implement new system" (Ferede & Haile, 2015:41). Many have argued though that the traditional system was rigid and was incongruent with modernisation (Kebede, 2006). In the traditional system, one could not question anything likened to the earth and God. The adoption of modern education meant adopting a flexible secular system, albeit a colonised system.

Pankhurst (1972) writes about the educationally destructive nature of Italian invasion in the 1940s in Italian East Africa. He points out that this region became 'educationally bankrupt' with no trained teachers, no school textbooks and only a few suitable schools. Italian education was merely to glorify Mussolini and brainwash the Ethiopian learners. The Ethiopian learners were also taught to be loyal to the Italian royal family and the Duce, Mussolini. Therefore, according to Richard Pankhurst (1972), Ethiopia, under the brief Italian Fascist education, became decrepit. The fall of Ethiopian traditional education largely came because of Emperor Menelik's desire to modernise Ethiopian education. Various missionaries had entered Ethiopia and the Emperor had sent several young Ethiopians to study in Europe. Because of this, new Western schools were established in Ethiopia in the early 1900s under Menelik. The Italians' intentions were clear in their desire to colonise Ethiopia and alienating the Ethiopian learner from his/her history and culture. Pankhurst (1972:364) cites Festa who addressed the Second Italian Congress in Florence in April 1934:

> Schools for Ethiopians aimed at "forming the new generation" and had well defined aims. The 'native child', he declared, had to be 'acquainted' with a little of our civilization in order to become a 'conscious propagandist' for Italian culture. He had therefore to "know Italy, its glories, and ancient history, in order to become a conscious militia man in the shade of our flag".

It is remarkable to observe the similarity of colonial education's objectives all over Africa. The above quote by the Italian representative is reminiscent of George Grey, a British Colonialist in South Africa who was quoted saying to Parliament in 1855:

> If we leave the natives beyond our borders ignorant barbarians, they will remain a race of troublesome marauders. We should try to make them a part of ourselves, with a common faith and common interests, useful servants, consumers of our goods, contributors to our revenue. Therefore, I propose that we make unremitting efforts to raise the natives in Christianity and civilization by establishing among them missions connected with industrial schools.
>
> Rose & Tunmer, as quoted in Christie, 1988:37

Western, colonial education was not neutral and all over Africa, colonists wanted to dominate and domesticate the indigenous people. In several instances, as we see in the case of Ethiopia, the coloniser sought to indoctrinate the 'natives' as was the case in South Africa under the British. In Ethiopia, the education for 'natives' was to lead them in serving the coloniser, making them loyal to the Fascist flag. Although the Emperor Haile Selassie later reiterated the need to defend Ethiopian legacy, in practice nothing was done. The Emperor did nothing to integrate traditional Ethiopian education and Western education. Kebede (2006) cites Selassie's speech when he pointed out that Ethiopia has her own cultures and these are more than just history, they define their Ethiopianness: "We do not want our legacies and traditions to be lost. Our wish and desire is that education develop, enrich and modify them".

Yet, there was no attempt to integrate traditional Ethiopian education to the Western education. This major blow led to the domination of Western education over traditional education. The Italians, in the five years they were in Ethiopia, continued with what started earlier in 1908 when Emperor Menelik II was in power. Otherwise, before this, Ethiopian education focused on the Bible, Astronomy, and Philosophy. The embedded Indigenous Knowledge Systems in traditional education were not limited to the material aspects but included regular communication with the spiritual and non-spiritual, the material world of existence (Dei, 2014). In 1908, Ethiopia witnessed the first involvement of Western experts who developed the curriculum and fund for education. During the Menelik II period, the French language dominated in both curriculum design and management of the school. Later though, when Haile Selassie was at the helm, education shifted first to Great Britain and later to Americans. During 1974-1990 when the socialist government came to power, the system of education was shifted to the Eastern socialist block. The main objective of education during the socialist government was the dissemination of Marxism and Leninism's imported ideology.

The Language Dilemma in Ethiopian Education

For many language experts in Ethiopia, the language question is critical, similar to other countries like South Africa and Nigeria. The call for a decolonised system in South Africa also demands for a review of language policies that would ensure that indigenous languages in South Africa also need to be spoken. We know it has not been easy; many researchers point out that English and Afrikaans continue to dominate (Msila, 2019). Amharic is traditionally a lingua franca in Ethiopia although there are 90 various Ethiopian languages or dialects. Until 1994, primary schools taught learners in Amharic because the government was promoting indigenous languages. The learners whose mother tongue was not Amharic though, were at a disadvantage and the English language was introduced in later years in primary schools (K12 Academics, 2004). The English language brought with it clashes between indigenous cultures and Western cultures. The K12 Academics (2004) capture the dilemma brought by English language succinctly:

> Politically, some Ethiopians regard English medium instruction with English textbooks, as replacing Ethiopian culture with Western values and loss of identity. The failure of Ethiopia to modernize was because modernisation was based on modern values rather than renewal within the Ethiopian tradition. Educational systems foster national unity by inculcating social, cultural and political ideas and these need to become Ethiopian by replacing English instruction with instruction in Ethiopian languages.

The introduction of English has created several problems in Ethiopian education. English has been proven to have a negative effect in Ethiopian education from primary school to tertiary education. K12 Academics (2004) cite results of a study conducted in Gedeo and Sidama zones where Grade 5 learners' English was so poor that they were not able to learn in classrooms. Furthermore, the teachers' English was poor and there was a lack of English teaching materials (K12 Academics, 2004). Western education was an obstacle to learning because the Ethiopian system decided to marginalise indigenous languages of Ethiopia. English has such a colonising effect and dominance that some learners are not proficient in writing a short essay in Amharic (Terefe, 2017). Therefore, as English dominated, the indigenous languages lagged behind. Like elsewhere in Africa, the role of English (as is the role of French and Portuguese) is to undermine the indigenous local languages whilst upholding the European powers that speak these languages. Yet, in various countries, research has demonstrated how language affects the progress of learners. Foreign languages usually create problems for learners who might first struggle understanding the questions before attempting to write answers in workbooks. Language is the crux in decolonisation because the learners try to interpret the world in a language that's not their own. The re-introduction of indigenous languages in Ethiopia should be a critical point in demarginalising the marginalised languages or else education will barely make sense for hundreds of learners.

Negash (2006) comments about what she refers to as the "curse of English language" as a medium of instruction. She contends that English as a medium of instruction from Grade 7 upwards brought many challenges for learners and teachers and this was known as early as 1983. The standards and the quality of education fell because of the lack of proficiency in English. Negash also argues that the replacement of English by Ethiopian indigenous languages could enhance the survival potential of the Ethiopian political community. Negash (2006:33) adds a profound statement when she points out, "attending all classes in English is tantamount to the wholesale adaptation of the culture that the English language represents at the pride of one's native language and the values that such a language contains". African countries need to find ways of how to treat languages within the realm of social justice and fairness. In a country like South Africa, there are still challenges for indigenous languages, which are not used, as much as Afrikaans and English in schools. In Nigeria, there are concerns that English usage will lead to re-colonisation through the gradual extinction of languages like Yoruba (Fabunmi & Salawu, 2005). These writers also point out that language loss brings an emotional state hence language endangerment needs to be addressed well (Fabunmi & Salawu, 2005). English should not destroy the Ethiopian local languages. In fact, local languages should also not treat other languages with disdain for that would be inimical to decolonisation.

In Ethiopia, decolonisation also needs to address the concerns over Amharic language dominance over other indigenous languages. The Ethiopian Ministry of Education is usually blamed for adopting measures that restrict the use of teaching and learning in Oromo language. Research shows that education is posing challenges for learners who are not mother tongue speakers of Amharic language in many Ethiopian schools (Ikome, 2019). Ikome adds that using Amharic as the only language of learning and teaching prevents many learners who are mother tongue speakers of other indigenous languages. These learners do not develop psychologically, socially, and cognitively. A policy of including languages in a multilingual sense is necessary. The Ministry of Education needs to explore ways in which teachers from initial teacher education would have been prepared for multilingual classrooms that accommodate languages other than Amharic. For an ideal decolonisation there needs to be some justice in the use of indigenous languages for discontent will have negative impact on nationalism. Zahoric and Teshome (2009:99) state, "Language will always, have, besides its linguistic and social aspects, a remarkable political nature, especially in these countries characterised by a strong diversity".

Historicides and Culturecides: The Killing of a Rich Culture

Linked to the damage caused by linguicides (killing of peoples' indigenous languages) as cited by the editor' preface of this book (Ndlovu-Gatsheni, 2018), are historicides and culturecides. Historicides refer to the killing of the history of the people and culturecides refer to the killing of the cultures of the people. In addition, of course these are accompanied by epistemicides, which are linked to the killing of knowledges. The linguicides led by the English language lead to all the others because language expresses a culture and some forms of knowledge. Therefore, not using Amharic or any other local language has a negative impact on the education of the Ethiopian children. Terefe (2017) points out how vast portions of Ethiopian history was neglected in her school, thus ending up knowing more about Western countries than her own. This is so unfortunate considering the fecund history of Ethiopia. The learners could learn so much from the various epochs including their nation's association with the magnanimous King Solomon from the Biblical story. The Black Consciousness leader in South Africa, Steve Biko (1987) and Walter Rodney (1973) from Guyana, also wrote about the challenges of schools in avoiding historicides. Both writers highlighted the disaster caused by historicides where learners ended up knowing more about the West rather than their own countries. When learners are thus restricted, by curriculum, they will not experience epistemic freedom and education will only alienate them. Decolonisation is about inclusion and should be able to engage learners in a dialogue that would lead to critical learning as discussed in chapters 1 and 3. Without a dialogue in class, there can be no critical learning and linguicides, historicides, and culturecides can be obstacles to meaningful learning. Schools should not alienate, but colonial education will always alienate the learners as demonstrated in chapter 1 on how apartheid and colonial education in South Africa alienated the learners because they were learning about irrelevant education based on social injustices.

Woldeyes (2017) argues that Ethiopian education is presently far from the mark because it has shifted away from its rich culture and history. This writer points out that, before the advent of Western education, it was an endless journey and not a means to an end. However, the Western approaches changed education's objectives as the country sought to mimic the Western values. Furthermore, Woldeyes (2017) underscores the Ethiopian frame of reference even if the learners are learning a variety of knowledges. Focusing education on local priorities is vital in the introduction of enriching education process. Terefe (2017) points out that Woldeyes' study "shows that decolonising education across Africa will require an investigation of how indigenous epistemologies were violently discarded. It will also entail a critical study of the modes of scholarship previously sidelined as 'traditional'".

Bishaw and Lasser (2012) contends that the irony of creating a great nation among other nations ended up leading to epistemicides. The Emperor Menelik II sought to build Ethiopia as a 'modern state'. The Emperor saw the shortcomings of traditional schools in facing the demands of the international, political atmosphere. The Emperor also did not want to see his country an isolated nation, as he imported teachers after opening a school in Addis Ababa in 1908. The Ethiopian Church was however opposed to foreign teachers. Languages were promoted as the main objectives of education, therefore, French, Italian, Geez, Arabic, and Amharic were highly emphasised between 1908 and 1935 (Bishaw & Lasser, 2012). When the foreign languages were introduced in Ethiopian education, they presented several challenges, the French language for example is a case in point: "The application of French methods to Ethiopian students presented some challenges. For instance, the assessment methods used during this period were alien to the Ethiopians. The monarchy had depended on a non-native-Ethiopian curriculum which did not consider local peculiarities" (Bishaw & Lasser, 2012:55).

Foreign languages in traditional African education have always brought problems as seen above with the challenges brought by English language in Ethiopia. Generally, the foreign languages brought cognitive dissonance amongst Ethiopian learners. During the time of British domination, a foreign teacher observed that there was nothing Ethiopian about the curriculum and education was not responding to societal challenges (Bishaw & Lasser, 2012). In 1962, a study was conducted in Ethiopia to assess schooling and education. Several problems identified are linked to the killing of the rich Ethiopian culture. This means that education continued to marginalise the indigenous knowledges of Ethiopia. Five problems identified from the study were:

1. The Ethiopian Education system lacked a philosophy and its aims and objectives were not properly articulated.
2. Curriculum materials, teaching methodologies, and approaches were based on foreign countries, and instructional materials had to be adapted for Ethiopians.

3. Ethiopian needs, with respect to culture and language, were not well treated by the education system.
4. The social needs of Ethiopian students were not clearly reflected in the curriculum, and the goals of education system had been equally hazy.
5. The inequalities in education opportunities in the past had to be evaluated.

Bishaw & Lasser, 2012:60

The Future of Ethiopian Education

Melese, Tadege & Agosto (2019) claim that Ethiopian education system was influenced by the French, Italian, British, American, and socialist countries. Furthermore, this French-oriented system sought the learners to master different languages hence critics were against labelling these schools as simply language schools and nothing more.

Currently, Ethiopia has put in place plans to transform their education system to address some of the gaps they find, including the decolonisation of education. Melese et al. (2019) point out that the government has now developed a new education and training policy with new major and specific objectives. These authors state that the important qualities of the policy include the reorganisation of the curriculum and the introduction of indigenous languages as medium of instruction. Some aspects the decolonisation in Ethiopia has to oppose or resist are those pertaining to gender; education for the future has to depatriarchise as it opens doors for women. Girls as young as 14 are usually pressured to marry and start bearing children.

Gender-based violence is also a hindrance to girls' success. Patriarchy may thwart the initiatives to lift women's education in Ethiopia. It is useful to focus on the educational reform programme popularly known as Ethiopian Education Development Roadmap. This roadmap is comprehensive and can have huge implications for decolonising Ethiopian education. The Ministry of Education in 2018 declared that various aspects of the roadmap would be implemented over a period of five years (Dibaba, 2019). Dibaba also argues that Ethiopia needs to "come up with a stable home-grown and country-oriented education system". Various foreign countries were behind the system of education in the past; the French, the British, and the Americans – the Derge combined these and ended up with the Russian model (Dibaba, 2019). What is so crucial for a decolonised system is the envisaged involvement of the youth and parents in education. The roadmap magnifies the role of parents in Ethiopian education. Furthermore, the focus on the needs of the country and interests of the youth has far-reaching implications for decolonisation. Dibaba (2019) adds:

> This unstable transition from dependence of the education system of the country from one country to the other has prevented the country from developing its own education system. That is why the education system in Ethiopia has always been plagued with untold distortions and irrelevance. The roadmap stresses on the importance of focusing on the needs of the country and interests of students in career development.

The roadmap document examines the thorny issue of language and it draws recommendations for the future because as we have discussed above, language has implications on culture. The Ministry of Education's document states that trilingual education is critical for inter-regional mobility and unity, and promotion of local languages for communication, education and research (Ministry of Education, 2019:98). The recognition of local languages is critical for decolonisation and relevance. The Ministry of Education (2019) roadmap document goes on to stress that primary and secondary education would be taught in local/national language and English given much focus as lower primary education for internationalisation. The envisaged new system of education in Ethiopia is referred to as 6-2-4 education system. This means learners will be in primary school for six years, in junior school for two years then high school for four years. In the past before 2019, the system was 8-2-2 meaning learners spent eight years in primary school, then two years of general secondary school and two years preparatory for higher education.

All reforms in education usually have good intentions of improving the future of a country. One hopes that the UNICEF Education Strategy 2019-2030 will address the improvement of Ethiopian education. More children are in Ethiopian schools in 2019 more than ever before, but arguments are that duty-bearers who are supposed to lead the rights of learners to get effective education "are effectively failing to improve learning, and this failure is deep and broad, and has significant consequences. Many learners lack the knowledge and skills to realise their full potential and maximise their contribution to their communities" (UNICEF, 2019:4). The above is critical to shape the future of Ethiopian education.

It is conspicuous how the traditional education was transformed by self-colonisation, hence reforms in Ethiopia cannot avoid addressing the decolonisation of education. The language issue for example is a huge colonial question where foreign language dominate local languages and, in the process, alter the thinking of the learners in schools because of the values that accompany any language. There even comprehensive education reforms would not be effective if they are based on culturecides and linguicides. Furthermore, education should be biased towards social justice and democratic principles. In addressing culture, language, history, and epistemology, there should always be the thinking of using social justice and democratic principles as pillars. Ethiopian education would lose if it completely escapes from the traditional education that comprised certain epistemologies and values. Decolonisation in this instance would mean inclusion of the traditional education into the 'modern' education, which is sympathetic to Western education.

Concluding Comments

Demarginalisation of the marginalised knowledges in Ethiopia calls for intense involvement of all Ethiopians. Woldeyes whose book, *Native Colonialism: Education and the Economy of Violence Against Traditions in Ethiopia*, explicates the 'self-colonisation' that Ethiopia embraced as he discusses the challenges and opportunities in Ethiopian education.

Additionally, Woldeyes (2017) recommends that the decolonisation processes should be the community-wide project that would involve the ordinary Ethiopians. Therefore, elders, traditional leaders, and various other role players need to take part in a huge way in transforming education. Like Bulti in chapter 7, Woldeyes argued for decolonisation to combine the local with Western knowledges. However, like elsewhere in Africa, if Ethiopia is to demarginalise the marginalised, it needs to magnify the history, culture, and languages of the country. Decolonisation should focus on the philosophies and centuries' ways of life of the Ethiopians. There is no reason why Ethiopians cannot use traditional practices and their beliefs as a basis for their education.

A decolonised system of education would bestow epistemic freedom to Ethiopians and empower learners who will value their history and their culture. Woldeyes (2017) perceived education not as a means to an end, but part of an endless journey of knowledge seeking. Finally, it is crucial to contend as Msila in the Preface and Bulti in chapter 7, that to decolonise Ethiopia we neither need to follow Eurocentric models nor Afrocentric models, but what we need is an anthropocentric model that would "soar over all continents" (OSSREA, 2002).

References

Asante, M. 1995. The Afrocentric Idea in Education. In: F.L. Hord & J.S. Lee (eds.), *I Am Because We Are: Readings in Black Philosophy*. Amherst: University of Massachusetts.

Bishaw, A. & Lasser, J. 2012. Education in Ethiopia: past Present and Future Prospects. *Arican Nebula*, 5:53-68.

Christie, P. 1988. *The Right to Learn: The Struggle for Education in South Africa*. Braamfontein: Sached/Ravan.

Dagne, H.G. 1970. The Ethiopian Orthodox Church School System. In: S.H. Selassie & T. Tamerat (eds.), *The Church of Ethiopia: A Panorama of History and Spiritual Life*. Addis Ababa: EOTC.

Dei, G.J.S. 2014. Indigenizing the school curriculum the case of the African university. In: G. Emeagwali & G.J.S. Dei (eds.), *African Indigenous Knowledge and the Disciplines*. Rotterdam: Sense Publishers. https://doi.org/10.1007/978-94-6209-770-4_13

Dibaba, S. 2019. Ethiopia's Education Road Map for a Better Future. *The Ethiopia Herald*, 31 August. [Online]. Available: https://bit.ly/30FpABr

Etkind, A. 2013. Colonising Oneself. *Eurozine*, 25 June. [Online]. Available: https://bit.ly/30KlI22

Fabunmi, F.A. & Salawu, A.S. 2005. Is Yoruba an Endangered Language? *Nordic Journal of African Studies*, 14(3):391-408.

Ferede, W. & Haile, G. 2015. Re-africanizing the Educational System of Ethiopia. *African Journal of History and Culture*, 7(2):38-43. https://doi.org/10.5897/AJHC2014.0203

Ikome, L.B. 2019. Using Afan Oromoo as Primary Language of Learning and Teaching in Selected Schools in Addis Ababa: Policy, Problems and Strategies. Unpublished Doctoral Thesis. Pretoria: University of Pretoria.

K12 Academics. 2004. *Language Issues*. [Online]. Available: https://bit.ly/3d1I0if

Kebede, M. 2006. The Roots and Fallouts of Haile Selassie's Educational Policy. UNESCO Forum Occasional Paper Series. Paper no. 10.

Killbride, D. 2014. What did Africa Mean to Frederick Douglass? *Slavery & Abolition: A Journal of Slave and Post-Slave Studies*, 36(1):40-62. https://doi.org/10.1080/0144039X.2014.916516

King Jr, M.L. 1995. Black Power. In: F.L. Hord & J.S. Lee (eds.), *I Am Because We Are*. Amherst: University of Massachussets.

Kiossev, A. 1998. *The Self-Colonisation Cultures*. Bulgariaavangarda: Salon Verlag.

Melese, S., Tadege, A. & Agosto, V. 2019. The Ethiopian Curriculum Development and Implementation Vis-à-vis Schwab's Signs of Crisis in the Field of Curriculum. *Cogent Education*, 6(1):1-16. https://doi.org/10.1080/2331186X.2019.1633147

Ministry of Education. 2018. *Ethiopian Education Development Roadmap (2018-30): An Integrated Executive Summary*. Addis Ababa: The Author.

Msila, V. 2019. Rethinking Babylon: The Language Dilemma and the Search for Social Justice in Africa. *English Academy Review*, 36(1):100-112. https://doi.org/10.1080/10131752.2019.1587829

Nayyar, N.A. 2016. The Mind as Colony. *Literati*. December 4. [Online]. Available: https://bit.ly/2zxEVc2

Ndlovu-Gatsheni, S.J. 2018. *Epistemic Freedom in Africa: Deprovincialization and Decolonization*. London: Routledge. https://doi.org/10.4324/9780429492204

Negash, T. 2006. *Education in Ethiopia: From Crisis to the Brink of Collapse*. Discussion Paper 33. Uppsala: Nordiska Afrikainstitutet.

Pankhurst, R.K.P. 1968. *Economy of Ethiopia*. Addis Ababa: Haile Selassie University.

Pankhurst, R. 1972. Education in Ethiopia During the Italian Fascist Occupation (1936-1941). *The International Journal of African Historical Studies*, V(3):361-397. https://doi.org/10.2307/217091

Organization for Social Science Research in Eastern and Southern Africa (OSSREA). 2002. *Indigenous Knowledge Systems in Ethiopia. Report of Ethiopia National Workshop*. [Online]. Available: https://bit.ly/3d73qdQ

Rodney, W. 1973. *How Europe Underdeveloped Africa*. London: Bogle-L'Ouverture Publications.

Snapp, S. 2019. *Did African Americans Enslave Liberian Africans?* [Online]. Available: https://bit.ly/3efoFLK

Spicer, C. 2015. The Perpetual Paradox: A Look into Liberian Colonisation. *The Corvette*, 3(2):36-52.

Terefe, M.T. 2017. Ethiopia was Colonised. *African Arguments*, 21 June.

Ullendorff, E. 1968. *Ethiopia and the Bible*. Oxford: University Press for the British Academy.

UNICEF. 2019. *Every Child Learns: UNICEF Education Strategy 2019-2030*. New York: The Author.

Woldeyes, Y.G. 2017. *Native Colonialism: Education and the Economy of Violence Against Tradition in Ethiopia*. Trenton: Red Sea Press.

Zahoric, J. & Teshome, W. 2009. Debating language Policy in Ethiopia. *Asian and African Studies*, 8(1):80-102.

Chapter Eleven

Lost in Translation? Revisiting Language Decolonisation Project in Nigerian Education

Oluwaseun O Afolabi

Introduction

Education is an important instrument in the development of a society. It is a means of transmitting knowledge, experience, and instruction from one generation to another. Education is also is one of the yardsticks of measuring the growth and development of a country. It is one of the ways of understanding the world. Most of the time, acquiring and imparting knowledge through one's indigenous/native language helps retention. Evidence shows that students comprehend better when they are taught through their mother tongue or indigenous language. However, in a situation where the indigenous language is jettisoned for colonial language as a medium of instruction, it creates an endemic colossal loss of the richness that is embedded in the indigenous language. Thus, such a society will witness a situation whereby students cannot boast, speak, or write in their indigenous languages. Hence, the knowledge, experience, and instruction that is supposed to be transmitted from one generation to another gets lost in transit. This is the situation of the Nigerian education system. The government and stakeholders in education pay more attention to the colonial language education system than the indigenisation of Nigerian indigenous languages in education.

The National Policy on Education (2014) states that the government will ensure the medium of instruction is principally the mother tongue or language of the immediate community to teach students from early childhood to the first three years in primary education. However, this is just a policy on paper that is not enforced by either the government or those in the education sector. Thus, this chapter seeks to examine the loss in translation of indigenous language for the colonial language in the Nigerian education system. Why lost? Can African (or Nigerian) language(s) be used as a medium of instruction? Can the English language be decolonised? The chapter will also examine the prospect of indigenous languages in Nigeria.

Pre-colonial Education Language

The pre-colonial education language deals with the era when indigenous language was used as a medium of instruction for students in informal educational settings. It should be noted that many scholars (Majasan, 1967; Occiti, 1973; Fafunwa, 1974; Tiberondwa, 1978; Taiwo, 1980; Ozigi & Ocho, 1981; Omolewa, 1981; Datta, 1984) have written on the pre-colonial era of African education, which was based on the functionality of the society and the preservation of Africanness (i.e. African culture, language, and identity).

During this period, each ethnolinguistic group used its language for children's education, which was culturally contextualised. Hence, the content of traditional educational systems emanated from the physical, social, and spiritual situations of pre-colonial African society. The physical environment influenced the content of the curriculum in that what was taught in the local language was meant to assist the child to adjust and adapt to the environment in order to exploit and derive benefit from it. Castle (1966) argues that whether the child's habitat was dominated by mountain, plain, river, or tropical forest, he had to learn to combat its dangers and use its fertility. To come to terms with the physical environment, the growing child learned about landscape, the weather, and about both plant and animal life. Thus, the intention of education in the traditional African society was to set afoot a student with functional skills that would help the student in contributing his/her quota to the overall development of the community.

Okoro (2011) argues that African traditional education emphasises social responsibility, job orientation, political participation, spiritual, and moral values. Traditional education is a lifelong education and functionalism was the main guiding principle. Functionalism refers to practical-oriented, felt-need education that is aimed at identifying and providing solutions for societal needs, as well as the empowerment of the educated. African societies regarded education as a means to an end and not as an end. Fafunwa (1991) states that children and youth learned by participatory education through demonstration, recitation, ritual ceremony, and imitation. In traditional African education, the method of teaching emphasised learning by doing. For instance, the subjects are wrestling, dancing, drumming, racing, local history, proverbs, riddles, and storytelling. The traditional system of education was integrated in such a way that unemployment was minimal. Wagner (1999) states that the indigenous education in Kenya, Nigeria, and other African countries brought about skill acquisition and apprenticeship training system began as a part of the wider education process in which the African indigenous societies passed on their cultural heritage from one generation to the next. The skill owned by a family was highly valued and in some professions such as native medicine, secrets were jealously guarded as they are indeed today. Learning a craft often began with personal service to the master. Young boys would become house servants to a closer relative who would feed and clothe them and after some years of promising usefulness, they would then gradually be introduced to the craft of the guardian. Given the above, education being of great importance to all nations of the world is not an invention brought to Africa from Europe as claimed by the Europeans (Omolewa, 2001; Osokoya, 2003).

Invariably, the traditional language education system in Nigeria aims at equipping individuals with necessary skills; attitudes and linguistic abilities that would help them function effectively in the society. The linguistic ability helps in providing functional training and experience in artistry, farming, fishing, and other vocational skills, which are needed for the survival of the society. Every responsible member of the community serves as a transmitter-teacher and trainer of the societal norms and skills to the younger generations. They are looked upon as models of good virtues to be emulated by the young ones. The system has demarcated learning experience for each age grade which culminates in the acquisition of desired values and attitudes, and the specialisation of individuals in some specific vocations. Thus, the pre-colonial language education in most parts of Nigeria trained individuals to fit usefully by learning and producing economic skills for self-sustenance, adapting to the role expectations and contributing to the development of the society.

Therefore, the forms of knowledge acquired during this period made Africans to be unique as a continent. Education was transmitted using African languages to preserve the originality of the knowledge of different types of occupations that existed during the pre-colonial era. Thus, African traditional education was culturally, religiously, socially, and occupationally based on the needed skills that kept the society active. Hence, the education offered is African-oriented. Also, in the absence of recognisable institutions like schools, acquisition of knowledge was taught in an informal setting in which home, community, and the society formed the theatre of learning. The school was the society and the individual was taught through the oral tradition of the norms of the society.

Conclusively, the pre-colonial period of the education system in Nigeria produced intellectual life and activity in the society. It is important to note that intellectual life/activity does not depend on literacy. Intellectual life or intellectual activity in any society is a function of the intellect, i.e. "the power of the mind to grasp ideas and relations and to exercise dispassionate reason and rational judgment" (Falola, 2017:192). Thus, has Edward Shils (1968) and Falola (2017) rightly said that this can be present in any human society, be it literate or illiterate, and that every society has its intellectuals. Primitive societies also have their intellectuals or at least their proto intellectuals. Intellectuals, based on this context, are the aggregate of the persons in the society who employ in their communication and expression with relatively higher frequency than most other members of their society symbols of general scope and abstract references concerning man, society, nature, and the cosmos. Hence, indigenous language creates an atmosphere of intellectualism and distinction, which edifies the society.

Postcolonial Education Language

Several scholars (Bowen, 1857; Burns, 1929; Graham, 1966; Taiwo, 1980; Datta, 1984; Ajayi, 1984; Freeman, 1968; Kupferman, 2013) have examined the advent of Western education in Nigeria. This period ushered in the use of English language as a medium of instruction, by displacing indigenous language. However, this study examines the place of indigenous language during the postcolonial period. It should be noted that in the early phase of colonial administration, some missionaries in Africa believed that they were bringing education to entirely uneducated peoples, a supposition which would have been valid if education were equated with literacy and formal schooling. Detailed accounts of African peoples by anthropologists leave one in no doubt that African societies did possess a kind of customary education, a system that worked reasonably well, given the limits imposed by society within which it had to operate.

The day-school curriculum of Western education in Nigeria includes reading, writing, arithmetic, and singing. The schools were maintained with grants from the missions, donations from groups and individuals outside the country, contributions by local Christians and children's parents, and with the fees of the children. The annual, fixed, unconditional grants made to the missions by the government since

1877 till the period of inauguration of the Phelps-Stokes Commission, were used to promote mushroom multiplication of small schools. However, the Africans were critical of the denationalising tendencies of the education introduced by the missionary. Because of this, a bill was proposed for the promotion and assistance of education in the Gold Coast Colony. The bill was passed into an Ordinance for the Promotion and Assistance of Education in the Gold Coast Colony on 6 May 1882 (Hussy, 1930). The subject taught in all these schools include scripture, English composition, English grammar, arithmetic, geography, music, singing, reading, writing, dictation, catechism, ciphering, dictation, algebra, geometry, Latin, Greek, English history, Roman history, Greek history, book-keeping, physiology, geography, Bible history, Yoruba reading, and Yoruba composition. Sewing and needlework were taught to girls. The medium of instruction in the infant classes was Yoruba and in the elementary schools English.

From the aforementioned analysis, it is glaring that the Education Ordinance and the curriculum were Western-oriented without considering the language background of the children. The subjects taught functioned as a kind of indoctrination on the African children, which serve as a form of physiological, and mental exploitation for, indirectly, their advantage – propagating Western culture and civilisation to the detriment of Nigerian indigenous languages. Besides, there was no provision for the teaching of local languages despite the spadework already done by the missionaries and the fact that English, the main subject and the medium of instruction, was foreign to the student. Also, the 1882 Ordinance was enacted at a time when African nationalism was being awakened and whipped up. The process of English education had been going on for 40 years in the Lagos Colony and produced Nigerians who had assimilated European ways of life. Many of these Nigerians had become disillusioned with the attitude of Europeans toward them and Europeanised Africans generally. They realised that, no matter how well fluent they were, there was racial discrimination against them in social relationships and even in the Church. Africans were looked down upon as inferior and African institutions were down-rated and condemned.

Briefly, Sanda (1972) asserts that Western education was not designed to be particularly functional for Africans; it was in its inception designed both as an instrument of alienation and as a vehicle for exploiting the governed, as well as for the realisation of the coloniser's cultural imperialism. The nature of restructuring of African societies, which followed the advent of Europeans, was derived from the objectives of three main categories – missionaries, merchant traders and administrator – either of colonisers that came to different parts of Africa together or in succession. The missionaries were openly committed to the spread of the gospel and hence their immediate needs were for interpreters and indigenous lay preachers who could read, write, and teach the words from the Bible. The merchant traders were mainly concerned with exploiting the natural resources of the continent, but they needed intermediaries, as well as clerks and elementary teachers who would keep records, make simple additions and subtractions, and re-interpret commercial policies in ways that would placate the dynamics of the African population. And the administrators were mainly concerned with keeping the flag of the home country flying in the African colonies as well as in 'civilising' the supposedly uncivilised 'natives' even though the economic and military-strategic potentials of the different colonies were also sufficient incentives. All three categories of colonisers were not in any way or at any time working in isolation from one another; in fact, each represented a part of the whole process of colonisation.

Hence, colonial education in Nigeria, operated jointly by the church and the state, was meager, both in terms of quantitative and qualitative standards. Colonial education was characterised by a pronounced European bias. This was reflected in the provision for the medium of instruction and the curricula. Teaching was generally conducted in the language of the colonial power. Thus, students were prevented from expressing themselves in their mother tongues within school premises (Datta, 1984). Furthermore, the colonial language policy was not aimed at developing an indigenous language system that would be linguistically and economically responsive to the needs of the Nigerian population. Rather, colonial schools were created to serve European economic and political interests. The use of European languages and European-based curricula were necessary conditions for this endeavour (Alidou, 2004).

Despite the above assertion, the practice of Western education has not been without challenges. Nearly two centuries of the practice of Western education has been greeted by sporadic calls for educational reforms in Nigeria; it has been found, that while Western education has served to globalise Africa, its processes and contents suffer from partial incongruity with African realities when thoughtlessly operationalised within the Nigerian environment. The pragmatic needs of the colonisers, therefore, dictated the spread of literacy and general education, an emphasis on de-traditionalisation or de-Africanisation of the African. That is why Sanda (1972:77) argues:

> [...] indirect rule of the British [...] exhibited [...] elitist orientation in their colonial education policies [...] The monetary incentive (wages) which is the strongest base of this new educated class created a basis for subsequent

> social divisions of African societies not only into the literate and the illiterates or the educated class and the uneducated class but also into the wealthy, culturally distinct, spatially segregated, educationally distinguishable class and the poor, uneducated, 'primitive' tradition-oriented and socially alienated class of peasants.

Therefore, the spread of Western education in Nigeria not only involved the spread of religion, but also the transmission of foreign language and elitist orientation of colonised Nigerians. Besides, this also brought about the linguistic division in which the English language superimposed on Nigerian indigenous languages. Those who can speak and write in a colonial language get access to more opportunities than a typical Nigerian. However, as time goes by, the rate of unemployed westernised graduates increased in which those that cannot secure a job now become dependents on those that are literate in indigenous languages. This shows the gap between pre-colonial education language and Western education language systems. As mentioned earlier on, with pre-colonial education, language makes students fit into the society – culturally, linguistically, and professionally because the skills needed are taught in indigenous languages. This makes them independent and innovative, contributing meaningfully to society. In addition, it should be noted that the needs of the society could only be met when the problems are understood indigenously. Thus, a foreign language cannot either explain the indigenous problem or bring a solution. Nigerian education problems can only be solved through Nigerian indigenous languages. However, Western education language produces white-collar employees and income earners instead of building on the existing foundation laid by the African informal education language of producing employers of labour that are specialised linguistically in different professions. Hence, this shows the pitfalls in the Western education language system.

Challenges of Language Decolonisation in Nigerian Education

After independence, the choice of language for education and administration became problematic due to the multi-ethnic setting of the country. Since the English language has become the dominant means of communication in all spheres of the country, Nigerian elites found it difficult to replace colonial language with any of the three major ethnic languages (Yoruba, Hausa and Igbo). Moreover, because each ethnic group is fighting for supremacy, no ethnic group would succumb to another ethnic group in making use of its language as the official language.

Thus, the retention of colonial language as the official language of government becomes the most practical, linguistically and politically preferred choice, and by extension medium of instruction in education. Invariably, the challenge of language decolonisation in Nigeria started from the post-independence period.

Alidou (2004) examines some challenges faced by African countries over the retention of colonial languages. Some of the challenges that are peculiar to Nigeria will be considered. The first major challenge is the lack of corpus planning (including orthography). Nigerian indigenous languages lacked a long tradition of literacy right from the time they were spoken. The language(s) were only spoken; they were not codified early enough before the arrival of the colonial language. Thus, most Nigerian indigenous languages did not acquire orthography early enough before the postcolonial period and publications in indigenous languages were scarce during this period. Despite the fact, the government and policymakers on education stated in the National Policy on Education (2004) that "[…] will ensure develop the orthography of many more Nigerian indigenous languages, and produce textbooks in Nigerian indigenous languages", this has not be achieved to its optimum level. This brought a setback in the actualisation of formal and literate Nigerian indigenous languages or mother tongue environments that can be used as a language of convenience in place of colonial language in politics, economy, and education spheres. Thus, Nigerian indigenous languages suffer international deficits from being elevated to official status. In other words, this affects the Nigerian children in developing literacy skills and eager to learn or to be taught in Nigerian indigenous languages. Moreover, access to job opportunities, gaining admission into the universities and all forms of business opportunities is only possible through colonial language. However, Nigerian indigenous languages can fulfil this role through the proper implementation of the policy on the development of orthography of Nigerian indigenous languages and the production of textbooks in Nigerian indigenous languages.

The need for languages of wider communication that could allow Nigerians to engage with the international world is another challenge. Because Nigeria is a developing country, including its education sector, access to foreign education, scholarships, fellowships, grants, and aid are only possible with the acceptance and usage of colonial language. Nigerian students cannot compete with their fellow counterparts in the developed countries without fluency in the English language in reading, writing, speaking, and listening (even if such students cannot speak a complete sentence in their mother tongue). In addition, since the English language is one of the international languages in the comity of nations, the medium of teaching and learning can only be carried out through the colonial language. Hence, the impact and effect of globalisation on medium of instruction policies is evident in Nigeria whose national languages are not among the major languages. This posed a serious challenge in decolonising education language in Nigeria. However, Nigeria can overcome this challenge by first carrying out the process of Africanisation of Nigerian education language. When this is done, its development to be part of the global languages will be possible because teaching and learning will be carried out using Nigerian indigenous languages. Curriculum planning, textbooks, and all materials related to education will be based on the internationalisation of indigenised education. By so doing, the Western world would be forced to reckon with this form of education that is very African-based.

It is important to note that sub-Saharan African countries that have maintained colonial languages in education continue to be among the poorest, illiterate, and most poorly educated countries in the world (UNESCO, 2000). UNESCO's experts report extremely poor student performance all over Africa. Concerning student performance on tests taken in English in Nigeria, for example:

> In Nigeria when researchers administered cognitive tests of literacy, numeracy and life skills to fourth graders as part of the Monitoring Learning Achievement project, the results were described as generally poor. The mean percentage of scores was 32% in numeracy, 25% in literacy and 33% in life skills. In one test item, pupils were instructed to copy a five-line passage into a given space. Only 8% of them were able to do so accurately, and 40% were unable to copy a single word or punctuation mark.
>
> UNESCO, 2000:34

To address such problems, in 1990, UNESCO, the World Bank, and the European Community sponsored the World Conference on Education for all in Jomtien, Thailand. Most developed and developing countries were represented. All governments and development agency representatives at the meeting recognised that educational provision is qualitatively and quantitatively inadequate in sub-Saharan Africa. The conference highlighted the need in Africa to develop quality education that is socially equitable and culturally relevant. The promotion of African languages as media of instruction was announced as one of the best strategies for promoting effective learning in formal basic education. The 10-year action plan developed after Jomtien by the national ministries of education anticipated the expansion of the use of national languages in all elementary schools in these countries. Unfortunately, since 1990, little public debate has focused on popular reaction to the use of national languages for formal basic education. Since Jomtien, African governments have held only two major conferences on language policy in education and development (in Cape Town, South Africa, and Accra, Ghana). These gatherings were academic and political, re-emphasising the need to invest in the development and use of African languages. Unfortunately, at the national level, most policymakers are reluctant to implement a new medium of instruction policy. Therefore, bilingual schools in sub-Saharan Africa merely remain experimental projects (Alidou, 2004).

Another factor in the challenge of language decolonisation is the lack of specialisation in bilingual education in schools. This depicts to lack of infrastructural facilities. Nigerian Colleges of Education and tertiary institutions lack both teachers and students that can specialise in this area. And the needed instrument and materials are not available. There is the dearth of libraries and laboratories schools in achieving bilingualism. It should be noted that such an area needs to be considered by the policymakers in the education sector and the government. This is because such an area can bring synergy between the colonial and Nigerian indigenous languages. It can improve the status of indigenous languages in teaching and learning. This will aid students in Colleges of Education to be fluent in the English language and Nigerian indigenous languages. This will add up to the quality of education that graduates eventually possessed after their period in the tertiary institutions. By so doing, the Nigerian indigenous language system will achieve quality literacy both colonial and indigenous languages. Concisely, adequate financial resources and willingness on the path of the government to promote indigenous languages as a medium of instruction will render bilingual education realisable in Nigeria.

Privatisation of Nigerian education has hindered language decolonisation. Private schools, both at primary, secondary and tertiary school levels, outnumber public schools in Nigeria. Additionally, many of the private schools are faith-based establishments. These schools are fashioned toward propagating Westernisation, creating a colonised generation that is misinformed about Nigerian indigenous languages. Such an action has succeeded in producing a set of new class of students who are deeply separated from their communities. These students failed in acquiring mastery in colonial languages and yet lost fluency in Nigerian indigenous languages. Owing to this, the government needs to strengthen the National Education Policy by insisting that all private school institutions give paramount attention to Nigeria's indigenous languages. This will be in terms of speaking, writing, and teaching. Furthermore, all higher education institutions should establish a bilingual centre to underscore the critical nature of indigenous languages.

Alidou (2004) argues that there are three main sets of factors (economic, political and pedagogical) that trigger the problem of medium of instruction in African schools. Economic factors include the retention of textbook markets for Western publishing companies. Political factors include African elites' reluctance to implement a language policy that may reduce the gap between two unequal social classes – a tiny privileged minority of educated Africans who have access to political and economic power and the underclass of non-educated masses deprived of economic and political resources. Pedagogical factors include inadequate preparation of school personnel in bilingual education, ongoing corpus planning (the codification of African languages), and the need to develop qualified human resources in publishing educational materials in African languages. These three sets of factors devalued the essence in Nigerian indigenous languages and the inability to become a developed country. This is because no country can be fully developed using only a foreign language as a medium of instruction.

It should be noted that the medium of instruction is the most powerful means of maintaining and revitalising a language and a culture, additionally it is the most important form of intergenerational transmission (Fishman & Fishman, 2000). The political, social, and economic forces shape the choice of medium of instruction. The medium of instruction policy is an integral part of educational policy and pertains to educational efficacy. Thus, equipping Nigerian education with indigenous language as a medium of instruction, put the country abreast with the developed countries. This will not only make Nigerian indigenous languages to have value in the labour market but will assist in globalising Nigerian indigenous languages and the decolonisation project.

Conclusively, the challenge of language decolonisation is due to irresponsiveness to the call of the project by the stakeholders in education. This is because colonial language has perpetuated every aspect of the government. Besides, the government does not see the need and the possibility of getting off the grip of the colonisers owing to lack of political will and taking decisive steps towards developing Nigerian indigenous languages. The lack of political will comes from the fact that political elites do not see the advantages that are inherent in the development of indigenous language. In addition, they are not willing to go through the rigorous process (such as overhauling the curriculum, producing bilingual materials, codification and standardisation of Nigerian indigenous languages, funding, etc.); it takes a lot of time and such agenda cannot be achieved within the minimum of 4-year political tenure of a government. In fact, due to the tribalisation of the country, Nigerians might find it difficult to believe in any government that might want to take such a step. However, the challenge of language decolonisation is surmountable when there is a collective effort by the government and the masses to indigenise local languages in education for globalisation output. Such an output will bring global economic advantages and recognition.

Decolonising Nigerian indigenous Languages: Steps taken thus Far and Why They Have Failed

In 1970, an educational research project was carried in developing a curriculum where the mother tongue would be used to teach students in schools. The Ford Foundation funded the project. The project was called Ife Primary Education Research Project and lasted eight years (1970-1978). The aim of the project included training bilingual curriculum specialists, the production of relevant educational materials in Nigerian indigenous languages and English as a second language, and systematic initial and in-service training for all bilingual classroom teachers. The project, which was carried out by Fafunwa and his team, was successful. Unfortunately, the activities of the project were abruptly brought to an end when funding from the Ford Foundation terminated. The Nigerian government and educational agencies failed to carry on with the project with necessary funding that might have improved not only the quality of education and producing bilingual teachers, but also in decolonising and decentering the English language as a medium of teaching and learning in schools. The government forced Fafunwa and his team from the University of Ife (now Obafemi Awolowo University) to reduce their activities to teacher training and curriculum development for mother tongue education. With this singular action, the project was lost and since that time, neither the government nor the academia in the country ever revived a similar project (Fafunwa, Macauley & Sokoya, 1989).

From the above analysis, the chapter examines factors that have hindered decolonisation of Nigerian indigenous languages, which include:

Lack of commitment on the part of the policymakers: Less than 30% of Nigerian budget goes to education though Nigeria has invested heavily in Western education and language to the detriment of bilingual education that fit the system. Pennycook (2002:91) observes:

> The spread of western knowledge and values was of equal, if not greater, importance to securing goodwill toward the colonizers and producing a loyal working force. Consequently, formal education was made available

> by colonial governments through the indigenous languages (to a greater or lesser extent), either as an alternative or as a transitional medium of instruction. No matter whether the colonial language or the indigenous languages were used as the medium of instruction, the goal remained the same – to subjugate the colonized.

This assertion is in line with the fact that the government prefers that Nigerian indigenous languages should be subjugated under the Western epistemology. In addition, they see it as the only means to bring neutrality among diverse languages. This non-committal attitude is motivated by avoiding ethnic conflicts, the economic agenda of exploiting the market of postcolonial countries, and the socio-political agenda of protecting the interests of the elite. Thus, the government does not see any need to make policy concerning decolonisation projects because Nigerian policy itself is suppressed under Western policy.

Lack of continuity, parochialism, and inadequate resources for implementation: The 1970 educational research project was supposed to be a continuous exercise. After the first successful attempt, a similar project should have been carried out in other parts of the country by testing the validity and reliability of the instrument used. However, this was not the case. The project was stocked and the student that was experimented using Yoruba language later found it difficult to cope in the tertiary institution because the English language is the sole medium of instruction. Invariably, the project was futile. In addition, government and private establishments do not see the political and economic gains in funding such a project. This leads to inadequate resources for achieving bilingualism for the efficacy of indigenous languages in teaching and learning.

Lack of codification and standardisation of indigenous languages: Standardisation is not possible without codification of all Nigerian indigenous languages. It is only through standardisation and codification that Nigerian indigenous languages could be used in the domains of education, law, and government. However, the scarcity of teaching materials in indigenous languages and the lack of enabling environment for professionals, make standardisation and codification of Nigerian indigenous languages difficult to realise. Moreover, the age-long low status attached to indigenous languages as not modern and the prestige accorded to the English language gave rise to reluctance in speaking indigenous languages. These surmountable challenges have been the excuse of government and policymakers for their non-committal stand toward the introduction of mother tongue education.

Nonconformity and ineffectiveness of the National Policy on Education: National Policy on Education of Nigeria (2004), Section 1 and Section 4 state:

> Government appreciates the importance of language as a means of promoting social interaction and national cohesion, and preserving cultures. Thus every child shall learn the language of the immediate environment. Furthermore, in the interest of national unity, it is expedient that every child shall be required to learn one of the three Nigerian indigenous languages: Hausa, Igbo, and Yoruba [...] ensure that the medium of instruction is principally the mother-tongue or the language of the immediate community [...] The medium of instruction in primary school shall be the language of the environment for the first three years. During this period, English shall be taught as a subject.

However, these sections of the policy are not implemented. English language is used exclusively as the medium of instruction at pre-primary school and the first three years (Grade 1-3) in primary school, in either public or private schools. This renders not only the policy ineffective, but weakens the value of Nigerian indigenous languages as a key in the education sector and as a means of communication that students can boast about. The prestigious status of English is most evident by the way students and teachers take pride in it than their mother tongue or indigenous languages. It should be noted that the English language is one of the compulsory subjects that must be passed before a student can be promoted from one class to the next across different levels of education. It means that students can fail any of the three major Nigerian indigenous languages as a subject, but must pass the colonial language. It shows the higher status the government and policymakers give to colonial language to the detriment of Nigerian indigenous languages. Thus, we are not only faced with class-based inequality but also faced with language-based inequality.

Other reasons why the decolonising of Nigerian education project failed are the gradual decline of enthusiasm for African languages and cultures. In addition, this is encapsulated in the belief in the lack of political, economic, and global values of Nigerian indigenous languages. This belief is not only deep-seated in the minds of the English-speaking elite, but also among the policymakers, and even the native speakers due to the long-standing low status of Nigerian indigenous languages. Regardless of the well-crafted National Policy of Education, Nigeria's education sector has failed to enhance the values of indigenous language. It has also failed to produce learners with multilingual skills that could make them fit into the African society.

Prospect of African Language in Teaching and Learning

The prospect of African language in teaching and learning lies in dealing with the challenges of language decolonisation and addressing the reasons why previous projects have failed to achieve its set out objectives. In addition, writers, linguists, and local publishing companies should work hand-in-hand in codification, standardisation, full orthographies, grammars, and dictionaries of all the Nigerian indigenous languages. They should promote and produce all types of literary work and invest in the production of materials that will enhance indigenous languages. This will help the development of a literate culture of indigenous languages. Also, materials produced must be of high quality linguistically, culturally, and pedagogically. Literary works, books, and textbooks that will be produced should not be a mere translation of Western works which will eventually undermine African language and culture. In addition, writers and publishers should desist from describing African culture and language as archaism while tagging Western culture and language as modernism. African language is classic and evergreen; books written in African language should be viewed from an analytical pedagogical standpoint that is necessitated in challenging Western and African elite dominance. In addition, they should consider that African education seeks to develop global learners and workers who are globally competitive. This complexity should be reflected in the textbooks produced in national languages (Alidou, 2004).

Conclusion

The loss in the transition of local languages in Nigeria illustrates the endemic phenomenon and the supremacy of the English language. It shows the unwillingness on the path of government and the lack of unity amongst diverse ethnic groups due to the conflict that might ensue in the future if such a step is taken (i.e. conflict of language hegemony); the social status of the elite, and the Nigerian economy that is determined by the West. Thus, for the English language to be decolonised in teaching and learning lies on the concerted effort by the government, policymakers in the education sector, academia and all concerned citizens in actualising the project for the benefit, preservation, and globalisation of Nigerian indigenous languages.

It should be noted that globalisation and decolonisation are two different concepts. Edward Shizha (2005) argues that globalisation is consistent with colonisation or neo-colonisation in that it seeks to 'universalise' and 'internationalise' the

Western concept of knowledge and science, thus continuing the marginalisation of Indigenous Knowledge Systems. 'Global' technologies have condensed time and space to create a postmodernist consciousness that has accelerated Euro-American political, economic, social, and cultural processes at the expense of other cultures. Globalisation has tended to universalise, validate, and legitimate Western knowledge while trivialising Indigenous Knowledge Systems. Therefore, to achieve language decolonisation, Africans must first de-globalise every trait of Euro-American globalisation in the African education system and create African globalisation (or Africanisation), i.e. globalisation that evolves from the African continent (that includes indigenous economic, political, social, and cultural homogenisation), serving as African international worldview. It would be a kind of a benchmark that would be acceptable worldwide. This huge step will place the continent from a unique perspective from the rest of the world because Africa will be rebranding itself from its worldview, rather than the Euro-American worldview.

Recommendations

The study recommends the following:
1. Provision of universal education through the medium of Nigerian indigenous languages. This will ensure that these indigenous languages are not only being used in a formal setting but give prominent status in the education sector. It will also increase publications in indigenous languages.
2. The development of a literate environment and literate culture using Nigerian indigenous languages. This will elevate indigenous languages beyond local usage. It will be a medium of communication among both the illiterate and literate classes. It will also help people to freely identify with their language without being ashamed.
3. The government should be committed to policies that will give strong value to Nigerian indigenous languages and multilingualism and must ensure the conditions for implementation are satisfied.
4. There must be concerted efforts by elites in the major ethnic groups in the realisation of the decolonisation project of Nigerian indigenous languages so that the richness that is embedded in each ethnic groups' culture and language are transmitted to the next generation through decolonised education.
5. Providing material and teaching resources for indigenous languages medium of education so that teachers will be well equipped with the instrument that is needed to impart indigenous knowledge to the students.
6. Indigenous language should be made compulsory as a medium of instruction in nursery and primary school education and as an added prerequisite for secondary school students in gaining admission into tertiary institution regardless of their choice of study. This will ensure that students, regardless of their background, will not have any choice than to be literate in their indigenous language. It will put abreast

indigenous language with the English language. It will give strong value to it in the global world. Fellowships and grants will be placed on those that can intellectualise Nigerian indigenous languages.
7. There should be bilingual training programmes in colleges of education in such a way that prospective teachers will specialise in indigenous languages.
8. Establishment of bilingual primary and secondary schools in all the six geo-political zones. The major language of the geo-political zone with the English language will be studied in depth. This will ensure that every part of the country is carried along in decolonisation of the Nigerian indigenous language. Thus, the national curriculum must be indigenised and overhauled.

References

Ade Ajayi, J.F. 1965. *Christian Missions in Nigeria, 1841-1891*. London: Longman.

Adeyinka, A.A. & Kalusa, W.T. 1996. Introduction to History and Philosophy of Education. Unpublished Manuscript. Lusaka: University of Zambia.

Ajayi, S.A. 1984. The Development of Free Education in Western Nigeria, 1951-1960. An Historical Analysis. An Unpublished Dissertation in the Department of History. Ibadan: University of Ibadan.

Alidou, H. 2004. Medium of Instruction in Post-Colonial Africa. In: J.W. Tollefson & A.B.M. Tsui (eds.), *Medium of Instruction Policies. Which Agenda? Whose Agenda?* New Jersey: Lawrence Erlbaum Associates Publishers.

Bowen, T.J. 1857. *Adventures and Missionary Labors in Several Countries in the Interior of Africa*. Charleston, South Carolina: Southern Baptist Publication Society.

Burns, A.C. 1929. *History of Nigeria*. London: Allen & Unwin.

Datta, A. 1984. *Education and Society: A Sociology of African Education*. London and Basingstoke: Macmillan Publishers.

Edward S. 2005. Reclaiming our Memories: The Education Dilemma in Postcolonial African School Curricula. In: A.A. Abdi & A. Cleghorn (eds.), *Issues in African Education Sociological Perspectives*. New York: Palgrave Macmillan.

Fafunwa, A.B. 1974. *History of Education in Nigeria*. London: George Allen and Unwin.

Fafunwa, A.B. 1991. *A Keynote Address by the Honourable Minister of Education at the National Conference on National School Curriculum Review, Implementation Committee on National Policy on Education*. 2-6 September.

Fafunwa, A.B., Macauley, J.I. & Sokoya, J.A.F. 1989. *Education in Mother tongue: The Ife Primary Education Research Project (1970-1978)*. Ibadan: Nigeria, University Press Limited.

Falola, T. 2017. *The Collected Works of J.A. Atanda*. Austin: Pan-African University Press.

Federal Republic of Nigeria. 2004. *National Policy on Education*, 4th edition. Lagos: NERDC Press.

Fishman, J.A. & Fishman, S.G. 2000. Rethinking Language Defense. In: R. Phillipson (ed.), *Rights to Language: Equity, Power and Education*. Mahwah, NJ: Lawrence Erlbaum Associates.

Freeman, T.B. 1968. *Journal of Various Visits to the Kingdom of Ashanti, Aku and Dahomi in Western Africa*. London: Frank Cass.

Graham, S.F. 1966. *Government and Mission Education in Nigeria, 1900-1919*. Ibadan: Ibadan University Press.

Hussy, E.R.J. 1930. *Memorandum on Educational Policy in Nigeria – Sessional Paper No. 31. of 1930*. Lagos: Government Printer.

Kelly, M.J. 1991. *Education in a Declining Economy: The Case of Zambia 1975-1985*. Washington, DC: World Bank.

Kupferman, D.W. 2013. *Disassembling and Decolonizing School in the Pacific*. New York: Springer. https://doi.org/10.1007/978-94-007-4673-2

Majasan, J. A. 1967. Yoruba Education: Its Principles, Practice and Relevance to Current Educational Development. Unpublished Doctoral Thesis. Ibadan: University of Ibadan.

McCarty, T.L. 2004. Dangerous Difference: A Critical – Historical Analysis of Language Education Policies in the United States. In: J.W. Tollefson & A.B.M. Tsui (eds.), *Medium of Instruction Policies. Which Agenda? Whose Agenda?* New Jersey: Lawrence Erlbaum Associates Publishers.

Ocitti, J.P. 1973. *African Indigenous Education: As practised by the Acholi of Uganda.* Nairobi: East African Literature Bureau.

Okoro, N.P. 2011. Comparative Analysis of Nigerian Educational System. *International Journal of Business and Social Science*, 2(21):234-238.

Olamosu, B. 2000. *Crisis of Education in Nigeria.* Ibadan: Books Farm Publishers. pp. 5-6.

Omolewa, M.A. 1981. *Adult Education Practices in Nigeria.* Ibadan: Evans Publishers.

Omolewa, M.A. 2001. *The Challenges of Education in Nigeria.* Ibadan: UPL.

Osokoya, I.O. 2003. *6-3-3-4 Education in Nigeria, History, Strategies, Issues and Problem.* Lagos: Bisinaike Educational Publishers and Printers.

Ozigi, A. & Ocho, L. 1981. *Education in Northern Nigeria.* London: George Allen and Unwin.

Pennycook, A. 2002. Language Policy and Docile Bodies: Hong Kong and Governmentality. In: J. Tollefson (ed.), *Language Policies in Education.* Mahwah NJ: Lawrence Erlbaum Associates.

Sanda, A.O. 1972. Education and Social Change: Some Problems in Class Formation. *Ufahamu: A Journal of African Studies*, (5):22-23.

Shils, E. 1968. Intellectuals. In: D.L. Sillis (ed.), *International Encyclopedia of Social Sciences*, 7:399-401.

Snelson, P. 1974. *Educational Development in Northern Rhodesia. 1883-1945.* Lusaka: Kenneth Kaunda Foundation.

Taiwo, C. O. 1980. *The Nigerian Education System Past, Present and Future.* Lagos: Thomas Nelson.

Tiberondwa, A.K. 1978. *Missionary Teachers Agents of Colonialism: A Study of their activities in Uganda, 1877-1925.* Lusaka: Kenneth Kaunda Foundation.

UNESCO. 2000. *Status and Trends 2000: Assessing Learning Achievement.* Paris, International Consultative Forum on Education for All.

Wagner, D.A. 1999. Indigenous Education and Literacy Learning. In: D.A. Wagner, R.L. Venesky and B.V. Street (eds.), *Literacy: An International Handbook.* London: Westview Press.

Chapter Twelve

Transforming Leadership: Towards the Advancement of Decolonisation and Social Justice

Itumeleng I Setlhodi
Philip M. Ramadikela

Introduction

All the chapters in this book have argued well to demonstrate why Africa needs decolonisation. The contributors have examined various crucial themes that would be vital for all African classrooms and learning sites. Furthermore, the topics in this book, whether on ethnomathematics, on decolonising language or on adult basic education, need progressive leadership that would not only understand decolonial debates but also have the ability to lead that transformation. In chapter 7 Bulti presents the vital nature of values-based leadership. He raises the need for approaches that combine the best from decolonial approaches as well as the best Western approaches to establish effective leadership. This is an idea advanced by several contributors in the book beginning with the preface where this is underscored. The understanding of decolonial thought calls for an understanding of what the future entails. The latter is an idea Bulti upholds in chapter 7 as he spells out the critical nature of values in leadership. In that chapter Bulti delineates how leading with values cam lead to positivity and high performance. Values such as spirituality and respect can enable many to lead successful organisations. Writers such as Mbigi & Maree, 1995; Mbigi, 1997; Broodryk, 2006; Msila, 2008; Letseka, 2012) have demonstrated the crucial importance of *Ubuntu* in leadership and management. Furthermore, *Ubuntu* has been shown to contain the positive values for a transforming organisation where African values are necessary. All workplaces need values that enable success.

Leadership values should enable leaders and followers to experience this success. Msila (2015) highlights the various ways in which workplaces can use *Ubuntu* in enhancing success.

Again, as seen in chapter 7, leadership is about learning from a variety of models. When we speak of decolonisation and leadership it is a search for decolonial values that would free the organisation from exclusive Western values. Grounded leadership would utilise important values for the success of the organisation. There are many values in leadership. Bright (2006) writes about forgiveness as an attribute of leadership. Bright (2006:173) refers to this as a virtue of integrity and "can be practiced continuously as a consistent demonstration of character". Glynn and Jamerson (2006) emphasise the importance of principled leadership. "Principled leadership is not simply about having the right values or principles, but also about being able to act on these principles when leaders find themselves in situations that may work against those principles and values" (Glynn & Jamerson, 2006:151). Different leaders emphasise a variety of values in their organisations. Decolonial leadership requires leaders and followers who intentionally follow principles and values that support transformation. In this chapter, we examine how leadership can help transform teaching and learning and how this can help advance decolonisation and social justice in workplaces and society.

Education in Africa is undergoing elaborate transformation as organisations also search for epistemic freedom, and leadership is pertinent in this regard. From basic education institutions to higher education institutions (HEIs), there is a need to align teaching, learning and leadership practices geared towards ensuring that leaders give direction as they lead strong accountable organisations that accommodate indigenous knowledges. Without scrupulous leaders who are decolonial advocates who believe in Afrocentric perspectives, many organisations will not be amenable to the current movements that advocate the overhaul of colonial and apartheid systems. A few chapters in this book have mentioned the critical nature of the Fallist Movements from #RhodesMustFall to #FeesMustFall whose role was immense in calling for a decolonial society free from imperialist domination and cultural imposition. The role of leadership in these movements was to chart ways for activists who wanted an overhaul of a system represented by the statue of Rhodes. Adeyemo (2009:4) cites President Bill Clinton of the United States of America when he says that the rest of the world needs the African continent. Yet, it is a strong Africa with able leadership that would realise the dream of flexing its strength in a fast, changing world. Without leadership, Africa will not be able to compete with other nations and will not be able to decentre the Eurocentric notions that have dominated the continent over three centuries.

This chapter examines the role of leadership in the African society. From the 1960s, Pan African leaders such as Julius Nyerere, Kenneth Kaunda and Kwame Nkrumah have dreamt of leading a unified Africa. Many of them like Nyerere wanted to lead a Tanzania that was self-reliant, hence he spoke of the philosophy of *Ujamaa* (Nyerere, 1967). *Ujamaa* is a Swahili word for familyhood or brotherhood and it is rooted in traditional aspects that support social and economic development (Nyerere, 1966). The questions we examine in this chapter are similar questions on leadership. We first define leadership and decolonial theory as we draw a framework. Then we focus on leadership teaching and African methodologies. Then we pose the question of what to teach in decolonial leadership programme before focusing on fostering leadership and finally unlearning to learn decolonial leadership approaches.

Decolonial Leadership Theory

Decolonised leaders liberate and empower others by upsetting the coloniality of control sustaining and promoting education spaces as "racial/colonial" ventures because they realise that education may be used as a colonial project (Garcia & Natividad, 2018). Setlhodi (2020:1) contends, "there is a need to rethink the social dimension of leadership preparation and development to deepen the construction for the social process of leading effectively in education settings". The social process in this chapter relates to decoloniality of individuated leadership. Leadership individuation is two pronged First there is submerged individuality that is unlimited, such as perpetuating the decoloniality and consciously pursuing a prescriptive qualification, through which transformative abilities can be developed because they know what to do, and therefore pursue decolonial leadership development through the practice of *Ubuntu*, *letsema* and communion. The second prong refers to allowing transitioning from an Afro-communal ethos to relating communally and allowing others to commune in developing leaders to advance just decolonial leadership (Metz, 2018).

The evolution of leadership theory stems from the various situations in the process of leading, informed by the situations within which leadership exists. This chapter frames leadership theory on African philosophies by incorporating it within the three approaches of existence; aesthetical, ethical, and spiritual existence (Storsletten & Jakobsen, 2014). Aesthetic refers to the sensed interpretation from sensual awareness that encompasses particular implicit understanding embedded in feeling and emotion (Hansen, Ropo & Sauer, 2007). There is lack of focus and stability, with no commitment and rather the leader follows what appeals at any given time (Storsletten & Jakobsen, 2014). The values seem inconsequential in this instance because the leadership aligns with what appeals at any given time and thus there is mere fluid attachment to values because leaders are mindful that meeting requirements is beyond reach. This could be traced to the state of being forced out of a sense of identity due to colonial dislodgement of the values of indigenous practice in this context.

Ethics focuses on the two pronged dimensions of leadership that are transformational: individualised consideration and idealised influence (Bedi, Alpaslan & Green, 2015). There is high sense of responsibility and striving for truthfulness informed by a heightened sagacity of morality. In the context of decoloniality, there is a moral sense to change the colonial practices that tend to undervalue African ways of leading and the notion that you are because I am, underpinned in the principle of *Ubuntu/Botho*. Transformation generates the importance of change in people and institutions (Pasovska & Miceski, 2018). In this instance the change is towards a decolonised leadership that embraces African practices and purposely follows the principles and values that support transformation. Ndlovu-Gatsheni (2016) maintains that pushing for decolonial theory enables decolonisation of being, knowledge and power. Leaders are at the centre of driving the process of decolonisation and placing at the centre the beliefs and values that represent African practices, thereby helping to transform teaching and learning and bringing about social justice in education.

The values of *Ubuntu*, *letsema*, and communion among others should be placed at the core of decolonisation of leadership to enable informed transformation of learning, teaching and leadership. Nussbaum, Palsule and Mkhize (2015) echo that African leaders are yet to claim African values and place them where they should be. We maintain that propagating *Ubuntu* initiates the essence of being for African people and is a salient way of moving from the aesthetic level to bestowing ethical practices and enabling commitment to a higher purpose within the decolonisation agenda. Hence the need for leaders to infuse the values of *letsema* and communion as well. *Letsema* (a Sesotho word meaning 'working together') enables collective effort and streamlines the notion of humaneness, 'you are because I am' (Setlhodi, 2019), which the decolonial leadership needs to forge. In Tanzania, *letsema* is termed *Ujamaa*, a project that was led by the then President Julius Nyerere to spearhead the nation building agenda, such as the decolonisation programme in this context. It is a way of offering one's service for the good of a collective, particularly with an intention to advance a specific course. Communion, however, refers to the notion of being relatable towards improving the 'life-force' and enhancing *Ubuntu* to define an ethical claim (Metz, 2018). The wellbeing of African people lies in the recognition of their being and putting practices at the centre of all policies and laws regulating education and recognising their communal approach in operations to achieve desired results. Communion brings about unity and deepens relationships with the aim of gaining harmony and strengthening collaboration. *Ubuntu* serves as an overarching philosophy permeating through *letsema* and communion, hence its significance in understanding spiritual existence.

Spiritual existence refers to the transcendental and cultic, going beyond life expectancy (Khoza, 2011; Setlhodi, 2019). It is a commitment to a higher purpose. Letseka (2012) defines spiritual existence as a fundamental metaphysical essential for African socio-economic and cultural-political way of governance and highlights humaneness, state of being and people's moral fibre as integral tenets in considering African beliefs. African cultures are transcendent and inform being within many cultural folds, which becomes compelling for leaders to recognise and enable practices that accommodate spiritual existence.

In his book, *Ubuntu: Life Coping Skills from Africa* (2006) Broodryk presents an African worldview from which we can learn leadership skills. This world combines traditional ways of life, religion and various values and philosophies such as *Ubuntu*. Humanness, caring, sharing, respect and wisdom are some of the qualities that Broodryk mentions as critical in African leadership. Mbigi and Maree (1995) refer to *Ubuntu* as the spirit of African transformation management. Mbigi and Maree, like Broodryk above, list a number of characteristics vital in supporting decolonial African leadership and these include cultural diversity and African solidarity. They refer to this African transformation management as a reflection of the African soul in business. Mbigi (1997) refers to *Ubuntu* as an African dream in management. Mbigi and Maree (1995:9) opine, "*Ubuntu* can help organisations to develop corporate citizenship. By building the solidarity spirit of *Ubuntu* it is possible to build co-operation and competitive strategies by allowing teamwork to permeate the whole organisation". We perceive *Ubuntu* as a form of decolonising leadership and is part of Indigenous Knowledge Systems. Decolonised leadership utilised several aspects from African management approaches and some of the theories mentioned above reflect this practice. Mbigi (2006:23) points out:

> Compared with Western management theory and practice. African management is characterised by flatter structures, which stress inclusion, interdependence, democracy and broad stakeholder participation. Rather than formal, uniform policies, African managers call for an emphasis on

> flexibility in relation to policies, which can be easily initiated, changed and transformed through a broad-based collective, mass-scale consensus and participation of many stakeholders. Instead of the tendency towards impersonal relationships in Western management theory within an organisational context African culture calls for highly personalised relationships. [...] Finally, African management tends to prefer a web of interdependence of roles relationships and competences and is less concerned with structures and function than Western management.

Mbigi (2006) succinctly points out that this African worldview puts a deliberate emphasis on people and human dignity and the African cultural paradigm. All these ensure that the organisation embraces certain key values, which help the organisation to care for not only production but social justice as well. Broodryk (2006) highlights skills necessary in *Ubuntu* and these are the skill of sharing, the skill of sympathy, the skill of happiness, the skill of sympathy, the skill of empathy and the skill of respect. Mbigi (2006) points out that there are five key dimensions:

1. respect for the dignity of others
2. focus on group solidarity
3. teamwork deeply valued
4. service to others and
5. interdependence.

Msila (2015) also lists a number of crucial elements necessary for an *Ubuntu*-inspired workplace. Collective vision, caring, loyalty, honesty, transformational leadership and dependability are some of the qualities raised by this author. Khoza (2012) mentions several critical aspects of leadership: connectedness, compassion, integrity and humility are among these. Furthermore, Khoza (2012) adds:

> A leader who forms deep and lasting reciprocal relationships within the community can step boldly into an uncertain future with the certainty that the followers will lend their support behind. Leadership is about insight into and harmony with the followership [...] leadership is achieved not given. The leader's moral authority is fashioned in the encounter with community.

The literature above shows the decolonial theory that is embraced by models of decolonised leadership. There are some qualities shared with Western ways of leadership for some qualities are universal. However, African societies also contained various aspects that are uniquely African, which are sometimes overlooked or marginalised by Western approaches. Decolonised leadership strategies seek to address the colonial violence that disregarded the African models in leadership. As evident in the literature above, *Ubuntu* is the cornerstone of decolonial leadership strategies. The decolonial strategies support the idea of a community in an organisation. These strategies are opposed to isolation and silos that are found in many organisations. Decolonised leadership models call for the use of indigenous knowledges. Zand (2018:21) supports the above when he posits that the indigenous knowledges framework that informs indigenous leadership models accommodate relationships with self, family, community, nations "and creation as integral to leadership development…[and] is contextual, decolonising, empowering, ethical, and beneficial to the community". Furthermore, Zand summarises the differences between Western and indigenous leadership models as follows:

Table 12.1   Zand's Western and Indigenous Leadership Differences (Zand, 2018:21)

Western	Indigenous
Transactional	Transformational
Capitalistic	Based in local knowledge
Decisions based on expense and gain resources and power	Linked to self-governance and self-determination
Emphasis on individual	Emphasis on community and family

In addition to the above, Mackie (2016) explains how decolonised leadership looks like in theory and practice. She points out that when people draw up a leadership curriculum they should include relevant ways of knowing that accommodate decolonising leadership. In designing a decolonising leadership, the following should be distinct:

o   Alternative to the traditional western school system
o   Input of what's worth knowing from the community
o   Style of schooling would value 'community knowledge' over more hierarchical styles of information dissemination
o   Formed around local indigenous philosophy
o   Indigenous content infused in all curricula

Similar to Zand's (Table 1) Western and indigenous differences is a table by Bolden and Kirk (2009) who portray the shift of leadership from being individualistic to communal. This is very similar to the shift that African leadership models are introducing to society. Bolden and Kirk tabulate the differences as follows:

Table 12.2   Changing Perceptions and Meanings of Leadership (Bolden & Kirk, 2009:80)

From	To
Leadership is...	**Leadership is...**
Intimidating and inaccessible	Desirable and achievable
Beyond my capability	Possible within the capacities I have and what I have learnt
Exclusive (for men, elders, the select few)	Inclusive (for women, young people, everyone)
Distant/aloof	In touch with local concerns
For senior people in politics and organisations	For everyone in all communities
About being the best	About being engaged
For personal gain	For the benefit of the community
About heroic/charismatic individuals	About groups of people working together
Exercising personal power	Mobilizing action within the community
Influencing from a position of hierarchical authority	Influencing from wherever you are in the system
About dictating	About connecting
About maintaining order and control	About embracing chaos and uncertainty to let new things emerge
Individualistic	Collective and interconnected
Based on who and what you know (elitism)	Based on who and what you are (autheticity)
About making decisions and setting rules	About stimulating a dialogue
About problems we currently face	About creating a more positive future

As in Table 12.1, the characteristics listed in Table 12.2 show the salient differences between Western and indigenous approaches to leadership. The discussions above have highlighted several of these differences.

These are among qualities that would enable people to realise that all people have cultural capital. Conscientious and transformative leaders would work towards innovative models that promote indigenous knowledges. Decolonised leadership is linked to transformative change. Murfitt (2019:88-89) states that leadership of transformative change requires a "multi-dimensional understanding of leadership theory and an overarching belief in the process of conscientisation and resistance leading to transformative praxis with an in-depth understanding of the context in which leaders lead". Such leaders build social justice in their organisations. Murfitt (2019) also emphasises the importance of critical consciousness in understanding decolonised leadership. Various chapters in the book have explained the need for critical consciousness in education. This is a Freirean concept that means that a person does not only understand himself or herself but is able to critically look at society and understand inequalities; it enables people to understand their conditions. Critical consciousness begins with knowing oneself through deep reflections of one's own position within the dominant discourse "framing society's behaviours towards marginalised peoples" (Murfitt, 2019:75).

Conscious Leadership, Critical Consciousness and Decolonised Leadership

Today numerous programmes prepare educational leaders to work for social justice. This has called for the development of critical consciousness (Bradley-Levine, 2012). Yet, apart from critical consciousness, there is what some leaders of thriving organisations use referred to as 'conscious leadership'. Rosales (nd) writes about the need for conscious leadership stating that conscious leaders use entire selves into a leadership position and, as in *Ubuntu*, do not merely focus on themselves but on the entire organisation. Rosales describes conscious leaders as follows:

> Their vision far extends beyond their immediate to-do lists for the day. When approaching things this way conscious leaders automatically create a reliable and robust culture of trust within the organisation, which has a tremendously powerful impact on morale and by extension productivity. This high level of consciousness and self-awareness, though rare, is achievable through practice […] When a higher level of consciousness is achieved, people can transcend the reaction trap and begin focusing on what's truly important - generating outcomes.

Conscious leadership is purpose-driven and leaders want to utilise the interdependence of all team members. Jackson (2015) points out that conscious leaders inspire others to work in a positive environment. Furthermore, she lists five qualities that help conscious leaders to motivate their teams:

1. Self-awareness - conscious leaders need this to choose thoughts for positive emotions.
2. Win-win - new approaches of leadership seek to see everyone in the organisation win. This leads to compassion.
3. Everything is a learning opportunity – conscious leader are not judgemental. Employees are given the chance to think differently.
4. Recognising differences - conscious leaders are always aware of varying views.
5. Wisdom - conscious leaders use their intuitive abilities.

All the above are desirable qualities shown by conscious leaders. Bhatnagar et al. (2016) also list a number of attributes necessary for conscious leaders and these include sharing power, self-awareness, psychological empowerment of employees and intellectual ability. When Renesch coined the term 'conscious leadership' in the 1980s, he called it 'conscious' "because our circumstances call for a higher state of consciousness, a state of mind that includes a heighted awareness of what is needed for the whole of humanity and taking action as a result of that awareness" (Renesch, nd).

What is more linked to decolonised leadership in addition to the above is the utilisation of critical consciousness. Organisations today need culturally relevant leadership spurred by critical consciousness. Getlaf and Osborne (2010) point out that leaders who develop a critical perspective value respect for differences, inclusiveness, equity and social justice. Furthermore, they use their influence to enact these values in their organisations. Critically conscious leaders are able recognise and analyse systems of inequality and are able to view them critically. Paulo Freire was the first to use the concept conscientisation from which critical consciousness emanates. In his book, *Pedagogy of the Oppressed* (2005:199), he states, "Leaders who do not act dialogically, but insist on imposing their decisions, do not organise the people [...] they manipulate them. They do not liberate, nor are they liberated: they oppress." Having discussed *Ubuntu* and *letsema* above, we can say that both are indeed based on critical consciousness.

When Paulo Freire referred to critical consciousness, he meant a democratic vison of education based on reflection and dialogue. Therefore, when we argue for a leadership that embraces critical consciousness, we mean leadership that emphasises democracy and social justice. Gumede (2017) calls for the need of African leadership for Africa's development, highlighting the important for including indigenous African leadership. Gumede argues that thought liberation and critical consciousness have the potential to achieve a decolonised form of leadership. Additionally, Gumede (2017) contends that raising critical consciousness among Africans involves an endeavour to "deconstruct and reconstruct their sense of being". Gumede opines, "Critical consciousness in particular implies a thorough understanding of the obtaining reality and the ability to take fitting action to address the oppressive elements of that reality, as Paulo Freire (2005) had put it". In fact, Freire, when he speaks of critical consciousness refers to liberating action that supports democracy, liberation, anti-racism and dialogue (Freire, 2005). Gumede (2017:83) also underscores the crucial nature of African leadership models; this is what we refer to as decolonised leadership:

> Regarding African leadership, what is required is leadership that is centred on Afrocentric histories and African philosophies noting that historically there are multiple histories and philosophies in the African continent. There are different manners of knowledges and knowledge production. Moreover, Pan-Africanist orientations need to be taken into account while embarking on the further renewal of the African continent and the critical issue of unity.

Yet colonialism has made Africans forget the African methodologies hence the need for conscious decolonised leadership strategies. Colonialism over the years destroyed the indigenous cultures hence the emphasis is on Western methodologies today. The call for Pan Africanist and decolonial leadership approaches is a call to accommodate the indigenous knowledges.

Pan-African Leadership

Bolden and Kirk (2009) state that in pan-African leadership development initiatives the participants use their understanding of leadership to facilitate beneficial social change in their communities. Pan African leadership initiatives seek to introduce African leadership that decentres the Western approaches. Bolden and Kirk (2009) refer to the Western styles as having limits. In addition, Bolden and Kirk (2009:2) opine:

> A number of authors (e.g. Blunt and Jones, 1997; Wheatley, 2001; Jackson, 2004) have highlighted the manner in which Western management and leadership theory may represent a new form of colonialism – enforcing and reinforcing ways of thinking and acting that are rooted in North American and European ideologies. By doing this, there is a tendency to play down the importance of indigenous knowledge, values and behaviours, assuming instead a linear progression from the 'developing' to the 'developed' and/or the 'traditional' to the 'modern'.

Yet some have argued that, although Africa has much leadership potential – having produced illustrious leaders in the past, it lacks leaders of quality. Strategies (2020) claim that African leadership should meet the challenges of today and take into account climate change, diversity and inclusiveness as well as technology. Leaders ought to understand the African continent and its challenges but still be able to understand the global trends. Yet these African leaders need to be developed. Despite history, the USB-Ed (2018) contends that Africa currently has six challenges that have to be overcome for its potential to be realised:

1. Lack of ethical leadership.
2. Youth unemployment and poverty has spiralled.
3. Bridging the knowledge gap and fostering a culture of leadership.

4. Succession planning essential to develop tomorrow's leaders.
5. Closing the divide between vison and policy implementation.
6. Investing in education today.

The above shows how Africa needs the development of leadership using its epistemologies and cultures for this is what is entailed by Pan-Africanism that we are talking about. Afegbua and Adejuwon (2012) also highlight the leadership and governance crisis in Africa. These authors attribute Africa's failures to frequent leadership change and weak institutional systems. "The search for leadership in Africa is a search for social justice, which automatically eliminates social injustice. The principle of justice is to give each person or group what is his/her due and to demand the contribution of each on the basis of equal consideration" (Afegbua & Adejuwon, 2012:153). The search for decolonised models is a search for this pan-African liberation; it is a search for development of African leadership models which over the years have been replaced by individualism, corruption, selfishness and rivalries.

The new cohort of leaders should be developed in various approaches that reflect qualities of *Ubuntu, letsema* and *Ujamaa*. Igue (2010) claims that leaders in Africa should also strive for effective leadership through which the black continent would be able to play a key role on the global stage. New leaders must be developed and decolonial leadership models could bring back the respectability of leadership to heal the wounds of fragmentation and decay. Igue (2010) claims that leaders in Africa should strive for effective leadership, and the new generation should play a crucial role in restoring values to Africa so that communication and democracy could come back. According to Igue, new leadership should be able to repair the fragmentation of the political arena, the disintegration of historical conscience and address the challenge of epistemicides. Malunga (2006) asserts that *Ubuntu* principles can be useful in developing all leaders. He lists a number of critical lessons for leadership development, which include emphasis on values, planning leadership succession and viewing leadership development as a long-term endeavour.

Rethinking leadership in the Continent would salvage Africa from the many ills that she struggles under. The examination of several models and principles would help enhance African leadership models top advance decolonisation.

Conclusion

The process of decolonisation cannot succeed without resolute leadership abilities to direct the African worldview in all of life's avenues. Decolonial leaders in Africa should incorporate critical African values to enhance their influence. Therefore, effective communication, decisiveness, the practice of *Ubuntu* and the introduction of *letsema* will highlight the importance of decolonial approaches of leadership. Leadership trainers need to consciously draw from these African approaches at all times. Some have suggested the use of elements such as African proverbs (which are rich in various methodologies). Mkhize et al. (2016) submit that leaders should also focus on 'plurivocality' rather than 'monovocality' to achieve cognitive justice by steering the focus towards understanding that knowledge forms are incomplete. We argue, therefore, that the continuation of research in pursuance of adding to the existing body of knowledge regarding African leadership methodologies.

Surrendering colonial techniques of leading ought to be underpinned by: (i) a desire to enhance the capacity of decolonial leaders, (ii) support of their development, (iii) usage of development resources that are centred on decolonial leadership learning, and (iv) increased indigenous subject matter that equally considers sociological, political and philosophical paradigms. These should cut across key decolonial leadership programmes. Ndlovu-Gatsheni (2013) avers that the colonisation of knowledge works on people's minds, thus the ways of knowing and knowledge production as products of colonial epistemology ought to be decolonised through social evolution. New, innovative, African leadership should be part of this social evolution.

The discussion above has revealed that decolonisation does not imply only mere transformation, but also reclaiming identity and following one's own distinctive make-up to bring about social justice by embarking on an unlearning process. We argue that decolonisation should be a platform that enables leaders to accept the process of unlearning of exclusive old colonial practices so as to be able to learn previously marginalised decolonial strategies. *Mignolo* (2011) shows in his study that decolonisation is the undoing of the colonial power matrix. We argue that colonial domination needs to be addressed through the unlearning of its superordinate tendencies of parading its practices above other ideologies to enable pan-African knowledge, epistemology and methodologies to flourish.

Unlearning in this instance implies prioritising Africa's teaching modalities using what has been learned to further search for indigenous methods suitable for decolonial leadership learning within the African context. Mkhize et al. (2016:2) advance that African HEIs are undesirably impacted by the marginalisation of indigenous African manners of "knowing and being in the world" because of colonial interaction. It is therefore important for institutions, through rigorous research processes, to draw African knowledge towards the centre and deepen transformation of decolonial leadership development and training in Africa by entrenching her knowledge systems among other knowledge systems of the world. We can then summarise our arguments in this chapter by stating that decolonised approaches of leadership should:

o   Initiate the acceptance by African people to liberate themselves by embracing African identities in line with pan-African notions;
o   Develop theories that would liberate Africans from exclusive colonial tendencies that seek to marginalise African notions; and
o   Unravel and demystify colonial beliefs that oppose African belief systems and epistemologies.

Finally, we want to conclude with what Bulti emphasised in chapter 7. Decolonial leadership approaches should learn from other epistemologies from outside Africa. Julius Nyerere (1966:187) underscores this fact when he states:

> A nation which refuses to learn from foreign cultures is nothing but a nation of idiots and lunatics. Mankind could not progress at all if we all refused to learn from each other. But to learn from each other does not mean we should abandon our own [for] the sort of learning from which we can benefit is the kind which can help us to perfect and broaden our own culture.

References

Adeyemo, T. 2009. *Africa's Enigma and Leadership Solutions*. Nairobi: World Alive Publishers.

Afegbua, S.I. & Adejuwon, K.D. 2012. The Challenge of Leadership and Governance in Africa. *International Journal of Academic Research in Business and Social Sciences*, 2 (9):141-157.

Bedi, A., Alpaslan, C.M. & Green, S. 2015. A Meta-analytic Review of Ethical Leadership Outcomes. *Journal of Business Ethics*, 3(7):517-536. https://doi.org/10.1007/s10551-015-2625-1

Bhatnagar, P., Nigam, S., Prashant, P. & Caprihan, R. 2016. Desirable Traits of a Conscious Leader: An Empirical Survey. *The Delhi University Journal of the Humanities and the Social Sciences*, 3:71-91.

Bolden, R. & Kirk, P. 2009. African Leadership: Surfacing New Understandings through Leadership Development. *International Journal of Cross Cultural Management*, 9(1):69-86. https://doi.org/10.1177/1470595808101156

Bright, D.S. 2006. Forgiveness as an Attribute of Leadership. In: E.D. Hess & K.S. Camron (eds.), *Leading with Values: Positivity, Virtue, and High Performance*. New York: Cambridge University Press.

Broodryk, J. 2006. *Ubuntu: Life-Coping Skills from Africa*. Randburg: Knowledge Resources.

Freire, P. 2005. *Pedagogy of the Oppressed*. New York/London: Continuum.

Garcia, G. & Natividad, N.D. 2018. Decolonizing Leadership: Towards Equity and Justice at Hispanic-Serving Institutions (HSIs) and Emerging HSIs (eHSIs). *Journal of Transformative Leadership & Policy Studies*, 7(2):25-39. https://doi.org/10.36851/jtlps.v7i2.505

Getzlaf, B.A. & Osborne, M. 2010. A Journey of Critical Consciousness: An Educational Strategy for Health Care Leaders. *International Journal of Nursing Education Scholarship*, 7(1). https://doi.org/10.2202/1548-923X.2094

Glynn, M.A. & Jemerson, H. 2006. Principled Leadership: A Framework for Action. In E.D. Hess & K.S. Camron (eds.), *Leading with Values: Positivity, Virtue, and High Performance*. New York: Cambridge University Press.

Gumede, V. 2017. Leadership for Africa's Development: Revisiting Indigenous African Leadership and Setting the Agenda for Political Leadership. *Journal of Black Studies*, 48(1):74-90. https://doi.org/10.1177/0021934716678392

Hansen, H., Ropo, A. & Sauer, E. 2007. Aesthetic Leadership. *The Leadership Quarterly*. 18(6):544-560. https://doi.org/10.1016/j.leaqua.2007.09.003

Igue, J.O. 2010. A New Generation of Leaders in Africa: What Issues do They Face? *International Development Policy*. [Online]. Available: [https://bit.ly/3fAwz2g] https://doi.org/10.4000/poldev.139

Jackson, J. 2015. *5 Qualities of a Conscious Leader*. [Online]. Available: https://bit.ly/3ab5Ng0

Khoza, R.J. 2012. *Conceptual Framework for Interpersonal Relationships and Leadership*. Address to Nedbank Group Technology Leaders. 15 September 2012. [Online]. Available: https://bit.ly/3fzxCzx

Letseka, M. 2012. In Defence of *Ubuntu*. *Studies in Philosophy and Education*, 31(1):47-60. https://doi.org/10.1007/s11217-011-9267-2

Malunga, C. 2006. Learning Leadership Development from African Cultures: A Personal Perspective. *INTRAC Praxis Note 25*. [Online]. Available: https://bit.ly/2F3qqiN

Mbigi, L. & Maree, J. 1995. *Ubuntu: The Spirit of African Transformation Management*. Ramdburg: Knowledge Resources.

Mbigi, L. 1997. *Ubuntu: The African Dream in Management*. Randburg: Knowledge Resources.

Mbigi, L. 2006. A Vision of African Management and African Leadership: A Southern African Perspective. In: H. Van den Heuvel, M. Mangaliso, & L. Van den Bunt (eds.), *Prophecies and Protests: Ubuntu in Glocal Management*. Amsterdam and Pretoria: Rozenberg Publishers-Unisa Press. https://doi.org/10.1057/9780230627529_19

Metz, T. 2018. An African Theory of Good Leadership. *African Journal of Business Ethics*, 12(2). https://doi.org/10.15249/12-2-204

Mignolo, W.D. 2011. Geopolitics of Sensing and Knowing: On (De) coloniality, Border Thinking and Epistemic Disobedience. *Postcolonial Studies*, 14(3):273-283. https://doi.org/10.1080/13688790.2011.613105

Mkhize, N., Ndimande-Hlongwa, N., Nwoye, A., Mtyende, V.L. & Akintola, O. 2016. Editorial. *Alternation Journal*, 18:1-11.

Msila, V. 2008. *Ubuntu* and School Leadership. *Journal of Education*, 44:67-84.

Msila, V. 2015. *Ubuntu: Shaping the Current Workplace with (African) Wisdom*. Randburg: Knowledge Resources.

Murfitt, D. 2019. An Auto-ethnography: Decolonising Educational Leadership in Aotearoa/New Zealand. Unpublished Master of Education dissertation. Waikato: University of Waikato.

Ndlovu-Gatsheni, S. 2013. Decolonising the University in Africa. *The Thinker for Thought Leaders*, 51:46-51.

Ndlovu-Gatsheni, S. 2016. The Decolonial Theory of Life. In S. Ndlovu-Gatsheni, (ed.), *The Decolonial Mandela: Peace, Justice and the Politics of Life*. New York: Oxford. https://doi.org/10.2307/j.ctvgs0c16

Nussbaum, B., Palsule, S. & Mkhize, V. 2010. *Personal Growth, African Style*. Johannesburg: Penguin.

Nyerere, J.K. 1966. *Freedom and Unity/Uhuru na Umoja*: A Selection from Writings and Speeches 1952-1965. Dar-es-Salaam: Oxford University Press.

Nyerere, J.K. 1967. *Education for Self-Reliance: Freedom and Socialism*. Dar es Salaam: Oxford University Press. https://doi.org/10.1111/j.1758-6623.1967.tb02171.x

Pasovska, S. & Miceski, I. 2018. The Impact of Transformational Leadership in Improvement of the Organizational Capability. *International Journal for Innovation Education and Research*, 6(2):235-246.

Renesch, J. nd. Conscious Leadership-Transformational Approaches to Bringing about a better Future. [Online]. Available: https://bit.ly/3klVOZS

Rosales, P. nd. *What is Conscious Leadership and Why it is Important?* [Online]. Available. https://bit.ly/2DjH6SD

Setlhodi, I.I. 2019. Ubuntu Leadership: An African Panacea for Improving School Performance. *Africa Education Review*, 16(2):126-142. https://doi.org/10.1080/18146627.2018.1464885

Setlhodi, I.I. 2020. Deconstructing Leadership: Engaging Leading through a Socially Constructed Process. In: H. Şenol (ed.), *Educational Leadership*. [Online]. Available: 10.5772/intechopen.90630

Storsletten, V.M.L. & Jakobsen, O.D. 2014. Development of Leadership Theory in the Perspective of Kierkegaard's Philosophy. *Journal of Business Ethics*. https://doi.org/10.1007/s10551-014-2106-y

Strategies Team. 2020. *Finding African Solutions to African Problems Begins With African Leadership*. [Online]. Available: https://bit.ly/3ihRSaJ

USB-ED. 2018. *Six of African Continent's Biggest Leadership Challenges*. Online [Available] https://bit.ly/2C4QtEU

Zand, A. 2018. *Decolonizing Capacity Building and Leadership Development for Indigenous and Newcomer Youth through Intercultural Dialogue: A Case Study of Surrey, British Columbia. Capstone Report.* Master of Community and Regional Planning Student (Class of 2018) School of Community and Regional Planning. The University of British Columbia 20 April 2018.

Chapter Thirteen

Western Thought and African Presence in Biblical Interpretation

Joseph A. Agbogun

Introduction

The Synoptic Gospels usually have similarities in most of the narratives of Jesus' life and ministry. The cumulative result and conclusion of the life and ministry of Jesus are suffering, death, and resurrection, which translated into the completion of salvation and redemption for humankind according to the Bible. Complexity of content and the antiquity nature of the Bible, coupled with the fact that the Bible came from a particular culture and written in ancient and foreign language later translated, calls for necessity of interpretation. The interpretation of the New Testament commenced long ago under certain cultures that dominated it. Without doubt, the culture, history, and experiences of the interpreter matter a lot in arriving at an acceptable and valid conclusion. Those who brought Christianity to Africa came along with biblical interpretation centred around their socio-cultural lifestyle, which never put biblical events in their proper perspectives. The Eurocentric and American biblical interpretations are unfair to Africa and Africans in that they look down on Africans in matters of ancient historical and biblical events.

The task, among others, confronting African biblical scholars is refuting the bias interpretations of passages against Africa and Africans. The New Testament passages must be placed in their appropriate perspectives to mirror them with African culture, history, and experiences. This will permit adequate contextualisation, which will bring about their meaningfulness and relevance to Africans, making Africans at home with Christianity. Africa has had her own culture from ancient times and had been participating in ancient civilisations. This study points out how Western thought has misled people in biblical interpretation; defining Africa and Africans in the New Testament; Simon of Cyrene; and the role of African interpreters in teaching and learning the Bible.

How Western Thought Misled People in Bible Interpretation

Western imposition of thoughts can be seen in every facet of African life and activities. Metan (2015) decries this as concerned democracy when he said that Western imperialism has always been sold under the pretext of spreading freedom and democracy. Obviously, there are several ways by which Western thought has misled people in historical texts such as the Bible. One such way is the 'de-Africanisation' of the Bible. This concerns the mindset of the Eurocentric Biblical scholars to reduce Africa and Africans to slavery when they admit their presence at all or much earlier deny the entire presence of Africa and Africans in the Bible.

According to Adamo (2005:4), "this denial of African presence and influence is so strong because for the past centuries, the thrust of biblical scholarship has been in the hands of Western scholars." An examination of various books on introduction to the Old Testament, histories of Ancient Israel, and Bible Atlases show that American and European scholars dominate the field of biblical studies. Whenever they made any submission against Africa and Africans, there is no reply in defence of Africa.

Perhaps, de-Africanisation is foundational to the concept of slave trade and colonisation. Several movements to remove African presence from the Bible can be pointed out in Speiser's commentary on Genesis, the moment he called the identification of 'Kush' with Africa a mistaken identity (Speiser, 1979). Though Speiser did not specifically locate Kush with a particular region geographically, he totally condemned the idea of identifying it with Africa. This gave room for other scholars to search for possible alternatives about the locality of Kush in the world. Accordingly, George Raulison and Claus Westernman argue that instead of locating Kush (in Genesis) in Africa, it should be located in Mesopotamia. Western civilisation originating from Greece, Rome, and Palestine was the prevailing tendency at the beginning of the development of science history. Again, Aalders (2018) is an example of Western scholars who were out to de-Africanise the Bible by his denial of the possibility of African location Kush.

There are other scholars who accepted the presence of Africans in the Bible but vehemently denied or reduced their worth and influence. Adamo (2005:2) claims, "Everywhere the presence of Africans is identified in a text; such personality is reduced to nothing but a slave. Thus, Ricardo and Kalouche (2002) identify the

Kushite man in King David's army as a Negro slave". Hammershaimt (2018) in his commentary on Amos says that the dark-skinned people from Africa were held in contempt by the Israelites. Israelites regarded Africans as slaves.

These submissions by different Eurocentric scholars are aimed at dehumanising the entire Africa nations. To Adamo, (2005) there are several reasons why Africans are to challenge biblical and other kinds of academic racism, neo-colonisation, and the policy of de-Africanisation of the Bible as practiced by the majority of Eurocentric scholars. Challenging and reputing the Eurocentric scholars' inhuman actions in academic world was neglected or made impossible because perhaps the Africans were lagging behind in the examination of texts.

The situation became worse as all Africans in diaspora were never allowed to participate in literacy and intellectual development process. Adamo (2005) points out: "I believe that the situation of de-Africanisation would have improved if Africans in the Diaspora have been taught how to read and write very easily. Unfortunately when they were taught and given the opportunity to be educated, they were given inferior education." Let me illustrate this as far as Africans in their homeland are concerned. In the late 60s and 70s, some Africans were allowed to go to one of the universities in Europe. They were given the so-called special education and given special degrees and diploma in a few years. On the degrees/diploma/certificates were written, "For work in Africa only".

This means that even when Africans were given some education, they were given inferior education. The slave owners were aware that some enslaved people were intelligent and were deliberately denied and excluded from successful and worthwhile living. The white men then knew that if the enslaved people had been taught how to read and write or allowed into the higher institutions very early, they would have dominated as scholars and intellectuals globally. To this end, Joseph Enuwosa (2017) states that it is the duty of modern biblical scholars to rise to break Western domination in biblical interpretation. By implication, supposing the early African Americans had been allowed into the major seminaries and divinity institutions very early, the domination of the biblical scholarship by the Eurocentric scholars would have been impossible.

Although the Hebrew Bible is primary the record of and a witness to the revelation of the act of God within a particular nation (Israel), it also recognises God's involvement with other nations, such as Africans (Ethiopians), Africans, Babylonians, Edomites, Syrians, and others. This is because ancient Israel interacted with these nations. The New Testament, like the Old Testament, is also a record of God's revelation concerning the great redemption He has accomplished through a particular group of people (Jews). However, the New Testament is not limited to the Jews, but extended to other nations. God did not only use the Jews, but also other nations for the spread of the Gospel of redemption.

While the role played by many nations has been examined and articulated, those of Africa and Africans have not been adequately researched. Although there is research on Egypt in the Old and New Testaments by Western scholars, it was actually done with the presupposition that Egypt is not part of Africa and presumably the idea that nothing good can come from Africa, especially the South of the Sahara. This makes documents handed down to modern biblical scholars imbalanced, thus undergoing criticism. The kind of education impacted into Africans during the colonial period was the kind that made them feel inferior. Adamo (2005) asserts that even those who studied abroad at the dawn of postcolonialism were given what was not useful for the future development of Africa. Accordingly, Imam (2012) posits that in the colonial era, the British educational policy did not address the aspirations of Africans leading to frequent clamour for change in the post-independence era. Additionally, Umez (2016:7) argues:

> [...] those I looked up to, namely, my mentors, educators, and leaders were busy teaching me and other youths, probably inadvertently, to feel inferior and remain inferior. Essentially, I was taught, just as many youths in Nigeria are being taught today, to feel inferior and develop low self-esteem. Here are few examples. I was thoughtlessly taught (and children are still being thoughtlessly taught today), that *oyibo bu ndi muo*, (white men are naturally spirits), *oyibo bu agbara*, (white men are wizards by nature), and *America ilu oba* (which suggests that white man's country is naturally the land of kings). Similar phrases such as *dan bature*, (which implies that white men are by nature civilized), and 'or buter' (which symbolises the natural lead of white men) are very common all over Nigeria. I was thoughtlessly taught (as children are still being thoughtlessly taught today) that almost anything 'black' is inherently evil. In fact, to our 'educators', it is perfectly okay to use the word, 'black' (the ascribed name to people with African decent), to describe evil. In accordance with this teaching, a bad person is the 'black sheep of the family', and should be 'black listed.' In accordance with this teaching, illegal market is 'black market' (as if only black people do business in such market). In according with this teaching, Satan (no one has ever seen) is 'black' in colour. In fact, to our 'educated' teachers, frequent use of 'black' to describe evil demonstrates a mastery of the 'Queen's English,' deserving an 'A' in English essay composition. What an education! It is a pity! Indeed, Nigerian African children and the public are being taught, directly or indirectly, self-hatred and how to develop a sense of low self-esteem. Without question, there are deadly consequences resulting from this kind of miseducation, and to them, I now turn.

The British curricula that brought about miseducation is difficult to wipe out of Africa. Even if Africans try hard to change it theoretically, in practice, it undoubtedly lives on. Therefore, a conscious and concerted effort must be made continuously to reorient all Africans.

Umez (2016:36) did not mince words pointing out the consequences of making do with the wrong education. He further states the reasons why Africans accepted such miseducation from the colonial educators and the possible solutions, thus:

> There are grave consequences in the inferior miseducation given to Africans. We often agree that the mind is a terrible thing to waste. I must add that the mind is a terrible thing to pollute. The minds of so many African children and that of the general public have been grossly polluted and destroyed by a powerful force largely unseen by naked eyes. That powerful force is inferiority complex (also called 'mental slavery'). Here is a brief illustration of the destruction caused by inferiority complex/lack of self-confidence in Africa and among Africans: we prefer anything made in the Global North; we respect or honour the white; most African leaders are very proud to invest African money and resources in non-African countries. Why? In their miseducated minds, Africa is 'unsafe heaven', while America is the 'safe heaven'; and almost making them lords.

In his book, *How Europe Underdeveloped Africa*, Walter Rodney (1973) traces the plunder of colonialism and ways colonialism affected the mind of the African. Colonialism was a philosophy based on miseducation and it was convenient for this philosophy to make the African believe in his/her inferiority. For centuries European scholarship supported numerous misleading notions when it comes to indigenous epistemologies versus western epistemologies. Rodney (1973:25) writes about how European scholars supported the myth that underdevelopment of Africa was ordained by God and making all believe that Western countries are more developed because westerners are "innately superior, and that the responsibility for the economic backwardness of Africa lies in the generic backwardness of the race of black Africans".

From the above, all corrupt practices that bring about underdevelopment are inherent in this miseducation. Effective and critical education liberates the mind. Unfortunately, many Africans are consumed by colonialism and may not always realise what is wrong with the Western education meant for Africans. Ignorance makes them to take pride in attaining the kind of education. Only a liberated mind is capable of liberating others. Decolonising of African minds should be a more lasting struggle for all.

Defining African and Africans in the New Testament

The word 'African' is not mentioned in the Testament as such. Its wild usage is recent. According to Enuwosa the Greeks referred to the African continent as *Libya* and the Romans called it *Africa* in antiquity. Perhaps African is derived from the Latin word *African* meaning 'sunny' or the Greek *Aphrike'* meaning 'without cold'. It was mainly applied to the Northern coast of the African continent, which was regarded as the Southern extension of Europe.

Africa is also the Arabic transliteration of the word *Ifriqiyah*. Africa was known in antiquity under the name Libya and this referred to that portion opposite the coast of Greece and west of Egypt. Old Testament Hebrews were very familiar with Egypt in Africa and referred to Libya as *Lehabim* (Gen. 10:13) and *Lubim* (2 Chron. 12:3). Other parts of Africa know to Old Testament Hebrews were 'Cush or Ethiopia and put' whose inhabitant were regarded as the Hamitic stock. In this way, we use the term Africa as the land of the blacks and Africans for the citizens of the black continent as was known to the ancient Greeks, Hebrews and the Romans. Thus, at the time of the New Testament, Africa was well known to the Jews, Greeks, and Romans. The Hebrews called Africa by the various names of tribal groups. These names, as found in the New Testament, are *Aiguptoj/Aiguptiej* (Egypt/Egyptians, Matt. 2:13-19; Acts 2:10), Aiqioy (Ethiopian, Acts 8:27), and *Niger* (Niger, Acts 13:1).

Aigu,ptoj (Egypt/Egyptians)

Aigu, ptoj (Egypt) is one of the terms used in the New Testament for Africa and Africans (Matt. 2:13-19, Acts 2:10; 7:9-10; 13:17; 21:38, Heb. 3:16; 8:9; 11:26-29; Jude 5; Rev. 11:8). While Egypt appears 24 times in the New Testament, Egyptian surfaced five times. According to Brown (1974), the Greeks word *aigu,ptoj* is derived from the Egyptian *hwtkpth* which is pronounced *ha-ku-ptah*. It was the term ancient capital of Egypt opposite modern Cairo. Brown (1974:52) says that the term was later used for both the country as well as its capital.

Josephus and the Old Testament treat Egypt as the land of Ham (Josephus, Antiquities 1, vi, 2: Gen. 10; Ps. 78:51; 105:23; 27; 106:21) Josephus described the Egyptians as following: "for the four son of Ham. Time as not hurt the name Chus; for the Ethiopians over whom he reigned are even at this date, both by themselves and by all men in Asia are called Chushites. The memory also of the Mesraites is preserved in their name for all that inhabit Judea call Egypt/Egyptians Mestre/Mestreans".

Some scholars agreed that Ham was the ancestor of the Egyptians and Egypt was the land of Ham. According to Walter Arthur McCray, the name 'Ham' means 'hot, heat' and by implication 'black'. This implies that the Cushites, Egyptians Putites and Canaanites were Africans because they were sons Ham. In the New Testament era, Egypt played host to not fewer than a million Jews. They became very prosperous, influential and well cultured in Egypt especially in the city of Alexandria where some Jews held important state officials under the Ptolemies.

Libuhj (Libya)

One of the terms also used in the New Testament to refer to Africa and Africans is Libya (Acts 2:10). Libya or Libyans are translated from three distinct Hebrews words as follows:

o   *Kub*: the King James Version has 'Chub' and LXX translated it Libues.
o   *Lubim*: this is the translation in King James Version AV and RSV (Libues, Phual).
o   *Put*: LXX has Phout, KJV Phut and RSV Put.

Put is identified in Genesis 10:6 as one of the sons of Ham and the brother of Cush, Egypt and Canaan. J.E. Harris stated, "Put was the founder of Libya. He called the inhabitant 'Putites'". Old Testament references to Libya links it with Egypt, Ethiopia (2 Chron. 12:3; 16:8; Ezek. 30:5; Dan. 11:13; Nahum. 3:9).

The New Testament also links Libyan cities in antiquity with a large Jewish colony almost like that of Alexandria. Greek and Roman historians and poets used the word Libyes to refer to the inhabitants of North Africa. C.O.G. Ndubukwu said that Herodotus (480-425 BCE) used Libya for the whole continent of Africa. Diodorus (60-30 BCE) employed the term Libya to denote Africa of the Nile as far as Egypt.

The New Testament mentions some Cyrenians of Libya such as Simon of Cyrene, Alexander and Rufus (Matt. 27:32; Mark 15:21; Luke 23:26; Acts 13:1) We also have Cyrenius who was the governor of Syria and might have been an African from Cyrene.

Aiqioy (Ethiopia/Ethiopians)

Ethiopia is another term used in the New Testament (Acts 8:27). It references to the black people inhabiting the lands south of the Mediterranean coast of Africa. Homer in his poem was the first Greek writer to use the term Ethiopian.

Ethiopia was a Greek word derived from Aethiops who was the son of Vulcan, the Greek god of metal work and fire. It was the Greek counterpart of the Ethiopian god Bes. Aethiops means 'the Glowing' or 'the Black'. D.T. Adamo applied the term for people considered to be burnt or 'black' and of African origin both at home and in diaspora. Following the environment theory, Copher (2018) says "that the dark colour of their skin where as a result of the intense heart of the south sun." He also cities an inscription discovered by A.H. Sayce and G.C. Griffith in 1914. It reveals that the Ethiopians described their land as the land of Qevs, Kesh. This is not identified with the Egyptian word *Kesh* and the Hebrew word *Cush* which where designations applied to Ethiopians by Egyptians and the Old Testament for thousands of years.

The ancient Egyptians knew Ethiopia and its people under a variety of names. The earliest known record is the inscription on the **Palermo** stone (ca. 3000 BCE) in it, the region immediately south of Egypt was designated as, "There were other names with which Ethiopia was known in Egypt". This includes the Egyptian words *Khent* (border land) *Ta-sti* (land of the bow) and *Nub* (gold). This indicates that Ethiopia was known as the land of bowmen, the land of gold, as well as of blacks.

Hebrew and Asian sources have indicated that the term Cush and Cushites which also used for Ethiopians. The Old Testament identifies Cush as one of the four son of Ham (Gen. 10:6-8; 1 Chron. 1:8-10; Ps.7). Harris cites Josephus who said that "Of the four sons of Ham, time has not at all hurt the name of Chus: for the Ethiopians over whom he reigned, are even at this day both by themselves and by all men in Asia called Cushites." In the light of this evidence, it appears conclusive that Ethiopia both in the Old and New Testament as well as classical literature to Africans South of Egypt.

Niger (Niger)

Another term used in the New Testament for African is *Niger* (Niger). The word is only used once in the New Testament (Acts 13:1). According to J.H.Thayer, the word Niger is a Latin name meaning black. Thayer considers Niger in Acts 13:1

as the surname of Simeon, whereas S.F. Pfeiffer (2018) regards it as the Latin name of Simeon. In the Old Testament, the most frequently used words with colour significance for the black person is *Cushite* (Cush). The Greek equivalence is *Aethiops*, whereas the Roman equivalence is Niger. Hence C.B. Copher (2018) said that Greek and Latin terms where use to trance late the Hebrew word Cush and related terms in the Old Testament terms for blacks.

Thus Niger translates the Old Testament word in the New Testament. In the New Testament, for the Hebrew term Cush and the Greek word Ethiopia. These terms where used by biblical and classical writers to describe Africans on account of their black colour and Negro characteristics. Lucius in Acts 13:1 used the word to describe the African prophet who was probably Simon of Cyrene.

Simon of Cyrene (Matt. 27:32, Mark 14:21, Luke 23:26)

The story of Simon of Cyrene who was forced to carry the cross of Jesus is one of the passion narratives that are common to the three synoptic gospels: Matthew, Mark and Luke. Source criticism maintains that stories which are common to the three gospels were drawn from Mark. For this reason, Mark is considered to be the first written gospel. They argued that Matthew and Luke improved on the work of Mark. Hence the synoptic gospels have common and similar works. However, three different people writing on the biography of one person in the same environment, age, period, and faith are bound to be identical. From the tradition of the early church, Mark was regarded as an interpreter of Peter from whom he collected his materials. This tradition is said to have been derived from three centres: Antioch, Rome, and Alexandria. The story appearing in the three gospels confirm that it was one of the popular stories told in the Christian communities of the early Church.

A careful examination of the facts surrounding Simon of Cyrene reveals that he was an African, not a Jew. According to Enuwosa and Edoisang, citing J. Strong, the name Simon or Simeon derived from the Hebrew word, *Shimone* or *Shawmah* which means 'to hear'. For J.H. Thayer, Simon was a Greek name meaning 'flat-nose'. Black dark skin, flat-nose, wooly hair, and thick lips are some the physical characteristics of Africans long recognised by scholars and classical writers. What we discover from the above point is that Simon might have been the Greek name of this African which indicates his black nationality and traits however the name was borne by Jew and non-Jews alike.

According to Isiorhovoja (2017) there is a strong reason to think of Simon the cross bearer as the same Simon, the evangelist, in Acts 13:1 because of the Latin name *Niger* which means 'Black'. Although W. Barclay considers him a Jew who moved in Roman circles, K.L. Barker and J.R. Hohlenberger, according to Barclay, consider him to be native of Cyrene in Africa. The term *Niger* (black) and, Simon (thick flat-nose) given to Simon in the gospel and the Acts confirms that he was an African and both the gospel and the Acts refer to the same person.

Another reason to think that Simon, the cross bearer, was an African is the very act of conscription. In ancient Roman society, a person of low status or who had strange somatic appearances, were given a contemptuous treatment such as thrashing. According to Onibere (2015), because of African early great civilisation and religiosity, Africans participated so much in early Christianity. Simon therefore might have been a proselyte with black appearance among the white Jewish population. It can be suggested that this combined with his low status might have made the Roman soldiers to conscript him. Pfeiffer (2018) related how Judaism attracted particularly the lower class, including women, as did Christianity in the beginning. This class of people was often ridiculed and denounced by people of high education breeding and wealth. Simon is one of those in the class of Jewish converts. Cyrene had a population that made up peasant, traders, Roman soldiers, and Jews.

Cyrene was a Greek colony in Libya that was founded in 630 BC. Libya, like Egypt, fell to raiders, invader settlers, as well as Greek and Roman influences and imperialism in the classical era. Nevertheless, despite the cross breeding due to inter-marriage, the Negroid characteristic of the native Libya have not been erased until date. Libya is descendant of Ham, the father of Africans. They are intrinsically linked with Egyptians and Ethiopians in biblical narratives (2 Chron. 12:3; 16:8; 14:9-15; Ezek. 27:10; 30:1-9; Neh. 3:9).

The New Testament shows that Simon was a native of Cyrene in Libya in North Africa. The King James Version refers to him in Mark as 'Simon a Cyrenian'. Phillip Modern English Bible used 'Simon a native of Cyrene in Africa'. Revised Standard Version and New international Bible have it as 'Simon of Cyrene' which indicates that he was an African (Matt. 21:32; Luke 23:26; Mark 15:13). Had he been a Jew, the gospel writers would not have hesitated to append the word, 'a Jew from Cyrene'. This was the pattern adopted by the gospel writers and Paul when they described person outside their native land. For example, the Samaritan woman in Samaria (John 4:9) identified Jesus as a Jew. If Simon was therefore a Jew, the gospel writers would have mentioned it.

The description of Simon in Mark 15:21 show that he was known to the church. It is probable to think that this African who was compelled to carry Jesus' cross by the Romans, must have followed up what befell the man he shared his last suffering with until resurrection. Furthermore, he might have followed the events that led to Jesus' crucifixion and discovered that he was an innocent great man.

The transformation received by Simon turned him to a popular black evangelist known by the gospel writers and other first century Christians like Luke. He witnessed Pentecost as one of the Libyans or Cyrenians who were present in the cut pouring of the spirit (Acts) Simon probably came to Jerusalem together with other proselytes from Cyrene and other parts of Libya. This Simon and his children Alexander and Rushs were Africans. He aided Jesus at a critical moment when no Jew wanted to help. Though he was compelled to carry the cross by the Roman authority, he did not resist or refuse to assist Jesus. The word compel translated to Greek is *avngareuvw*. It originated in Persia and was adopted in Latin and Greek languages. It was used for somebody conscripted by a King to go on a journey, bear a burden or to perform any other service. This African, therefore, bore the burden of humankind with Jesus.

Simon later became the preacher of the suffering and resurrection of Jesus to the word. He identified Jesus as the messiah and preached to his children into believing in the saviour of humankind. He evangelised both Jesus and gentile of his days. There could be no greater contribution to the Christian faith then that made by Simon of Cyrene, the African.

The Role of African Interpreters in Teaching and Learning the Bible

Teaching the truth from the Bible to influence practical living must come from an individual with sound understanding of the Bible. Sadly, it seems that Christianity has no strict method and system of indoctrinating their young ones, except few orthodox denominations. African interpreters who have a good foundation of African culture and are thinking in such lines are very rare. Even what such Africans write and say are seen to be scholastic and are not embraced with open mind by Christian teachers and learners.

The interpreter of the Bible is first the learner before being a teacher of little truth. In discussing some basic qualifications of a Bible interpreter, Nihinlola (2008) opines that the following are the basic qualifications, attitudes, and requirements for a Bible interpreter: experience of regeneration, dependence on the Holy Spirit, open mindedness, diligence, and prayer. As the interpreter of the Bible depends on the Holy Spirit, so must one approach the Bible with an open mind, a willingness to learn from God through reading, meditating, and studying. Without this, the interpreter may fall into the error of reading his/her own preconceived ideas into the meaning of the scriptures.

Therefore, Isiorhovoja (2017) contends: "since the Bible is God's word, the thing for us to do is to open our minds to it and let us say to us what it will". This sincerity of heart as we engage in Bible interpretation is required because a basic task "is to discover the meaning of the text in its proper setting; to draw from Scripture rather than reading one's presuppositions into it". To Ejenobo (2016), this open mindedness helps the philosopher or interpreter to lay hand on what other interpreters have postulated about the concept under discussion. It becomes almost imperative here for the interpreter to consult Bible dictionaries, commentaries, among others. Unfortunately, European interpreters carried out most of these works.

To throw a light on the role of African interpreters, Adamo (2005) defines African Cultural Hermeneutics, thus that African Cultural Hermeneutics in biblical studies is an approach to biblical interpretation, which makes Africa socio-cultural context a subject of interpretation. It means that African cultural hermeneutics, like any other third world hermeneutics, is contextual hermeneutics since it is always done in the perspective of a particular context. It means that the analysis of the text is done from the perspective of African worldview, and culture African cultural hermeneutics is re-reading the scriptures from a premeditatedly African centred perspective with the purpose of not only understanding the Bible and God in our African experiences and culture, but also with the hope of breaking the hermeneutical hegemony and ideological stranglehold that Eurocentric biblical scholars have long enjoyed in their interpretation of the Bible. This is a methodology that reappraises ancient biblical tradition and African worldview, culture, and life experience with the purpose of correcting the effect of the cultural ideological conditioning to which Africa and Africans have been subjected.

By this submission, every African biblical scholar owes it a duty to understand the socio-cultural worldview of Africa; clearly differentiating from that of the European Bible and any other, bringing home the message of any Bible text. It is obvious that the history and total experiences of the interpreter should influence the interpretation, thus all African teachers of Christian religion should have the method and tool of African cultural hermeneutics, if decolonising Bible reading will be possible. The advantages the Eurocentric interpreters have over Africans are based on their culture and experiences, which they imposed on Africans.

Furthermore, there was no consideration of African cultural heritage by the colonialists when they came. There was even neglect of the biblical culture, or still being replaced by the westerners as they interpreted and taught biblical truth. This brings about the reiteration by Adamo (2005:11) that "understanding African indigenous culture is absolutely important in doing African cultural hermeneutics. This is because African culture is part of African cultural hermeneutics. Despite the resemblance of the biblical and African cultures, there are still some distinct aspects of African culture. This distinctive African culture influences or dominates the interpretation of the Bible". This is one of the conditions for African cultural Hermeneutics given by Adamo. The neglect of culture brings about the misleading of people about the Bible truth by Western thought. Anyone who does not hold firm to his culture may be for lack of understanding or flexibility tends to abandon it for another. African scholastic interpreters of the Bible or Christian philosophers are expected to have deep knowledge of African culture so that everyone reading the Bible can be contextualised.

The contribution and value of African theology to the decolonisation of African thought and mind cannot be overemphasised. This is because theology as science is grounded on God's revelation in Christ and based on deep, thorough knowledge of human beings and the factors that conditioned their lives. It is in considering this that Tshibangu (2016) in his article titled, *The Task of African Theologians*, presented four obligations of African theologians which is applicable to all African teachers.

First, African theologians must be fully aware of the fact that their Catholic work calls for real spiritual commitment. There can be no theological effort without commitment. One must raise questions about one's own life and about the spiritual destiny of the people with whom one is associated. This presumes a real ability to ask fundamental questions. The theologian must be a person of deep faith and a solidly metaphysical life. The theologian cannot do any useful, worthwhile or relevant work unless he or she accepts personal involvement in the theory and practice of life while making every effort to maintain intellectual and moral sincerity and scientific objectivity. The example of great theologians in the past and present day are Lubac and Tillich who became great theologians because they tackled deep metaphysical questions and committed themselves wholly to their task. They accepted the demands of thought and action imposed by their own concrete situation. African theologians must be aware of this obligation to commit themselves to the situation and the issues of their rime and milieu.

Second, the African theologian must be equally conscious of the intellectual demands imposed by theological work. As I pointed out above, theology is a scientific discipline grounded on knowledge of revelation and its content and based on knowledge of the reality of human beings and the universe. This means, first, that the theologian must possess theological knowledge in the strict and formal sense. According to Nihinlola, Emiola (2008:31), Vatican I defined it thus: "Reason illumined by faith which, with the help of God, seeks to gain a deeper understanding of the mysteries. He does this by learning all it can by way of analogy from nature, by exploring the relationship between the different mysteries themselves, and by considering the ultimate end of humanity". It also means that the theologian must strive to possess the deepest and most accurate scientific knowledge of humanity and the factors that condition it. If African theologians want to be rigorous and to be taken seriously, they must be fully conscious of these intellectual obligations. They must be able to go beyond simple commitment. If the latter is correct, it may be intuitive and difficult to formulate. Theologians must be able to propose matters in a valid and convincing way to other human minds.

Third, African theologians have social commitment. They cannot live as beings apart because they must bear responsibility for their own personal destiny and that of others. They must be involved in their community and their social participation must be as active as possible. This participation will put them in a position to gain a deeper grasp of the cultural issues posed by their community and the living conditions of their contemporaries. Isiorhovoja (2017) opines that the social obligation of African interpreters will help them to pay due attention to the questions raised by the appearance of new values in a given society. Also, its characteristic perception and conception of things and events and by the facts and events related to its socio-cultural evolution and development are to be considered. If Christian thinkers are not wholly involved in the on-going process of their society, they can hardly claim to be authentic African theologians.

Closely associated with this overall commitment is the fourth obligation of ecclesial involvement. Ejenobo (2016) affirms that African theologians must live in fidelity to ecclesial truth. They must of course possess discernment so that they can know exactly what is defined as certain truth by the church. However, they must equally cultivate courage and take risks in exploring, pondering, and expressing the theological conclusions that derive from their authentic research. The churches of which African theologians are members also have a role to play. They must have confidence in their theologians unless there is good reason to feel otherwise. They must support them on the intellectual level and the level of religious practice, encouraging their research, avoiding hasty condemnations, and being careful not to voice fear and reservations for purely a priori reasons. If the above conditions are met, African theologians can undertake the research that faces us with a real chance of handling it successfully.

In attempt to decolonise Bible reading, every African Christian religion teacher should come to the awareness that his/her culture deserves to be at the centre, like Western epistemologies. On discussing the relationship between African and Biblical cultures, Umukoro (1978:366) submits: "African theologies have set about demonstrating that the African religious experience and heritage were not illusory and that they should have formed the vehicle for conveying the Gospel varieties to Africa". They showed that many of Africa's religious insights had a real affinity with those of the Bible.

On many respects, the African was much more on the wavelength of the Bible than the accidental ever was. The African understood more easily in his bones, as it were, the meaning of corporate personality, for instance than the individualistic westerners. In the view of Onibere (2016), it was shown time and time again that the African sense of the numinous, his awareness of the proximity of the spiritual, his attitude to death and diseases, in all these ways, he was far closer to the biblical thought patterns than the westerners could ever hope to be. Here, recognizing the closeness of African culture to that of the Bible people is to make sure that Africans contextualised the Bible's contents meaningfully. Though Adamo states that there are distinct between African and biblical cultures, but their affinity makes the Bible and its messages more relevant in Africa than as it was introduced by the colonialists. The areas of the Bible message that makes no sense to the westerners make most sense to the Africans when taught and applied appropriately.

Conclusion

Looking at the study generally, it is overt that Africa and Africans played vital roles in redemption work of Jesus Christ through his life and ministry as reflected in the Bible. Simon of Cyrene is unarguably an African who demonstrated African virtues – being one's keeper and hospitality. The fact that Simon of Cyrene did not hesitate when called to give a helping hand to Jesus goes a long way to say that Simon must have had compassion on the suffering and tortured Son of Man. Unfortunately, these facts and virtues of the African have never been mentioned or commended by the European and American interpreters before now.

Reference

Aalders, G.D. (2018). Commentaries on Mathew 27 in *Austin, Precept's Commentary*. [Online]. Available: https://bit.ly/3d5fsEq

Adamo, D.T. 2005. *Exploration in African Biblical Studies*. Benin-City, Nigeria: Justice Jeco Press and Publishers Ltd.

Ejenobo, D.T. 2016. *Insights into African Biblical Interpretation*. Effurun: Okiemute Publishing House and Press.

Enuwosa, J. 2017. *Toward Evaluation and Breaking of Western Hegemony in Biblical Interpretation*. Abraka: Delta State University Press.

Enuwosa, J. & Udoisang, F.P. 2002. Africa and Africans in the Synoptic Gospels. In: D.T. Adamo (ed.), *Biblical Interpretation in African Perspectives*. New York: University Press of America.

Copher, C.B. 2018. Commentary on Luke 23:26. In *Austin, Precept's Commentary*. [Online]. Available: https://bit.ly/3d5fsEq

Ejenobo, D.T. 2016. An African Interpretation of Paul's Understanding of The Holly Spirit. *European Scientific Journal*, 12 (32):426.

Hammershaimt, O.J. 2018. Commentary on Mark 15:21. In *Austin, Precept's Commentary*. [Online]. Available: https://bit.ly/3d5fsEq

Imam, H. 2012. Educational Policy in Nigeria from the Colonial Era to the Post-Independence Period. *Italian Journal of Sociology of Education*, 1(2):181-204.

Isiorhovoja, O.U. 2017. *Africans Biblical Interpretation in Contemporary Nigeria*. Sapele: MorningStar Publishers.

McCray, W.A. 1990. *The Black Presence in the Bible and the Table of Nations*. Chicago: Black Light Fellowship.

Metan, T. 2015. *Decolonizing Democracy from Western Cognitive Imperialism*. Langaa, Cameroun: RPCIG. https://doi.org/10.2307/j.ctvh9vw57

Ndubokwu, CO.G. 2002. *Egyptian Cult of Isis: The Mother Goddess*. Ughelli: Oputovu Books.

Nihinlola, E. 2008. *The Task of Bible Interpretation*. Ogbomoso: Scepter Prints Nig. Ltd.

Onibere, S.G.A. 2015. *An Evaluation of Africans' participation in New Testament Events*. Emevor-Isoko: Pentecost Christian Press.

Pfeiffer, S. F. 2018. Commentary on Luke 14:27. [Online]. Available: https://bit.ly/3d5fsEq

Ricardo R.L. & Kalouche, F. 2002. *Africa and other Civilizations: Conquest and Counter-Conquest: The Collected Essays of Ali A. Mazrui*, Vol. 2. Trenton, NJ and Asmara, Eritrea: Africa World Press.

Rodney, W. 1973. *How Europe Underdeveloped Africa*. Abuja/Lagos/Pretoria: Panaf Publishing.

Speiser, E.A. 1979. *Genesis: The Anchor Bible*. Garden City, N.Y.: Doubleday and Company.

Thayer, J.H. 2017. *Greek-English Lexicon of the New Testament*. Grand Rapids, MI: Zondervan Publishing House.

Tshibangu, T.B. 2016. The Task of African Theologian. In: N. Mushete (ed.), *History of African Theology*, 5(7):74-76.

Umez, B.N. 2006. *Educated to Feel Inferior: Harsh Realities of Low Self Esteem*. Baytown, Texas: GBS Publishers.

Index

Symbols

#RhodesMustFall ii, xxi, 80, 84, 167, 169, 226

A

Adamo, D 244-246, 250, 254-255, 257
Adult education 103-104, 107, 114, 116
Adult Education vii, xix, xx, xxix, xxx, 103-116, 119, 156, 177
African Renaissance ii, xiv-xv, xxvii, 8, 12, 125
Agenda 2063 iii, xiii
Apartheid v-vi, x-xi, xiv, xvi, xviii, 1-5, 8, 14-15, 33, 35-37, 43-44, 46, 52, 94, 105-107, 109, 112-114, 119, 142, 175, 198, 226

B

Banking Model v, 12, 45-46
Bantu Education 1-2, 4, 8, 43-44, 52
Basic Education ii, vii, xii, xvii-xviii, 5, 12, 14,-16, 33, 43-44, 50, 103, 107, 111, 113, 119, 213, 225-226
Bible xxii-xxiii, 188, 195, 209-210, 243-245, 252-255, 257
Biko, S 9, 104-105, 117, 119, 155, 159, 198
Black Consciousness (BC) 8-9, 105, 119, 198

C

Christianity 2, 191, 195, 243, 252-253
Christian National Education (CNE) 1
Cognitive Justice ix, xvi, 110, 120, 129, 143, 158, 161, 174, 176, 237
Collective Teacher Efficacy (CTE) xx, 126-127, 130-131, 136, 139, 141-143
Conscientisation xiv, 12, 45, 105, 109, 118, 177, 232, 234
Critical Indigenous Theory 23, 27-28
Critical Pedagogy xvi, xix-xx, 13, 31, 45-47, 50, 104-105, 107-108, 113, 115, 117, 119, 175, 177
Culture vi-vii, ix-xii, xv-xviii, xx-xxii, xxviii, 2-3, 7, 9-11, 14, 21-39, 44, 48, 50, 65, 69, 86, 89, 104, 108, 111-113, 117-118, 133, 143, 154-155, 158-159, 166, 171, 174, 177, 187-92, 194-202, 206, 209, 215, 218-220, 229-230, 233, 235-236, 238, 243, 253-255, 257
Culturecides x, 2, 106, 175, 180, 198, 202

D

D'Ambrosio, U 28-29, 31-32, 37
Dialogic Teaching v, 108-109
Distance Education xx, 149-153, 156, 161, 164, 167, 173-174, 178

E

Egypt 246, 248-250, 252
Eiselen Commission 44
Epistemic Freedom 1, 11, 106, 128, 166-167, 172, 174, 176-179, 187, 198, 202, 226
Epistemicide x, 2, 51, 175, 180, 198-199, 236
Ethiopia xxi, xxix, 187-188, 191-202, 248-251
Ethnomathematics xviii, 21-32, 35-39, 225
Eurocentrism ix, 7, 14, 21, 119, 158, 168, 176, 188

F

Freire, P v-ix, xiii, xx, 13, 45-46, 54, 105, 108-111, 117-119, 174-175, 177, 234

G

Gerdes, P 21-22, 31, 34-35
Ghana x, xi, 60, 67, 214
Grey, G 2, 194

H

Heutagogy xxi, 167-169, 171-180
Historicides x, 2, 106, 180, 198
Humanism xx, 3, 7-10

I

Inclusive Education ii, xix, 59-62, 66-69
Indigenous Games 22, 26-27
Indigenous Knowledge Systems (IKS) xiv, xviii-xix, xxviii, 28, 32-33, 44-54, 84, 173, 188, 193, 195, 220, 229

K

Kebra Nagast 192
Kush/Cush 244, 248-251

L

Language i-vi, x, xii, xv-xvii, xxi-xxii, xxxi, 2-3, 6-7, 9-12, 19, 23, 28, 33, 34-36, 39, 44, 48, 51, 60, 62, 79, 82, 89, 95-96, 105, 107, 109, 112-113, 116-117, 154, 157, 166, 169, 187-189, 193, 195- 202, 205-221, 225, 243, 253
Liberatory Teaching 3, 12-13, 45, 115, 167, 174-176
Linguicides x, 2, 106, 175, 180, 198, 202

M

Macedo, D xiv, 6, 44-46, 107, 175
Mazrui, A vi-xvi
Mbeki, T xiv
Mphahlele, E xv, xviii, 3, 7-10, 15

N

Ndlovu-Gatsheni, SJ vi, x, 3, 106, 143, 168, 177, 187-188, 192, 198, 228, 237
Nkrumah, K vii, x-xi, xxxi, 227
Nyerere, J xi, 16, 151, 227-228, 238

P

Pan-Africanism ii, xiii, 10, 236

S

Self-colonisation 188-190, 201-202
Self-directed Learning 176-177
Social Justice ix, xiii, xiv, xvi, xix, xxii, 3, 6, 8, 14, 16, 22, 24, 36, 39, 46, 51, 53-54, 108, 113, 115, 118, 129, 174-176, 179-180, 197, 202, 226, 228, 230, 233-234, 236-237
Synoptic Gospels xxii, 243, 251

www.ingramcontent.com/pod-product-compliance
Lightning Source LLC
Chambersburg PA
CBHW081203170426
43197CB00018B/2903